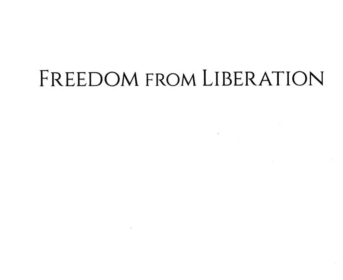

FREEDOM FROM LIBERATION

BLACKS IN THE DIASPORA
Herman L. Bennett
Kim D. Butler
Judith A. Byfield
Tracy Sharpley-Whiting
editors

FREEDOM *from* LIBERATION

Slavery, Sentiment, and Literature in Cuba

GERARD ACHING

INDIANA UNIVERSITY PRESS

Bloomington & Indianapolis

This book is a publication of

Indiana University Press
Office of Scholarly Publishing
Herman B Wells Library 350
1320 East 10th Street
Bloomington, Indiana 47405 USA

iupress.indiana.edu

Manufactured in the
United States of America

Portions of chapter 1 have previously
appeared as "On Colonial Modernity:
Civilization versus Sovereignty in Cuba,
c. 1840" in *International Relations and
Non-Western Thought: Imperialism,
Colonialism, and Investigations of
Global Modernity.* Edited by Robbie
Shilliam. New York: Routledge, 2011.

*Library of Congress
Cataloging-in-Publication Data*

Aching, Gerard.
 Freedom from liberation : slavery, senti-
ment, and literature in Cuba / Gerard
Aching.
   pages cm. — (Blacks in the diaspora)
 Includes bibliographical references and
index.
 ISBN 978-0-253-01693-5 (cl : alk. paper) —
ISBN 978-0-253-01705-5 (eb) 1. Manzano,
Juan Francisco, 1797–1854. Autobiografia.
2. Slaves—Cuba—Biography. 3. Slavery
—Cuba—History—19th century. I. Title.
 HT1076.M2835 O15
 306.3'6209729109034—dc23

                                    2015006243

1 2 3 4 5   20 19 18 17 16 15

For Miguel Ángel

CONTENTS

ACKNOWLEDGMENTS

This book has been long in the coming, and for this reason I would like to express my gratitude to many people for the roles that they played in helping me to elaborate this project. I first began to think about *Freedom from Liberation* while I was still teaching at New York University, where, in the Department of Spanish and Portuguese, I enjoyed the intellectual camaraderie of fellow Caribbeanists Sibylle Fischer and Ana María Dopico. I am grateful for Sylvia Molloy's reading of Juan Francisco Manzano's autobiography, which is nothing short of seminal. I am, moreover, indebted to her mentoring at a time when the research and thinking that I undertook for the book represented an advance in my maturity as a scholar. If there were a conversation and a number of dialogues that I consider pivotal for leading me to the philosophical reflections that inform my understanding of Manzano's paradoxical statements about his enslavement, they would be those that I enjoyed with my NYU colleague and dear friend Gabriela Basterra, whose work continues to be a source of inspiration and whose friendship I value deeply. I would like to thank the John Simon Guggenheim Memorial Foundation for the fellowship that it awarded me, allowing me to plunge into researching the history and geopolitics of slavery in Cuba in the late eighteenth and first half of the nineteenth century, the activities of British abolitionism in and around the island, and the Creole reformist bourgeoisie's struggle to free literary writing from colonial censorship. The fellowship also gave me the opportunity to deepen my knowledge of Hegel's master-slave dialectic and some of its commentators, which I frequently read in conjunction with and against my own readings of Manzano's account of his life.

Even though I had completed most of the book by the time I started teaching at Cornell University, I would still like to thank colleagues in the Departments of Romance Studies and Comparative Literature and at the Africana Studies and Research Center for their welcome, collegiality, and dialogue. Among them, I extend a special thanks to Jonathan Culler, Debra Castillo, Kathleen Perry Long, Richard Klein, Cary Howie, Karen Pinkus, Tracy McNulty, Natalie Melas, Tomás and Mónica Beviá, Salah Hassan, Leslie Adelson, Grant Farred, Riché Richardson, Judith Byfield, Kavita Singh, Alex Lenoble, Gustavo Llarull, Cristina Hung, and Valeria Dani. I would also like to thank Caribbeanists and Latin Americanists at other institutions for their enthusiasm about my research for the book, including Aníbal González Pérez, Nathalie Bouzaglo, Guillermina de Ferrari, Emily Maguire, Odette Casamayor, Francisco J. Hernández Adrián, Lena Burgos, Tomás Urayoan Noel, Khalil Chaar, and Gustavo Furtado. My heartfelt gratitude to George Yudice, Gema Pérez Sánchez, Pam Hammons, Mona El Sherif, Patricia Saunders, and Donnette Francis for your friendship and support during the roughest of times. I thank my colleagues from the Department of Modern Languages at the University of Miami for their warm welcome and professionalism. I am particularly grateful to Arcadio Díaz Quiñones for his always intellectually rigorous and gracious engagement with this project and, especially, for his kind words of encouragement just when I needed them. I am grateful to Raina Polivka at Indiana University Press for her acute insights and recommendations and to Darja Malcolm-Clarke and Jenna Whittaker for keeping our publishing schedule on track.

To my dearest friends, both old and new, I express my deep gratitude for your patient listening, your steadfast support and affection, and, most of all, for being family. Thank you Cathy Lenfestey, Dana Cordeiro, Sheila McManus, Françoise Hayet, Cecelia Lawless, Pierre Sassone, Émile Sassone Lawless, Adèle Sassone Lawless, Ardele Lister, Todd Senzon, Gabriela Basterra, Edward Sullivan, Clayton Kirking, Almudena Rodríguez Huertas, José Luis Patiño, Pepe Reyes, Marcelo Pacheco, Sonia Velázquez, Hall Bjørnstad, Claudia Brodsky, and Kerry Quinn. For their friendship and timely questions about the book, I thank Troy Oechsner, Jeff Day, Hal Goodwin, and Carrie LaZarre.

For their unwavering love and support, I am immensely grateful to my parents, William and Ann Aching, my brother, Jeffrey, and my sister, Vanessa; to my other brother and sister, Clif and Cheryl; to my parents-in-law, Serafín Balsa Carrera and Joaquina Marín Fernández, and my brothers- and sisters-in-law, Tomás, Teresa, Nacho, Queta, Alejandro, and Josu; to my nephews, Ivan, Alejandro, Javier, and Miguel, and my niece, Lucía; to my other nephew, Luis Eduardo; and to my cousins, Coleen, Jenny, and Kimmy.

I dedicate this book to my husband, Miguel Ángel Balsa Marín, who supported my every endeavor with openness, intelligence, candor, and respect. I thank you for choosing to walk by my side through thick and thin, no matter what. You are beautiful through and through, and I am inexpressibly grateful for the time, life, and profound love that we shared.

FREEDOM FROM LIBERATION

Introduction

In choosing *Freedom from Liberation* for the title of this book, I examine ways in which individuals from the same society reflect on, desire, imagine, and strive for personal and collective freedoms. Because diverse strivings for freedom typically coincide and compete in the same place and time, rival struggles and the individuals who embody and articulate them engage in uneven competitions with one another. The thinking, debates, and literature about slavery that emerged in Cuba in the 1830s and '40s provide sufficient material to make the distinctions between interlocked yet competing struggles for freedom intelligible. This book will demonstrate that there were fundamental differences between how slaves, manumitted slaves, free blacks, masters, abolitionists, and local reformists of slavery thought about bondage and freedom during this period and that certain ways of thinking about freedom were more valued and promulgated than others.

Needless to say, "Freedom from Slavery" would have been an unequivocal title because it invokes the opposition between masters and slaves with which we are most familiar, but it would reveal only part of the story about freedom and bondage in Cuba at that time. By juxtaposing "freedom" and "liberation" in the first place, I aim to foreground the existence of competing notions of freedom as well as claim that enslavement does not represent the only threat to struggles for freedom. "Liberation," which refers to the action of being liberated, is not synonymous with the quality of enjoying or striving for freedom. I have chosen the book's title not only because it captures the inflections, nuances, and dynamics that are most relevant for my readings but also because "freedom from liberation"—that is, the quest to be free from an externally constituted definition, source, or act of liberation—distinguishes between the competing notions of freedom that I explore in this study. In the process of producing a language for subsequent forms of political activism and emancipation, the nineteenth-century history of Anglo-American liberalisms amply documents the extraction and uses of metaphors of bondage from accounts of the lived experiences and eyewitness observations of slavery. By contrast, Cuban reformists, who wanted to transform slavery on the island but not immediately end it, overwhelmingly employed such metaphors to express their struggles for degrees of political autonomy from Spain. My goals, therefore, are to bring to light notions of freedom that the Creole, reformist bourgeoisie formulated and to compare their ideas about freedom with others that slaves articulated or that were attributed to slaves in the literature of the period.[1]

The notion of freedom from liberation makes sense when we can begin to decipher how the *subject* who strives to enjoy a certain freedom is, at the same time, the *object* of a conception of freedom that an external agent determines and assigns. Consequently, the relations between slaves, reformists, and abolitionists cannot be understood simply as a dichotomy between freedom and enslavement but also need to be examined in light of the slaves' and the reformists' respective reflections on freedom, both on their own terms and in competition with one another. In this book, I examine the writings of Juan Francisco Manzano, an enslaved poet who had been cajoled into writing his autobiography while he was still a slave, and those of the group of Creole reformists for whom he initially wrote the autobiography. Manzano's autobiography, which is the only slave narrative that has thus far surfaced in the Spanish-speaking world, was immediately taken as a model for an autochthonous literary expression in the Creole reformists' struggle for greater but not necessarily complete autonomy from Madrid; it was later submitted as parliamentary evidence against the persistence of the slave trade in Cuba that the British Anti-Slavery Society required as it internationalized its movement. As such, it is evident that two liberationist agendas recruited Manzano's reflections on bondage and freedom in order to describe his position and prescribe theirs. Yet, do these appropriations of Manzano's writings negate his status as the subject of his own view of freedom? The answer to this question can be found in reading against the grain of these attempts at commandeering his predicament and voice for political projects that were not specifically his.

JUAN FRANCISCO MANZANO'S *AUTOBIOGRAFÍA DE UN ESCLAVO* AND CREOLE REFORMISTS

The slave narrative that inspired the reflections in this book is significant not merely because it is the only such account to have surfaced in the Spanish-speaking world to date but principally because of the kind of story that it tells. There may be close to two thousand slave narratives in the United States, but, thanks to the determination and intrigues to smuggle Manzano's *Autobiografía de un esclavo* (Autobiography of a Slave) out of Cuba, translate it, and have it delivered to the British Anti-Slavery Society in London, the description that the former slave and poet provides of his life in bondage exists as both an account of the experience of being enslaved in Cuba and a challenge to abolitionist notions of what a slave narrative ought to say. Manzano wrote the autobiography under peculiar circumstances and completed it in 1839, when he was around forty-two years old. Whereas Anglo-American abolitionist circles gave rise to a transatlantic readership and facilitated a network of venues where former slaves could read or narrate episodes from their lives to a rapt antislavery public, Manzano had no such outlet or audience for his autobiography in Cuba. The island was still a Spanish colony when he penned the account of his life and would remain so for almost another sixty years, and slavery would not be abolished there until 1886. Most significantly, the colonial government prohibited the public discussion of slavery and anticolonialism, which were intimately related throughout the nineteenth century, and censored even indirect or camouflaged allusions to both to the extent that it could perceive them in the press, academia, and other forums.[2] Unlike his poetry, which he had begun publishing as early as the 1820s and because of which he became a public figure in Havana despite his enslavement, Manzano's autobiographical writing would have been destined to move and remain in clandestine

circles had it not been for the fortuitous temporary alliance between
two influential men: a wealthy local patrician whose literary circle met
secretly at his mansion in order to discuss what the Cuban novel should
look like and slavery's role in it, and an Irish abolitionist who had been
stationed in Havana in order, among other things, to gather evidence
of the cruelty of Cuban slavery for the abolitionist cause in England.
Yet what is perhaps the most unusual circumstance of all for the writing
of Manzano's account of his life is the fact that the idea for the autobiography had not originated with him. It had been Domingo del Monte,
the local patrician who subsequently became the poet's protector and
mentor, who requested the autobiography in 1835, when Manzano was
still enslaved. Aware of del Monte's great wealth and influence, the poet
was in no position to ignore the patrician's request.

The letters that Manzano wrote to del Monte about the difficulty that
he experienced in writing the autobiography offer a sense of the challenges that the former faced in his efforts to furnish the patrician with
an account of his life. Poetry was the medium with which Manzano felt
most comfortable. As a child, he had displayed a gift of gab, a facility for
rhyming, and a prodigious memory for reciting poetry, sermons, and
speeches from Masses and plays that he attended as his mistress's page.
According to him, there came a point in his youth when he could no
longer recall all of the poems that he heard or composed, so he taught
himself to write by tracing his young master's handwriting late at night
after the household retired, using materials that he procured from the
tips that he saved. This secretly acquired skill allowed him to write down
his verses and thereby ease the burden of having to memorize every new
composition.

Writing an autobiography presented Manzano with new and complex
challenges. Unlike writers of slave narratives who were aware that abolitionist circles provided them with sympathetic readers, no discussion
between del Monte and Manzano seemed to have taken place about
who the latter's readers might be beyond the literary circle to which the
patrician introduced the poet. With respect to the autobiography's content—and fortunately for contemporary readers—Manzano was left to
his own devices. Even so, writing about his life stirred two important
anxieties. First, del Monte's request effectively obliged him to break one

of the most significant rules of thumb to which slaves adhered in order
to protect themselves, which was never to be overheard speaking ill of
their masters. In order to comply with del Monte's request, Manzano
would have needed to place sufficient faith in the patrician's ability to
shelter him from his last mistress, who, because he had run away from
her household, was still in a position to stake a claim on his freedom. It
will occasionally become evident that Cuba's insularity under colonial
rule played an important role in the experiences and dispositions of individuals that I describe in this book. For Manzano, there was no underground railroad north that would have delivered him from bondage, and,
given his extensive training since childhood as a domestic slave, he was
ill-prepared to survive as a runaway in some remote part of the island.
Second, and more significantly for his autobiographical writing, the poet
stated in his correspondence with del Monte that he had great difficulties
selecting which episodes of his life he should detail and claimed that he
had given up on writing the account on at least four occasions. The multiple fits and starts are not surprising. An abolitionist reader at the time
would have found the descriptions of some of the brutal treatment and
punishments that Manzano received at the hands of his enslavers and
their plantation managers useful, for such scenes furnished the movement with the documented evidence that it required in order to speak
on behalf of slaves in distant government halls. Yet, Manzano was also
attempting to relate another story, in which he wished to minimize and
censor the scenes of physical violence to which he had been subjugated
in favor of demonstrating his dignity as a human being who possessed
valuable skills. He insisted that the cruelties that he had suffered failed to
distort his spirit and the essence of who he was. In light of the abolitionist movement's practice of gathering reports of slavery's barbarisms—
reports that frequently limited the representation of slaves to helpless
victims—Manzano's eagerness to transcend bondage by means of the
very skills that he had acquired while he was enslaved is a story that
abolitionists seldom highlighted. What makes Manzano's autobiography
intriguing is precisely this effort to view the ways in which enslavement
impeded the development of his full potential as a skilled worker in an
economy that also relied on the many trades and services that the island's free black and mulatto population provided as they garnered the

economic resources, but not the political rights, of a petty bourgeoisie. In other words, as a slave narrative, Manzano's autobiography describes the worthiness of its writing subject to enjoy a freedom that would result not from open rebellion or abolition but from his status as a free and proficient laborer.

As a publicly recognized but enslaved poet in Havana, Manzano also acquired liberators. When del Monte introduced him to the literary circle that met clandestinely at his mansion, the enslaved poet's recitation of his sonnet "Treinta años" (Thirty years) so moved his listeners that they immediately began a collection among themselves and other members of the Creole reformist bourgeoisie to purchase his freedom. In order to make sense of this act of liberating Manzano, it is necessary to ask who these reformists were and why they valued literature and literary writing to the degree that they would meet for discussions of both in secret and at great risk to their social standing on the island. The answer to the first question is easier to provide at the outset. The Creole reformists constituted an influential minority within the larger and very wealthy Cuban bourgeoisie. The island's burgeoning sugar production and trade after the Haitian Revolution generated such affluence that the Creole bourgeoisie's wherewithal resembled that of similar classes in Europe, the United States, and other parts of the globe. However, what distinguished the Creole reformists from the broader Cuban bourgeoisie were their efforts to forge the political culture of an "enlightened," antislavery class that was also willing to critique (but not necessarily reject) their colonial status and to influence the fate of slavery on the island.

Reformists such as del Monte belonged to some of the island's wealthiest families, but this minority, whose members called themselves the "young liberals," sought to encourage the broader local bourgeoisie to examine and denounce the deleterious effects of slavery on slaveholders and on the future of their community. Nevertheless, unlike abolitionists, whose agenda included the abolition both of the slave trade and then of slavery, Cuba's Creole reformists were eager to rid the island of the commerce in slaves, which had been outlawed since the Anglo-Spanish treaty of 1817, and believed that they could do away with slavery in the long run by eliminating the trade and convincing Madrid to adopt a vigorous policy of white immigration.[3] Their notion of reform, therefore, included an analysis of their particular socioeconomic context and aimed at ending slavery on terms that would satisfy future demands for labor by transforming production from a reliance on African slaves to the use of white immigrant labor. A certain economic logic thus characterized Creole reform, but race and antiblack racism not only lay at the heart of some of the tensions between Madrid and the reformists on the question of slavery but featured prominently in the future that the reformists attempted to define for themselves.

In addition to reaping the economic benefits of keeping Cuba consistently supplied with African slaves, even if illicitly, Madrid and its colonial administrations knew full well that the island's Creole bourgeoisie would be hesitant to share political power with the black and mulatto population in an independent nation. Authorities successfully exploited the fear that Cuba might turn into another Haiti—that is, into another independent, black-ruled nation—as a way of dissuading the local bourgeoisie from entertaining any serious thought of striking out for political independence. Throughout the nineteenth century, the term *el peligro negro* (the black peril) was often employed to conjure this fear. Having lost most of its colonies in the first three decades of the nineteenth century to Creole insurrections and independence movements, Spain was determined to retain its last colonies and hold on to its status as a European empire. In the case of Cuba in the 1830s and beyond, Spanish ministers understood that maintaining a large supply of slaves on the island was tantamount to undermining the potential for Creole insurgency. This policy was not lost on the Creole reformist bourgeoisie, whose ideologues were among the first to recognize how any discussion of the island's political status and future hinged on the question of slavery. In other words, if Madrid employed slavery to maintain its hold on the island, the reformists saw the elimination of the slave trade as a first step toward an eventual whitening of the island that they associated with civilization, progress, and the potential for greater political autonomy. As far as successive colonial administrations were concerned, antislavery ideas invariably bred anticolonialism. Yet such were the reformists' evolving and ambivalent attitudes toward independence with a large black population on the island that they oscillated in the 1830s between two alternatives: Cuba's continued status as a Spanish colony, so long as

Madrid carried out economic reforms to liberalize the island's trade, or annexation to the United States as a slaveholding territory, which was an idea that the Creole bourgeoisie entertained then and up to the American Civil War and that several U.S. presidents genuinely considered.

Distinguishing themselves from Anglo-American abolitionists, whose goals they considered too radical and ruinous for the Cuban context, and from Creole slave owners who preferred the island's status as a Spanish, slaveholding colony, the Creole reformists, who were also slave owners, sought to provide themselves with a social space that would allow them to critique slavery and argue for its gradual elimination in favor of new labor sources and regimes. From a purely local, economic perspective, the reformists displayed foresight: technological advances in sugar production were demanding more laborers at a time when abolitionism, backed by British naval power, was making the acquisition of slaves more difficult and expensive; and the demand for the slaves' increased productivity on plantations—a goal that more often than not included negotiations between plantation managers and slaves about daily tasks—was already meeting with more frequent instances of unruliness, strife, and rebelliousness. As far as the Creole reformists were concerned, what lay at stake in their attempts to have their views heard on the island and in Madrid was the posterity of the greatest wealth-producing colony in the world at the time. Yet because slavery was central to Spain's colonial policy in Cuba, the reformists met with the unrelenting adversity of colonial officials and the members of the Creole bourgeoisie that supported them. Given the censorship of all public discussions of slavery, the reformists had no choice but to pursue their interests in secret. It also became evident that in order to make any headway with reform, they would need to recruit supporters from among the broader Creole bourgeoisie.

The instrument that the reformists chose in order to foster their class's assumption of a critical attitude toward slavery was didactic, literary narrative. Before del Monte formed his secret circle of writers, literary activities normally took place under the auspices of the Comisión Permanente de Literatura, the literary branch of the pro-Spanish Sociedad Económica or Sociedad Patriótica de Amigos del País. The Sociedad was an intellectual institution of French encyclopedist bent that viewed the educational and cultural advancement of the island in terms of its

agricultural and industrial progress. Through secret negotiations that
involved cohorts who had access to the royal court in Madrid, thereby
circumventing the colonial administration, del Monte and his fellow reformists received permission in 1834 to reconstitute the Comisión as the
autonomous Academia Literaria. Nevertheless, despite the reformists'
determined and, for some of them, hazardous efforts, the new Academy
was short-lived because it could not survive the dogged adversity that it
faced from powerful members of the Sociedad Económica and the colonial government. In a countermove, del Monte opened his home to the
reformists' discussions about what would constitute Cuban literature
and how they would go about creating it. One of the consequences of del
Monte's counsel and influence—he has been called Cuba's first literary
critic—and especially of the reformists' access to his important personal
library was the consensus that no such literature could be imagined
without including depictions of slavery and the island's slaves and free
colored population. Abolitionists often incorporated poems, Romantic
narrative, and essays when they denounced slavery in Parliament. When
it came to considering the uses of literature for their respective causes,
the reformists once again differed from the abolitionists, whose quest for
documented evidence of cruelty against slaves in the transatlantic world
from the late eighteenth century forward generated the view that slave
traders and owners could, despite the European financing of the trade,
be isolated and treated as the principal agents of slavery's inhumanity.
With the British, abolitionist bourgeoisie simultaneously serving as a
model of enlightened economic and moral progress in the Americas, the
reformists believed that only slavery and its adverse effects on the local
bourgeoisie prevented their class from fully joining the ranks of its ostensibly progressive European counterparts. However, unwilling to accept the immediate abolition of slavery, such as had been introduced in
the British West Indian colonies in 1833, the reformists aimed to recruit
the Creole bourgeoisie to their cause through the didactic use of sentiment in the narratives that they wrote. Cuba's first novels thus came
into being clandestinely through a discussion of slavery that was meant
to foster empathy for the slaves' conditions among a local bourgeoisie
whose experience of colonialism should theoretically have provided it
with an uncommon understanding of its slaves' plight.

THE STRATEGIC USES OF SENTIMENT

In an examination of the liberal spirit that arose in Western Europe
in the late eighteenth century and its tendency to be pulled in two di-
rections, appropriately connoted by the titles of two of Adam Smith's
books, namely, *The Theory of Moral Sentiments* (1759) and *The Wealth
of Nations* (1776), David Brion Davis begins his analysis with an observation about the use of metaphors of bondage in early Western literatures:
"The literature of Hellenistic and early Christian times is saturated with
the paradoxes of human bondage: man was a slave to sin or to his own
passions; his incapacity for virtuous self-government justified his external bondage; yet he might escape his internal slavery by becoming
the servant of universal reason—or of the Lord. Emancipation from
one form of slavery depended on the acceptance of a higher and more
righteous bondage."[4] Turning his attention to the specific paradox of human bondage in the late eighteenth century, he argues that even though
unresolved tensions existed between sympathetic benevolence and individual enterprise, both denounced slavery as an "intolerable obstacle
to human progress."[5] For heuristic purposes, Davis alludes to a "man
of sensibility," who assured himself that he was virtuous by alleviating
the suffering of innocent victims, and to an "economic man," who favored a society that not only permitted but also justified and fostered
individual self-interest. In the historian's view, progress beyond these
tensions followed a script to which many philanthropists and reformers
subscribed: first, slavery was morally unjustifiable, and, because slaves
could not be held responsible for their bondage, they came to represent
nature's innocence; second, this innocence had its psychological counterpart in the "natural and spontaneous impulses" of the man of feeling,
for it was his compassion that would invoke an analogous sentiment in
the slave, so that at the same time that the former found a tangible way
to recognize and be recognized for his benevolence, the slave "would be
lifted to a level of independent action and social obligation"; and, finally,
bonding in this manner would then produce a love capable of cleansing
the world of avarice and evil.[6]

Literary invocations of sentimental exchanges between abolitionists
and slaves along the lines that Davis mentions abundantly informed abo-

litionist advocacy. Examining the relationship between slavery and the Romantic imagination in the writings of Keats, Shelley, Coleridge, and Wordsworth, Debbie Lee employs the term "distanced imagination" to demonstrate how these Romantics defined the imagination not simply as "expansive" in a nationalist or imperialist sense but as the means through which the self could "identify with and *feel for* another human being."[7] Similarly, Ian Baucom argues that the imaginative leap by which abolitionists could become sympathetic observers of the sufferings of others through melancholy Romantic literature is crucial for understanding the "alternate, long, Atlantic genealogy of the witness."[8] According to him, the great physical distance between Britain and its colonies meant that not only were the imagination and literary writing instrumental for communicating eyewitness accounts of slavery and generating sympathy among abolitionists toward distant lives but also they registered the historical remaking of the human as a sympathetic observer and a key figure in the discourses of cosmopolitan humanitarianism and occidental modernity. Interrogating what sentiment demanded of the slave, Adam Lively asserts that what the abolitionists brought to the discussion of sensibility was the idea that blackness could be associated with "truth-telling," a practice whereby humans are "stripped of the conventions of culture and civilisation," and with "authenticity."[9] This authenticity, he goes on to argue, brought about a "sentimental view of the African slave" that, through the Christian evangelism of the period, "exalted victimhood to a state of masochistic nobility."[10] Indeed, the evangelical and political demand for the "truth" about slavery toward the end of the eighteenth century and the beginning of the nineteenth encouraged British abolitionists to seek reportable, empirical evidence of all kinds from multiple sources at home and throughout the Atlantic in order to bolster their moral arguments against slavery. In fact, it was partly in order to satisfy this demand that Manzano's autobiography and some of his poems were submitted to the British Anti-Slavery Society as much needed evidence of the cruelty of slavery in Cuba that the Society required for the internationalization of its cause.

"Sentiment" in this study refers to the way in which affect is employed in literary representations of exchanges between masters and slaves in order to say something about the contradictions that mediate their rela-

tions. With the rise of abolitionist and reformist philanthropic humanitarianism, the frequent and purposeful articulation of affect to negotiate
and specify intellectual and moral distancing from the horrors of chattel
slavery became germane to a charged field of self-representation in both
literary writing and Parliament. I want to argue that the abolitionist and
reformist insistence that sentiment be employed and emphasized in literature and testimonies in order to provide access to the "truth" about
slavery had less to do with discovering that slavery was cruel and inhu-
man than with the desire to calibrate the critical stances that their humanitarian and philanthropic efforts seemed to require. Consequently, I
take sentiment to designate strategies for creating empathy for the moral
justifications, shelters, and alibis that would explain an individual's actions or failure to act in the face of slavery's dehumanizing practices. By
contrast, I employ "sentimentalism" and "sentimental literature" about
slavery to refer to the conventions to which writers resorted in melancholy, moral complacency or as reprieve from the tasks of deliberating
their intellectual and moral positions regarding human bondage. What
come to the fore in the analysis of the prescriptive uses of sentiment in
antislavery literature are the idealized accounts of master-slave relations
that abolitionists and reformists provide and perform for their own as
well as external consumption. In their writings, sympathy, benevolence,
compassion, melancholy, and stoicism come into play as some of the
means that they employed to expose and denounce the asymmetries
and antagonisms that defined master-slave relations. These accounts
were neither intentionally feigned nor cynical, and there were abolitionists and reformists who were moved to act out of genuine humanitarian
concern. However, the degree of insistent attachment to a sentimental
idealization of the slave on the part of both groups illustrates the extent
to which "elevating" the enslaved subject to become the master's moral
equal or superior became a way for both groups to negotiate their respective distances from the moral quandaries of human bondage.

The proximity of the Creole reformists to their slaves is a fundamental feature that distinguishes them from abolitionists and the intellectual and moral distances from which the latter advocated their cause.
Both Lee and Baucom identify the role of the abolitionists' physical distances from slaves, respectively, in the development of an imagination

that could produce empathy for the slaves' conditions from afar and in the historical emergence of the sympathetic observer as a vicarious or "imaginative" witness in abolitionism and subsequent discourses of cosmopolitan humanitarianism.[11] However, the Creole reformists refused to assume the abstract, moral disinterestedness of abolitionist, philanthropic humanitarianism that physical distances from plantation life could afford because, as I show in chapter 1, the young liberals believed that slavery in the Spanish colony was ultimately responsible for enslaving them. As slave owners who lived on the island, not only did they have direct experience with and empirical knowledge of human bondage that positioned their critique of slavery in the realm of economic self-interest, thereby foreclosing temptations toward abstraction, but the reformists' view that they were the principal victims of a strict colonial policy on slavery encouraged them to attend first and foremost to liberating themselves from it before considering any argument for freeing their slaves. Despite this very significant difference between abolitionists and reformists, their literary didacticism nonetheless coincided on a common liberationist script: the idealized elevation of the slave to a subject who would be willing to accept, as Davis puts it, "a higher and more righteous bondage" and who would "be lifted to a level of independent actions and moral obligation." Del Monte's literary circle read Manzano's autobiography and employed it as a model for sentimental, stoic, and submissive slave protagonists in its members' experimental novels and narratives. Yet none of these writings show the slightest influence of the poet's attempt to describe himself as efficiently prepared since childhood to aspire to wage labor and the free, black, petty bourgeoisie. Rather, as I demonstrate in chapter 4, the circle's writers consistently create slave protagonists whose fate is not to liberate themselves but to act as vehicles for the moral education of the Creole bourgeoisie. As I develop more fully in the second half of this introduction, the distinction between the slave's idea of freedom and that which his liberators imagine for him or her captures the most significant aspect of the "freedom from liberation" that I employ as the title of this book.

Orlando Patterson's concept of "perverse intimacy" is useful for critiquing how masters impute certain notions of freedom to their slaves and how the slaves' desire for freedom can be recruited for "lofty" agen-

das that may not be their own. Viewing slavery first and foremost as a "relation of personal domination," the sociologist employs "perverse intimacy" to define the "bond" that resulted from the power that the master
wielded over the slave and the manner in which the latter was obliged to
live "through and for his master."[12] To live subjugated as such meant that
slavery produced occasions of forced or violent intimacy between masters and slaves that often turned the spaces and conditions of physical
and psychological oppression into mundane experiences. The intimacy
of this violence is no less perverse when competing privileged struggles
for freedom, such as that of the Creole reformists to liberate themselves
from the colony's strict policy on slavery, harness the slave's desire for
freedom for their cause. In other words, the young liberals rallied to purchase Manzano's freedom not simply because he was enslaved; had this
been the case, they would have emancipated other slaves as well, which
would have brought them closer to being abolitionists than reformists.
They freed Manzano because he was also a poet, which, in their estimation, made him more recognizably human and worthy of their attention
than if he had been only a slave. Liberating the poet not only constituted
an act of enlightened paternalism—which, at the time, would have been
considered a virtue—but it provided the Creole reformists with the occasion to define themselves as "men of feeling" who could distinguish
themselves as morally superior to the rest of their class. That del Monte's
literary circle should make use of Manzano's autobiography as a model
for novels and narratives that were meant to foster the moral reeducation
of Cuba's Creole bourgeoisie is further proof of the perverse intimacy
through which the young liberals conceived of the poet's freedom.

THE STRUGGLE FOR THE FREEDOM OF SELF-MASTERY

Most literary historians and critics concur that one of Manzano's most
salient reactions to his enslavement is melancholy, and his stated reflections on the subject in the text help to substantiate this claim. Yet it is
precisely this psychological engagement with his oppression as well as
the contradictory ways in which he appears attached to his enslavement
that render the account of his life worthy of reflection as a slave narrative. Manzano's autobiography plays a significant role in this book be-

cause I believe that a fair reading of his self-representation asks us to shift our understanding of the struggle for freedom away from an overemphasis on or sole understanding of freedom as the elimination of external coercion and toward an analysis of the internal grappling with forms of coercion that constitutes the struggle for self-mastery.[13] All struggles for freedom entail resistance to external forms of oppression and their internalization.[14] However, because unambiguous and transcendent acts of resistance against external oppression possess the power to rally individuals to a cause and can convert such acts into symbolic values for an emancipatory politics, less critical attention has been paid to the less heroic forms of resistance that most slaves practiced on a daily basis. In placing Manzano's autobiography at the center of my discussion about the struggle for freedom, I contend that unless we are able to decipher his resistance to enslavement—especially at those moments when he seems to act against his own self-interest—we risk falling into the trap of blaming the slave for his bondage.

An example of the overemphasis on freedom as only involving the struggle against external oppression can be found in Paul Gilroy's reading of Frederick Douglass's tussle with Mr. Covey, a "professor of religion" in the Methodist church to whom Douglass had been contracted for a year and who cultivated a reputation as a "nigger-breaker."[15] According to Douglass, the two-hour physical fight with Covey ended triumphantly for him because he evened the odds in this struggle between master and slave: neither lost the fight, but, significantly, Douglass was never punished for rebelling. The latter explains this outcome by suggesting that because Covey's reputation and income depended on his ability to "break" slaves, he could ill afford bad publicity. Nevertheless, Douglass describes this moment as a "turning point" that rekindled his desire for freedom: "I now resolved that, however long I might remain a slave in form, the day had passed forever when I could be a slave in fact. I did not hesitate to let it be known of me, that the white man who expected to succeed in whipping, must also succeed in killing me."[16] In the context of slavery's systemic assault on the lives and humanity of slaves, how could Douglass's resistance not be acknowledged for the courage that he demonstrated and, subsequently, for the clarity that the outcome gave to his convictions? How could his actions not serve to inspire slaves

and abolitionists alike? Douglass's ability to even the odds long enough
for him to acquire a new sense of himself is symbolically transcendent
in Gilroy's view because it allows the critic to posit the "turning point" as
an example of the slave's preference for death over enslavement, which
is Gilroy's reversal of a key premise in the master-slave dialectic that
G. W. F. Hegel formulates as an integral part of his theory of the subject in *Phenomenology of Spirit* (1807).[17] Moreover, Douglass's physical
struggle against enslavement plays an important symbolic role in how
Gilroy's influential concept of the Black Atlantic engages with the way
in which the Enlightenment had been thought.

Even though Douglass's narrative details his personal courage, the account also describes a crucial reason why many slaves did not strike out
for freedom in the North: "It is my opinion that thousands would escape
from slavery, who now remain, but for the strong cords of affection that
bind them to their friends. The thought of leaving my friends was decidedly the most painful thought with which I had to contend. The love
of them was my tender point, and shook my decision more than all things
else."[18] I do not think it arbitrary that Douglass should have contrasted
the desire to cast off human bondage and "the strong cords of affection"
that bound slaves to one another. Rather than mere objects of a legal
condition, what makes his friends and him complex subjects is their
heartrending internal quarrel about whether they should strike out for
freedom by escaping to the North. We are less familiar with viewing the
slaves' decision to remain faithful to the love of friends and family at the
cost of their freedom from legal enslavement—what Davis might have
described as an example of a "higher and more righteous bondage"—as
a powerful illustration, when consciously undertaken, of agency and
psychological relief.[19] Consequently, the refusal to escape slavery does
not amount to masochistic servility; nor is it reducible to absolute terror. Douglass does not criticize his friends' decision or perceived need
to stay on the plantation as signs of moral weakness or inferiority. On
the contrary, he dignifies the complexity and difficulty of deliberating
between remaining in or escaping from legal bondage by calling the
love for and of enslaved friends the "tender point" that most challenged
his desire to escape. In other words, Douglass acknowledges how such
personal deliberations transform the slave into a reflective subject of and

in the struggle to be free. He demonstrates how the "turning point" and the "tender point" vied for dominance in his bid for freedom.

In order to appreciate how Manzano's self-representation as a melancholy, autobiographical subject registers his grappling with bondage and what tender points inform this personal struggle, it is necessary to take stock of the meanings that we ascribe to the terms and figures of "master" and "slave." This proposition is not as self-evident as it sounds. In this book, I want to argue that in addition to reading for epic turning points—those liberating, cathartic instances of consciousness and transformation that radicalize enslaved subjects and place them on the difficult road to self-emancipation—we need to examine the tender points, as sentimental as these attachments might be, as equally pertinent to the struggle for self-emancipation. Even though we possess a long and venerable tradition of demonstrating how masters and slaves, understood as autonomous actors, are locked in unequal and mutually antagonistic relations, we have paid relatively much less attention to showing how the struggle for freedom is also a contest that takes place with and within the self. To claim that the effort to cast off bondage also entails a struggle for self-emancipation is an obvious enough maxim in the contemporary period. However, it can also be argued that the vulnerabilities that this personal struggle exposes compromise the conception of slavery (and other forms of human oppression) as a strictly external source and application of coercion. Representing the master or oppressor as the wholly autonomous embodiment of this coercion possesses the advantage of a certain kind of political expediency in which it is easier to denounce slavery by rallying against the master as the incarnation of evil than to acknowledge evidence of his humanity. By the same token, this expediency also applies to the corresponding conception of the slave as an absolutely subjugated and helpless victim. Both representations are inaccurate, for they dehumanize the master and slave in obvious and arguably counterproductive ways, but they functioned well historically for the kinds of abolitionist humanitarian politics that arose and developed at a distance and intellectual remove from the European empires' slaveholding colonies.

Acknowledging that the master-slave dialectic, which Hegel refines from the metaphor of bondage, represents an internal struggle for self-mastery is useful for shedding light on the challenges that Manzano and

Cuba's Creole reformist bourgeoisie faced in their respective efforts to liberate themselves from oppression. Davis argues that by providing the dialectic with "such a rich resonance of meanings," the model "could be applied to every form of physical and psychological domination" and that its application allows us to come to "all the subtle stratagems, passive as well as aggressive; to all the interpersonal knots and invisible webs of ensnarement which are so much of the psychopathology of our everyday lives that they have been apparent only to a few poets, novelists, and exceptionally perceptive psychiatrists."[20] Colonialism and slavery locked masters and slaves into antagonistic relations, and the psychological and social consequences that emerged from these relations tell us a great deal about self-consciousness under some of the most ruthless and stressful conditions that have ever been imposed on human beings. Reading for evidence of internal quarrels and struggles, such as moral dilemmas, paradoxical reactions and attachments in the face of subjugation, or reasons that individuals intimate (consciously or not) for failing to act in their own apparent interests, affords opportunities for exploring the challenges of self-emancipation for those who strive for freedom in spite of the limits that circumstances or, unconsciously, they themselves place on their ability to act. Examples of what Douglass called the tender point become more visible in an approach that evaluates oppression not only as an external coercive force but also as an internal grappling with that coercion. In order to facilitate my approach to the corpus of texts that I read, it is necessary to take a closer look at the use of the metaphor of bondage in Hegel's master-slave dialectic because of the weight that it holds not only for interrogating the psychological struggle against oppression, which is what most interests me about Manzano's autobiography, but also for interpreting the meaning of freedom and the emancipatory politics to which it can give rise.[21]

Hegel's recruitment of the terms "lord" and "bondsman" (or "master" and "slave" in today's usage) to describe how relations of power function in his theory of the subject stimulated a rich but ultimately irresolvable problem of representation and, thus, of interpretation.[22] His use of "lord" and "bondsman" produces a conundrum in which history and philosophy are simultaneously invoked through the metaphor of slavery yet estranged when commentators approach the philosopher's master-slave dialectic as a strict reference either to "real" masters and slaves or to an abstract theory of the subject that emphasizes the acquisition of self-consciousness as an internal struggle between competing forms of consciousness.[23] Hegel drew his inspiration for the master-slave dialectic from observable and hypothetical relations of power between lord and bondsman in order to describe and interrogate the rivalry between an initially independent (lord) and a dependent (bondsman) self-consciousness in his complex theory of the subject. He made use of these figures because they captured the essential meanings of domination and servitude that he required for readers who would have been thoroughly familiar with the power that the lord/master exercised over the bondsman/slave in European and Europe's colonial societies during his time. Yet the disciplinary rift that often emerges *grosso modo* between historical and philosophical approaches to the relationship between the lord and the bondsman in Hegel's theory is arguably a direct consequence of how scholars interpret his metaphorical use of the terms. Philosophers identify two schools of thought by distinguishing between an *ontogenetic* and a *phylogenetic* reading of the master-slave dialectic. An ontogenetic reading assumes that the description of the relationship between the lord and bondsman is *intrapersonal*; that is, the dialectic is viewed as an *inner* struggle between two rival forms of consciousness. Hence, philosophers who subscribe to ontogenetic readings are more interested in working through the abstractions in Hegel's account of consciousness than in historicizing it. In the spectrum of the dialectic's interpreters, ontogenetic readers are the least likely to suggest that lord and bondsman should be understood literally as references to real individuals. By contrast, a phylogenetic or *interpersonal* reading posits the lord and bondsman as individual subjects and has been useful as such for most scholars outside the field of continental philosophy. Needless to say, whether or not Hegel meant scholars to pursue a solely ontogenetic or phylogenetic reading of the master-slave dialectic is unknowable. Those philosophers who engage in ontogenetic interpretations of the dialectic believe that Hegel was primarily interested in expounding an analysis of self-consciousness and the subject that would have universal applicability; this view probably has something to do with the reason why, as Sibylle Fischer asserts, there seems to be a consensus among philosophers and Hegel scholars

that the dialectic is unrelated to modern slavery.[24] A phylogenetic reading of the master-slave dialectic—the interpretation that informs most
conceptions of the struggle for freedom today—presumes that "lord"
and "bondsman" invoke a world of historically verifiable figures, events,
and facts and implicitly acknowledges slavery's relevance to Hegel's elaboration of a theory of the subject.

When Gilroy refers to the physical fight between Douglass and Covey
as their being "locked together in the Hegelian impasse," he focuses on
a critical moment in a phylogenetic reading of the master-slave dialectic when this interpretation holds out great promise for imagining how
bringing an end to externally applied oppression defines the whole idea
of freedom.[25] The impasse to which Gilroy alludes describes a point of no
return in Hegel's theory that the philosopher calls the "life-and-death
struggle" or "trial by death." In readings that posit lord and bondsman as
individuals, this impasse represents the perilous but worthwhile chance
to invert or, at least, transform the power relations between both figures;
it is a utopian and, for this reason, inspirational moment for emancipatory politics and movements that culminates in a radical if not violent challenge to forms of oppression that is undertaken at the risk of
self-destruction. According to this narrative, the bondsman's challenge
emerges as a definitive response to the failure or refusal of the lord to
recognize him as an equal. As inspiring as this opportunity to challenge and eliminate oppression might be, as essential a precondition as
this opportunity is for self-emancipation, the slave's successful rebellion
against externally imposed oppression does not bring the struggle for
freedom to a close, nor can it be considered the sole definition of what
constitutes freedom. I would argue that mundane internal struggles to
resist slavery, such as those that Manzano describes in his autobiography,
are destined to remain invisible in narratives that privilege the subject's
purported ability to transcend the life-and-death struggle between lord
and bondsman permanently and completely unscathed. Any suggestion that the poet may be characterized as a willingly submissive slave
derives from this misreading or limited interpretation of the impasse in
the master-slave dialectic.

In his bid to supplement Hegel's theory by reconstructing the history of modernity "from the slaves' point of view," Gilroy prematurely

transforms the slave into a subject who prefers death to enslavement and thereby reverses an important premise in the philosopher's explanation of subjectivity.[26] According to Hegel, it is the opposite that is true of the bondsman: the lord identifies with death because it releases him from life's enslavement, whereas the bondsman attaches himself to life because of his fear of transience and death. More significantly, death and enslavement are not presented in the philosopher's theory as viable options before the life-and-death struggle ensues because bondage is the internally negotiated *outcome* of this trial by death. In other words, it is the bondsman's fear of death that obliges him to accept servitude as a way of resolving a struggle in which he and the lord are intent on destroying each other at the cost of their own existence. In a phylogenetic reading, this apparent acceptance of servitude sets off alarms because it suggests that the bondsman is willingly servile. However, it is crucial to recall that the bondsman's forced labor in Hegel's dialectic constitutes a precondition for his eventual triumph over the lord. "In his work," Alexandre Kojève succinctly writes, the slave "trans-forms things and trans-forms himself at the same time: he forms things and the World by transforming himself, by educating himself."[27] Because he dominates the bondsman by confining him to unmediated labor, which means that he can enjoy the fruits of the bondsman's work only vicariously, the lord shuts himself off from any experience and knowledge of subjugation and the necessary presence of these factors for stimulating the desire for greater self-consciousness and self-mastery.[28] For the philosopher, then, true self-consciousness is to be found in the bondsman. When Gilroy privileges the trial by death over the efforts at self-mastery that take place afterward, he limits the idea of freedom to the contingencies of the impasse and elides Hegel's major contribution to a theory of the subject.

What is provocative about Hegel's theory is not the life-and-death struggle per se. For even if we consider him a long-distance witness of sorts to the slave rebellion that ejected France from its most important overseas colony, we would only be saying that he refined his notion of the trial by death from an historical event that preceded his conception of the term. Rather, the philosopher's significant contribution in the master-slave dialectic is the idea that the conscious, relentless striving for greater self-consciousness and freedom does not begin until *after* this

trial by death or impasse has taken place. Therefore, it is no surprise that
the philosopher does not even employ the words "lord" and "bondsman"
in *Phenomenology of Spirit* until after that struggle has transpired; that is
to say, there is literally no "lord" nor "bondsman" in Hegel's theory prior
to this feud, which favors the view that the master-slave dialectic should
be read ontogenetically and that the philosopher turns to metaphor in
order to make the aftermath of the trial by death between two forms
of consciousness intelligible to his readers. My principal proposition in
this book is that deciphering, recognizing, and attending to the internalization of oppression is just as essential for defining freedom as the ability to identify and act against external adversaries. It is my contention
that if Manzano's account of his life should have any value for us today, it
would be because it asks us to interpret and evaluate the internal struggle
for self-mastery as a way of attenuating exclusively triumphant or heroic
definitions of freedom and as an opportunity for reading against perverse intimacies that marginalize the slave as a thinking subject of the
struggle for freedom in favor of the slave as an object in someone else's
notion of what it means to be free.

⌐⌐

The following chapters provide an account of a slave's autobiography
and a literary circle's narratives when and where writing about slavery in
any fashion meant that lives and livelihoods would be placed in jeopardy.
Each chapter describes how this writing arises, not only as an urgent
desire to transcend unbearable limits on specific freedoms (such as the
freedom of movement or of expression), but also as a record of the inequality of the relations between the subjects and objects of abolitionist
and reformist emancipatory politics. I have attempted to throw light
on how all the actors in this charged milieu (the reformist bourgeoisie,
Manzano, the members of del Monte's literary circle, and Manzano's
abolitionist translator) imagined themselves as protagonists in their
respective bids for transcendence, self-realization, and empathy. I also
examine the consequences of their efforts at self-mastery for others. This
book would not have been possible without the scholarship of historians
and literary historians who not only provide us with archival research
but also engage with some of the complex problems of writing about

historical slavery. Nor would my readings of this literature have been enhanced without the reflections of particular philosophers, political theorists, and literary critics on freedom and its limits. A host of scholars on slavery in the Caribbean, particularly in Haiti and Cuba, and in the Atlantic world has paved the way for this study and facilitated both my examination of Manzano's autobiography in light of a model of slave narrative writing, such as Frederick Douglass's, and my comparative analysis of the politics and agendas of abolitionists and reformists throughout the study. However, there lies at the heart of this book an inquiry into the contexts, contingencies, perils, and daring of writing against slavery in a censored colonial environment—an inquiry that ultimately demonstrates how the struggle to be free of oppression is both a competition with rival bids for freedom and an unavoidable struggle for self-mastery.

In addition to providing historical contextualization for the study, the first chapter examines the Creole reformist bourgeoisie's conviction that slavery enslaved them in such a way that they could not respond adequately to the call for universal freedom and rights. Drawing from the scholarship of historians such as David Brion Davis, Manuel Moreno Fraginals, and David Murray, as well as archival material, the chapter describes the unstable relationship in the world's wealthiest colony at the time between liberalism's speculative discourses of freedom, on the one hand, and opportunities for greater economic liberalism that the local bourgeoisie attempted to secure from Madrid, on the other. The chapter shows how the clandestine struggle against colonial censorship to write about slavery emerged as a medium for articulating the reformists' dilemmas and ends with an analysis of Manzano's recitation of the poem that inspired the "young liberals" who frequented del Monte's literary circle to purchase his freedom. I examine this recitation as a point of empathetic exchange between the articulation of a slave's experience of bondage and the sentiments that the Creole reformists required in order to define themselves as an enlightened class of bourgeois "men of feeling."

On the basis of a close reading of Manzano's autobiography, chapter 2 analyzes the difficulty of writing an autobiography while still enslaved and makes a case for reading aspects from the former slave's account of his life as instances of unconscious resistance or the desire to transcend his bondage in seemingly counterproductive ways. Employing elements of Hegel's master-slave dialectic, Freud's "Mourning and Melancholy," Judith Butler's *The Psychic Life of Power,* and Gabriela Basterra's *Seductions of Fate,* the chapter interrogates Manzano's references to his melancholy and, in particular, to two occasions when he expresses affection for his enslavers. By comparison with the polished, inspiring narratives of Douglass and Equiano, or the transcription of Mary Prince's account of her life, which were texts that honed their messages to sympathizers with every new edition, Manzano wrote his autobiography without the aid of abolitionists or models for his writing or even a clear understanding of who his readers might eventually be. Given the absence of an organized abolitionist movement in Spain and Spanish America, the result was a rough-hewn, paradoxical, and all the more intriguing autobiography that articulates a subjectivity and master-slave relations that were often antithetical to the abolitionists' thinking and overseas strategies at the time, yet, unbeknown to Manzano, appropriate and timely as a model or source of inspiration for the writing of Cuba's first novels.

Richard Robert Madden's translation of Manzano's autobiography and poems into English is the subject of the third chapter. The Irish abolitionist, who testified in the famous *Amistad* case in the United States, was sent on a mission to Havana in order to gather evidence for the internationalization of the British antislavery cause. Among the documents that he submitted to Parliament and to the first human rights convention in 1840 were his own translations of Manzano's writings. Approaching Madden's translations from aspects of Walter Benjamin's seminal essay, "The Task of the Translator," the chapter examines decisions that the abolitionist took about the translatability of the poet's texts (especially in light of his treatment of Manzano's writings as parliamentary evidence) and the degree of freedom or fidelity to the original documents that he practiced in his translations. An examination of Madden's mission reveals the abolitionist's difficulty in coming to terms with the fact that he was no longer a distant, imaginative witness of slavery nor entirely impervious to being wooed into moral complacency by the seductive lifestyle of his wealthy Creole hosts. Even though Madden claimed to translate Manzano's autobiography literally and his poems liberally, the translations demonstrate the consistency with which generating empathy for the slave as an abstraction within an abolitionist readership took precedence over the former slave's subtler self-representation.

In chapter 4, I analyze the del Monte literary circle's writings as properly reformist antislavery literature. The abolitionists and reformists both valued didactic literature, but, in contrast to the former's emphasis on employing sentiment and philanthropy in order to promote the emancipation of slaves, the reformists placed greater emphasis on denouncing slavery for the ways in which it undermined the moral and political development of Cuba's Creole bourgeoisie. I argue that the disjunction between the voice and body of the enslaved protagonist in the narratives exposes the reformist bourgeoisie's failure to imagine the equality of whites and blacks in a single polity and demonstrates the desire of the Creole bourgeoisie as a whole to remain attached to fictions of the submissive slave at a time when there were growing indications that their slaves were claiming their right to freedom by either legal means or rebellion. I show that the enslaved protagonists in Félix Tanco y Bosmeniel's *Petrona y Rosalía*, Anselmo Suárez y Romero's *Francisco, el ingenio o las delicias del campo* (Francisco, the sugar mill or the delights of the countryside), and—even though she did not belong to del Monte's group, she contributed to this literary ferment—Gertrudis Gómez de Avellaneda's *Sab* embody the reformist bourgeoisie's critique of the contingent relationship between slavery and colonialism on the island just prior to the crisis of power that the colonial authorities preempted and resolved through the brutal oppression of the community of free blacks (to which Manzano eventually belonged) that has come to be known as the Escalera conspiracy. In this literature, the tension between the economically questionable but politically acceptable expendability of the slave protagonists' bodies anticipates this crisis, even as its writers failed to appreciate the extent to which it was the bodies of the free blacks and mulattoes who had begun to constitute a petty bourgeoisie that would receive the brunt of the violent colonial assault.

Overall, this study identifies two principal areas of inquiry and theoretical reflection that I elaborate in the epilogue. This book corroborates the philosophical tenets that freedom is not absolute, that it can be nei-

ther conceived nor practiced in isolation from others, and that, for this
reason, it is subject to both external pressures and internal compromises.
In light of the contexts of the autobiographical and literary writings that
I examine, the epilogue offers a final reflection on the subject of freedom
from the perspective of abolitionist and reformist, humanitarian emancipation as well as a proposition for evaluating the struggle for freedom
from within slavery. With respect to the first reflection, I investigate the
meanings and consequences of the physical, moral, and psychological
distances that separate emancipators from slaves (or, from a contemporary angle, humanitarians from the victims of injustice). Regarding the
latter, I reflect on Manzano's struggle for freedom from within slavery
as a valuable way to understand enslavement that nonetheless does not
lend itself to easy political appropriation.

ONE

Liberalisms at Odds

Slavery and the Struggle for an
Autochthonous Literature

In a letter that they wrote from New York on September 12, 1834, to the Creole patrician and liberal reformist Domingo del Monte and his cohorts, the Cuban exiles Félix Varela (del Monte's former philosophy professor and a priest) and Tomás Gener (a wealthy Catalonian plantation owner from Matanzas) strongly advised their colleagues against translating and publishing Charles Comte's *Traité de legislation*.[1] Comte, a respected law professor and permanent secretary of L'Académie des Sciences Morales et Politiques in Paris, published his treatise in 1826 on the natural and moral laws that determine the conditions and potential for the advancement of diverse peoples across the globe. Del Monte probably became familiar with some of the volumes from the treatise at the gatherings of Cuban intellectuals around Varela and José Antonio Saco, the most renowned of this group, in New York and Philadelphia in 1829. Apart from Comte's assertion that warm climates do not produce the effects on people that have been attributed to them and that the inhabitants of cold countries are generally no freer, no more active, nor more virtuous than those from warm countries, the most important section of the study for del Monte and his colleagues was the last book of the treatise, which tackles the subject of slavery. According to Varela's and Gener's letter, the idea behind translating Comte's study for Cuban readers was to bring the discussion of slavery into the open in order to educate public opinion and gain support for abolishing the slave trade. Writing about slavery in Cuba, especially during Captain-General Miguel Tacón's administration (1834–38), was practically outlawed.[2] Under such circumstances, it was necessary to articulate criticism indirectly, and even then with due caution. Leading intellectuals, such as Cuba's foremost poet, José María Heredia, and Saco, had been exiled because they dared to execute frontal attacks on Spanish imperialism and the slave trade. Hence, the translation of Comte's study was intended to bring about a change in public opinion about the slave trade employing an oblique approach through intellectual forums and discussion.

The importance of Varela's and Gener's letter lies in the clarity with which it points out the dilemma in which the Creole reformist bourgeoisie found itself at that time. In arguing against making Comte's study available to readers in Cuba, both men listed the reasons why the translation, instead of aiding the reformists' cause, would end up strengthening the arguments of those who wanted the slave trade to continue: the translation, they thought, would be censored; if not, any discussion of the extension of freedoms for whites would set a dangerous precedent for blacks and the free colored. The text, as a result, risked being considered incendiary, and, given the high regard that most Cuban Creoles had for their learning, fine manners, and well-being, Comte's view that the education of whites would be deficient so long as they were raised among slaves would be regarded as insulting and undeserved. Varela and Gener subsequently juxtaposed two statements that capture the Creole reformists' dilemmas about freedom and its limits and their concern about being misunderstood because, even though they belonged to the powerful local bourgeoisie, they rejected abolitionism. In the first of these, they maintained that "in many places, it is openly said that it is an injustice to claim freedom for whites and deny it to blacks," and, in the second, they asserted that in Cuba "the blacks' enslavement is the cause of the whites' enslavement. The people know it all too well, and the government knows it all too well."[3] I would like to take a closer look at Varela's and Gener's reference to the inequality of freedom for whites and blacks and illustrate the manner in which both statements are related, for the purpose of bridging what appears to be a gap between a broad ethical debate about the universal rights of man and the local stance within a colonial framework from which these reformists viewed and assimilated the debate. This explanation provides the context for my principal goal in this chapter, which is to show how del Monte's and his fellow reformists' efforts to emancipate local literary writing from colonial censorship constituted a response to the apparent incompatibility of two forms of liberalism that informed their class and its political aspirations—an incompatibility for which the reformists were partly responsible despite their remonstrance to the contrary.

This chapter's contextualization of the Creole reformist bourgeoisie's attitude toward chattel slavery challenges Hegel's claim in his introduction to *The Philosophy of History* that "what takes place in America is but an emanation from Europe."[4] The philosopher's statement fails to account for the ways in which the Americas, beginning as early as the sixteenth century, were regulated by a colonial jurisdiction that often contradicted legal and moral positions that European nations upheld for themselves on the other side of the Atlantic. According to Ian Baucom, the New World was "early occidental modernity's exemplary *space* of exception," which means that countervailing local circumstances, such as Varela's and Gener's suggestion that colonial subjugation complicated and impeded their readiness to subscribe to European abolitionist humanitarianism, were not just common but paradigmatic experiences in the western hemisphere.[5] Abolitionist humanitarianism—with its reliance on the ability of the abolitionists to become what Baucom calls "sympathetic observers" and, through the writing and reading of Romantic melancholy literature, vicarious "witnesses" to the sufferings of slaves from a distance—did not "emanate" from Europe and spread unchallenged throughout the hemisphere. Such concern and sentiment for the welfare of enslaved others emerged from the philosophical side of the Atlantic's culture of speculation; and even though this humanitarianism worked in conjunction with its speculative financial counterpart (economic liberalism), these liberalisms became highly incongruent for the Spanish colony's economically powerful Creole bourgeoisie in ways that stymied their ability to act decisively on the political front. Rafael Rojas argues that Cuban political culture in the nineteenth century was polarized between a fusion of economic liberalism and a national project founded on the technological modernization of agriculture, on one side, and the development of a theological and philosophical moral discourse—led by intellectuals like Varela—on the other.[6] Under these circumstances, the most radical elements of the local bourgeoisie chose

reform over cosmopolitan abolitionist humanitarianism. The first section of this chapter provides an account of how the Creole reformists,
who, in perceiving themselves to be enslaved by slavery, attempted to define their stances vis-à-vis two forms of related liberalisms. I explore the
way in which Varela and Gener imply that the Creole bourgeoisie could
not approach the universal and abstract dimensions of the debate about
freedom without first attending to the local implications of this debate.

The chapter's second section examines how the uncensored literary
reading, writing, and sentiments that Domingo del Monte failed to foment in a public institution but eventually encouraged in the literary
circle of reformists that met at his home provided the circle's members
with an opportunity to imagine and produce a literature that would praise
their local way of life and illustrate the difficulties of living under colonial rule. The literary, in other words, became the means by which the
reformists sought to reconcile both liberalisms for their own immediate context. Because the circle's activities took place in private, almost
clandestine, retreat from the colony's antagonistic political life and the
scrutiny of the reformists' powerful enemies in the colonial government,
the documentation to which we have access describing the discussions
that took place in del Monte's salon is scarce and can mostly be found
scattered piecemeal in the correspondence that the patrician received
from roughly 1834 to 1840 and that was posthumously collected. Nevertheless, these sources are adequate to form an idea of the Creole reformists' writing practices within and outside the literary circle; del Monte's
influence on the reading and writing that took place in their gatherings;
the circle's interest in and debate about literary Romanticism; and, last
but not least, the uncomfortable exchange between del Monte and the
young writer Anselmo Suárez y Romero concerning the kind of speech
that best suited the slave protagonist in the latter's novel. Despite the relative freedom that some of these activities granted the circle's members,
the stoicism that characterized the slave protagonists and characters in
their writings are related to the besieged political situation in which the
circle and the Creole reformist bourgeoisie found themselves.

In the chapter's final section, I describe the circumstances in which
del Monte introduced Juan Francisco Manzano to the members of his
literary circle and interrogate the resonances that the poem that the

enslaved poet recited there might have had for the gathering's members. Manzano, whose poetic voice del Monte must have considered appropriate for the occasion, recites his sonnet in a context in which the "eloquent complaint" was one of the most effective ways of appealing for justice under the slave code at that time.[7] The purpose of this exploration is to examine this event as an opportunity for mutual recognition and the fostering of empathy between a legally enslaved subject and a room of slaveholders, who also prided themselves on being what David Brion Davis might have called "men of feeling." In this last section, I show how the sonnet that Manzano recited for the members of the circle provides a bridge to the abstract dimensions of the debate about universal rights for all men.

COLONIAL LIBERALISMS

What were the two forms of liberalism that became dangerously incompatible for the Creole reformist bourgeoisie in Cuba? One of these liberalisms is informed by the modern discourse on the universal extension of rights, fruit of the emancipatory project of Enlightenment philosophies. By the 1830s, slavery was the subject of ongoing philosophical and legal deliberations among the political, commercial, religious, and intellectual elite of the Western world and was frequently understood as incongruous with the extension of these rights. The other liberalism emerges conjointly as the promulgation of strategies for liberalizing trade that is known as economic liberalism. Because of Cuba's rapid increase in sugar production after the Haitian Revolution, Spain alone could not absorb the island's economic boom, and the Cuban bourgeoisie looked increasingly toward establishing commercial ties with Britain, the United States, and France. Slavery was also a crucial issue with respect to economic liberalism in Cuba because not only did this regime of forced labor generate spectacular profits; according to Manuel Moreno Fraginals, the traffic in slaves was a commercial activity in which segments of the bourgeoisie had acquired extensive experience in important aspects of free trade.[8]

The social sustainability of the incongruities between these liberalisms constituted an important internal debate in modern nations at the time. The reformists, who were members of the Creole bourgeoisie that came on the scene because of Cuba's special trading status with nations outside of Spain, attempted to regulate this incompatibility to their advantage and sought to create a community based on a particular cultural notion of "civilized" but stateless nationhood. The reformists' eventual failure to manage the incompatibility between these liberalisms cannot be blamed entirely on their class and political persuasions: the ability of the island's Creole political, economic, and intellectual leadership to address the contradiction between both liberalisms in Cuba was rigorously circumscribed. However, it was also the idea of a unique local community that the Creole reformists eventually entertained—one that, as far as they were concerned, was negatively influenced by the proximity of a black republic in neighboring Haiti and the presence of a large black and mulatto population in their midst—that reproduced some of the incongruities that they sought to resolve. In order to approach the local incompatibility between these liberalisms, I would like to begin with the "universal" dimension of this issue of injustice and work toward Varela's and Gener's allusion to slavery's enslavement of whites in Cuba.

In the introduction, I alluded to Susan Buck-Morss's argument that slavery was more than a mere metaphor for Hegel, who kept abreast of the Haitian Revolution at the same time that he was writing *Phenomenology of Spirit*. Yet this call for the historicizing of philosophical ideas already represents an advance on views that tend to restate the Enlightenment's internal contradictions without providing a way to explain them. For example, in an extensively researched book, Adam Hochschild's *Bury the Chains*, one reads the following:

> The 1700s were, of course, the century of Enlightenment, the upwelling of ideas about human rights that eventually led to the American and French revolutions, expanded suffrage, and much more. Yet surprisingly few people saw a contradiction between freedom for whites and bondage for slaves. The British Parliament had never debated the morality of slavery or the slave trade. The philosopher John Locke, whose ideas about governments arising from the consent of the governed had done so much to lay the foundation for this century of revolutions, invested $600 in the Royal African Company, whose RAC brand was seared onto the breasts of thousands of slaves. In France, Voltaire mocked slaveholders in *Candide* and other works, yet when a leading French slave ship owner offered to name a vessel after him, he accepted with pleasure.[9]

Even though these facts are verifiable and their delivery well-intentioned, their arrangement as oppositions between historical figures—cast as wholly and consciously representative of liberal democratic thought— and their simultaneous involvement in some of slavery's brutal practices does not facilitate access to the motivations and forces that led to these apparent paradoxes. Presented in this manner, these paradoxes are misleading not simply because their selective juxtaposition sensationalizes the facts but mostly because the ethical questions that they are meant to raise get constituted as unwieldy oppositions between the material reality of chattel slavery and uncomplicated figures that stand in for the Enlightenment's ideals and epistemologies. Hochschild is interested in highlighting the frequency with which some of these important thinkers were apparently blind to the ways in which they participated in slavery, but he develops no hypothesis about the nature of this "blindness." Somewhere in this approach to the paradoxical coincidence of Enlightenment thought and the material reality of slavery lies the notion that these formidable thinkers possessed the intelligence to know better, or at least to avoid succumbing to the most hegemonic immoral institutions of their time. As this line of argument implies, these men fell from the lofty heights of their lucidity: how could their wisdom not have saved them from the pitfalls of this moral hypocrisy? According to Mary Nyquist, Locke's rejection of what she calls political slavery—in my study the analogy would be the reformists' critique of colonialism—at the same time that he defends the slaveholder's right to own slaves provides evidence of "antityrannicism's plasticity."[10]

A more compelling approach to the injustices to which Varela and Gener refer is Davis's argument that even though there was nothing new about New World slavery in the 1760s, what was unprecedented about this and the following decade was a shift in moral consciousness that affected "the ways in which Western culture had organized man's experience with lordship and bondage."[11] According to the historian, four interrelated developments in Western culture were responsible for this transformation, especially in the area of British Protestantism. They include the emergence of secular social philosophy, which sought to redefine human bondage for a modern rational world; the spread of an ethic of benevolence that the "man of feeling" came to personify; the growing importance of instantaneous conversion in evangelicalism; and a change in attitude toward the Negro's cultural difference among eighteenth-century "primitivists," who, in the travel accounts and descriptions of exotic lands that they read about and wrote, attempted to illustrate that man's virtue and creativity were inherent.[12] However, even as this shift in moral consciousness was under way, countervailing forces and activities were also at work. Assessing the whole, Davis avers that even as slavery always represented a moral contradiction, mainly because of the long Western tradition of arguments against the objectification of humans, moralists and social theorists found ways to rationalize the contradiction in their ethical systems.[13]

As Varela and Gener perceived it, what Davis calls a shift in moral consciousness regarding the relationship between lordship and bondage could be found "in many places" and not in Britain and Protestant spheres alone. Britain's power and influence extended across the seas not only in military and economic terms—on this score in Cuba alone, the British seized Havana in 1762 and occupied it for a year—but also in a wide range of social spheres. Davis affirms that in Cuba and the urban areas of Brazil at the start of the nineteenth century, there was a growing bourgeoisie that considered England "a model of economic and moral progress" and looked for ways to incorporate its form of commercial liberalism.[14] At the same time, progressive thinkers within this emerging class admired Britain's campaign against the slave trade and slavery and began distancing themselves from the more traditional planter oligarchies who, not surprisingly, considered abolitionism a foreign import and menace.[15] It should not be assumed, however, that abolitionism's moral imperatives (and the ways in which they facilitated local class constructions and divisions) constituted the major part of Britain's influence in Cuba at this time. Even after the abolition of slavery throughout the British Empire in 1834, Britain's commercial interests in Cuba were still powerful enough to come into open conflict with the abolitionists' humanitarian goals, especially on the issue of the contraband slave trade on the island.[16] In addition to this fact that Britain was identifiable with abolitionism as well as with British commercial interests in Cuba that continued to ply the slave trade, there was another more significant factor that skewed and compromised the broader "universal" debate about slavery for the island's Creole reformists.

Freedom for whites and enslavement for blacks did not begin and end as a solely racial problem. The injustice that gave rise to this difference in social positions was for all intents and purposes lawful: legal codes defined slaves as property, and property within commercial and economic liberalism constituted the very foundation of liberty. Naturally, this idea of proprietorship "obscured the conflict between human rights and property rights."[17] Hence, not only was this contradiction, which I have been tracing, a major obstacle for abolitionists in Europe and the United States who needed to come up with a way of separating slaves from the category of "property" while retaining the latter's sanctity for the bourgeoisie, it was also a dilemma that Cuba's Creole reformists experienced directly, especially in the 1830s and '40s, when they were purposefully barred from approaching the subject in any official capacity. Cuba, at the risk of reiterating the obvious, was a colony, which meant that, unlike abolitionists in Britain, France, and the United States, who deliberated about slavery within the halls of their own governmental institutions, both sides on the slave trade question in Cuba still confronted the added complication of getting their views aired in Madrid. In other words, the island's position as a slave-holding colony in which the immoral practices of chattel slavery were legally sanctioned and imposed meant that the question of freedom for whites and slavery for blacks could not be discussed as a purely abstract question of the universal extension of rights. Gener indicated as much to del Monte in a letter that he wrote to him from New York on May 11, 1832, in which he stated that it would not be enough to point out the slave trade's depravity nor the abyss to which it was leading the island because "no-one feels dishonored by a crime that everyone or almost everyone commits, nor is anyone alarmed or startled by dangers that no-one sees or wants to see."[18] Slavery in Cuba was a much more "universal" experience than the freedom to discuss it openly.

Yet Cuba was no ordinary colony. After the Haitian Revolution, the island's expanded sugar production turned it into the world's most important wealth-producing colony. Unlike the British and French West Indies, where sugar manufacturing was imported and then exploited by mostly absentee landowners, the sugar industry in Cuba originated and developed on the island, thereby creating an affluent bourgeoisie with considerable influence in the Spanish royal court and government. Given the fact that its Caribbean possessions and the Philippines were its last sources of overseas wealth during economic crises in the 1830s and beyond, Spain was reluctant to abolish the slave trade even though the British government had been consistently pressuring it to do so since the Anglo-Spanish treaty of 1817. Madrid was in the delicate situation of needing British loans to help it to overcome its economic crises, especially during the Napoleonic wars and the Spanish-American wars of independence, at the same time that the government could not afford to anger Cuban sugar plantation owners because they generated one of Spain's most significant sources of income. Before the American Civil War, Cuban planters frequently articulated their anger at Madrid for negotiating with London over the slave trade and the abolition of slavery as veiled threats of annexation to the United States. By 1848, José Antonio Saco could still write that if Spain did not want Cubans to fix their gaze on the "radiant stars of the United States' constellation" it should make "freedom's sun" shine on Cuba.[19] In any case, so economically powerful did the Cuban sugar-producing bourgeoisie become by the 1830s that it achieved particular reforms and concessions from Spain that Moreno Fraginals refers to as its "maximum legal conquest": the absolute censure of any governmental interference in the administration and creation of private wealth on the island.[20] Needless to say, this legal triumph also represents the local version of the obscured conflict between property and human rights that Davis cites as one of the greatest challenges that British abolitionists faced on the home front as well as abroad.

It would appear, then, that these achievements and concessions from Madrid facilitated the appropriate conditions for generating wealth on the island through trade liberalization and, by extension, for creating and developing a dynamic entrepreneurial class. There were definite indications that such conditions were in place: the sugar industry's technical needs and advances meant that its machinery and manufactured goods were increasingly being imported from British and American firms; the island was ready to build a railway line (the first in Latin America) for the transportation of sugar even before the railroad was introduced in Spain;[21] and Cuba's markets for rum and nonwhite sugar expanded beyond the metropolis to include Britain, France, and the United States—its products, in other words, were destined for the world market. In fact, free trade, in the specific form of the free commercial movement of slaves, became institutionalized in Cuba around 1792 because the British and American monopolization of the supply of slaves from Africa and other parts of the Americas obliged Spanish traders, who held the monopoly of supplying the island with slaves, to purchase them from these countries' merchants.[22] Not surprisingly, the bourgeoisie that emerged in these conditions resembled its European and American counterparts. For example, the Alfonso-Aldama-Madan clan into which del Monte married took full advantage of the sugar boom during the first four decades of the nineteenth century and became one of the island's wealthiest families. By 1860, this family's third generation had diversified its economic ties and interests; not only did it own forty sugar plantations with no less than 15,000 slaves, but it also possessed ten titles of nobility and married into wealthy European families, including the Bourbon royal house in Spain.[23] The wealth that they moved and their simultaneous leadership of the humanitarian effort against the traffic in slaves were analogous to the wherewithal of the Quaker businessmen in London, whose antislavery committee meetings took place after the Royal Exchange closed at the end of every business day.[24] In outlook and attitude, del Monte's family and similar clans acted like the bourgeoisie from other parts of world.

However, it was Cuba's status as a colony that hindered the formation of a more politically and economically autonomous, local bourgeoisie. The Cuban sugar plantation proprietor, as Moreno Fraginals consistently asserts in *El ingenio,* was not entirely bourgeois because he had one foot in a bourgeois future and the other in a distant slaveholding past.[25] Perhaps one of the first major socioeconomic setbacks that this emerging class experienced, "with its soaring bourgeois consciousness and its clipped wings," was the suppression of its endeavors to found Spanish America's first university chair in political economy in 1818.[26] The historian describes the local bourgeoisie's disillusionment at not being able to teach modern economics in the region in these terms: "Not being able to teach the true economics of the period in it demonstrates the terrible frustration of a class that tried but could not be bourgeois."[27] This initiative was undoubtedly forward-looking, if one considers that the first chair of political economy at an English university was established at Oxford in 1825.[28] This repressive economic policy and the Creole bourgeoisie's insistence on expanding free trade led to the steady erosion of colonial economic ties between Spain and Cuba. The economic and political situation in the metropolis was in part responsible for this deterioration. Rather than increase its manufacturing capacity for the raw materials that it received from its colonies, Spain mostly became a conduit for these commodities to other destinations in Europe in exchange for manufactured goods for itself and its colonies; this relationship created complex interdependencies that worsened as Cuba's sugar manufacturing volume grew and its sugar producers looked for more and larger markets for its products.[29] On the political front, the inability to resolve these structural economic problems (throughout the nineteenth century) and the further tightening of Fernando VII's absolutism domestically and in the colonies caused Spain to shift from its role as an economic metropolis and move toward a politico-military model of colonial rule.[30] Despite these structural weaknesses and political instability—and we arrive now at Varela's and Gener's reference to the cause of the "enslavement" of whites in Cuba—Spanish governments still possessed an effective impediment to the Creole bourgeoisie's bids for greater autonomy within its colonial status. Paradoxically, it was the continued supply and presence of slaves that both helped to generate enormous profits for the Creole bourgeoisie and permitted Spain to keep this class's political and economic ambitions in check.

Unlike the case of British abolitionism, which associated the end of the slave trade and the emancipation of slaves with domestic social reforms and a geopolitical agenda based on the expansion of markets that British supremacy on the seas afforded it, maintaining the slave trade was vital to Spain's own geopolitical agenda. What did Spanish governments stand to gain by adhering to this policy? The most radical political element within Cuba was not abolitionism but the reform movement among members of the Creole bourgeoisie, which was not anticolonial per se but had the potential to be if Spain refused to heed its demands for economic and political reforms. As Rafael Rojas asserts, there existed a bona fide colonial liberalism in Cuba (just as there existed monarchical liberalisms in the political cultures of England, France, and Spain) that did not seek independence from Madrid as its primary goal.[31] In the 1830s and '40s, the Spanish government consistently thwarted the reformists' main goal, which was to abolish the slave trade without emancipating the island's slaves, at least for the time being. While rejecting emancipation would ostensibly guarantee their labor supply for the immediate future, abolishing the trade made economic sense only once it was combined with the reformists' related plan of introducing white immigrant labor to replace black slaves. Saco, the reformists' most renowned ideologue, put it in these words in a letter that he directed to the Spanish Cortes in 1835: "It would be impossible for us, as we call for the abolition of the traffic in Africans, to stop advocating *white colonization*. On it depend agricultural progress, perfection in the arts, in a word, Cuban prosperity in all branches and the firm hope that the unsteady building whose ruin menaces us will once and for all settle on solid and indestructible foundations."[32] The reformists' sense of themselves as the members of a dynamic and influential class led them to imagine their leadership role in the creation of a "national" community, which, in light of the recent struggles for independence on the mainland and the Creole leadership that waged war against Spain, was no surprise. However, any idea of Cuban nationhood that the Creole reformists entertained was invariably influenced by both the local concern that Cuba's substantial black population could potentially transform the island into a black republic like Haiti and the general notion that pervaded Europe and the western hemisphere in the early decades of the nineteenth century that "civilized nations" could only be racially pure and preferentially white.[33]

By maintaining the slave trade, Spanish governments achieved the immediate goal of simultaneously securing a substantial black presence on the island—a definite obstacle to the reformists' plans for political reforms that would ready the island for autonomy at some point in the future—and rewarding the colonial officials who managed the trade. The Spanish minister, Calatrava, was reported to have said in 1837 that preserving slavery in Cuba was analogous to having an army of 100,000 men there to deter Cuba from seeking independence.[34] In an effort to circumvent the colonial administration's censorship, del Monte wrote a

letter to the Spanish government in which he detailed the three causes
that contributed to the continuation of the slave trade in Cuba. Although
he dispatched it with the British abolitionist David Turnbull, who had
been visiting Cuba in 1838, the letter never arrived.[35] The patrician describes these causes as, first, Spain's insistence on introducing African
slaves to prevent the development of any independence movement on
the island, which, in effect, blew the whistle on the Spanish government's
unofficial policy. The second and third causes he described as the greed
of the captains-general and other officials who grew rich from the bribes
that they received from slave traders and the insatiability of the traders
themselves. For example, Captain-General Tacón, the highest colonial
official on the island, received the modest sum of *media onza* for every
slave sold, which meant that he amassed roughly 100,000 pesos annually
in kickbacks. Considering the number of slaves that entered Cuba from
1834 to 1838, he left the island with what would currently amount to more
than $1.5 million dollars—a sum that he banked in London and Paris and
drew upon to purchase a grand estate near Palma de Mallorca, where
he spent most of his time after leaving Cuba.[36] For Spain, there was yet
another crucial advantage to continuing the slave trade: the contraband
traffic allowed it to empower and protect its own bourgeoisies in both
Cuba and the peninsula.

From 1820 onward, Spain encouraged the importation of slaves and
created a monopoly for mostly Spanish merchants who were loyal to
Madrid and the colonial government and who maintained economic relations with the Spanish bourgeoisie. The resulting antagonism between
Spanish merchants and the Creole bourgeoisie created the now familiar
split between both communities that marked Cuban history during this
period: the Spanish slave-trading merchants, whom the colonial government favored, and the patrician and bourgeois Creole sugar-producers
whose political and economic advances were closely scrutinized. If one
also incorporates details, such as the brisk pace with which Cuban rum
began replacing Catalonian spirits—one of this region's principal ex-
ports to the Americas—in large markets such as Nueva España (Mexico)
in the first decades of the nineteenth century, then it becomes possible to
discern how an important factor in the economic and political repression
that Cuba's Creole bourgeoisie experienced was the direct result of bitter

rivalry and competition from certain sectors of Spain's bourgeoisie.[37] Such rivalries between competing metropolitan and colonial bourgeoisies—an angle on Spanish colonialism in Cuba that is understudied— thus led to the apparent paradox that conservative Spanish governments moved against the slave trade while liberal governments protected the contraband traffic in slaves. In fact, del Monte observed this phenomenon and wrote that Havana was, relatively speaking, free in periods of despotism in Spain and enslaved in times of greater freedom in the peninsula.[38] The Creole bourgeoisie responded accordingly: it tended to favor absolutist Spanish administrations over liberal ones because the latter vigorously supported a trade that this Creole community aspired to eradicate.[39] Analogous to the way in which the specific contexts of colonial slavery generate paradoxes such as the simultaneously *legal* and *immoral* character of slavery, these contexts appear to give rise to grounds for questioning the applicability of terms such as "conservative" and "liberal," especially in relation to the slave trade.[40] According to Moreno Fraginals, however, the meaning of the term "liberal" remained consistent. For Spanish liberals and English Whigs around the middle of the nineteenth century, freedom did not refer to romantic liberalism but to the development of industry and capital free of state intervention.[41] In placing the contraband slave trade in the hands of their own loyal merchants, liberal Spanish governments positioned the metropolitan bourgeoisie to compete in the market at the expense of the its Cuban rival.

Varela's and Gener's claim that slavery was responsible for the "enslavement" of whites in Cuba indeed constitutes a response to the "universal" debate about human rights in the 1830s. Regarding the idea that freedom should be equally shared, they avoided treating the subject as an abstract ethical discussion and proposed, instead, that not all struggles for freedom ought to be considered equal. Their experience of the issues corroborates Davis's argument that there was "no automatic connection between a defense of natural rights and the imperative that slavery be abolished" even though the latter "at least in the abstract" was contrary to the spirit of the Enlightenment.[42] In responding in this manner, the exiled reformists prioritized their own struggle under colonial rule— that is, their attempts to overcome unfair economic competition and political oppression from the Spanish bourgeoisie on the island and in

Spain—over their slaves' desire for freedom. As a class, the Creole bourgeoisie refused to countenance the economic suicide of immediately
emancipating their slaves and tended to sidestep or remain silent about
the moral issues surrounding slavery. More essential for the reformists
was the end of the slave trade, for stopping this contraband would set
in motion a shift in power relations with the Spanish merchants on the
island and the attendant possibility of undertaking their dream of creating a more autonomous Cuban community. Even so, when the reformists
were in a position to cry out for freedom, Moreno Fraginals cogently
states, "they castrate it with an unavoidable proviso: freedom for white
men. Sugar, with its slave labor, made the genuine bourgeois concept
of freedom impossible on the island."[43] Looking toward the future, the
warnings that the reformists slyly communicated to Spanish governments tended to skirt the issue of Cuban political independence but consistently articulated the external threat (or desirability) of the island's
annexation to the United States.

What kind of freedom was this for Cuban whites if the reformists'
most potent rhetorical weapon never amounted to more that the threat
to abandon what remained of the Spanish colonial empire and to deliver
the island into the hands of the United States? Even Saco, in a comparative analysis between Cuba's colonial situation and that of Britain's
colonies, expressed his preference in similar terms for Canada's "light
chain of golden links."[44] In the final analysis, the reformists' ideal was
not political independence but the guarantee that the government that
ruled over them would foster the free trade practices that they required
for their advancement as a class, in Davis's terminology, of "economic
men." In light of this predilection for class interests above all else, it
becomes possible to reconcile how José Luis Alfonso, one of the most
prominent members of the Creole bourgeoisie and Domingo del Monte's
brother-in-law, led the annexation movement at the start of the 1840s as
a response to Britain's pressure on Spain to adopt an abolitionist agenda,
yet, once trade had been partially liberalized and the abolitionist threat
to the island eliminated toward the end of the decade, could be found
underwriting publications against the very annexation movement that
he helped to found.[45] The reformists' conviction that slavery "enslaved"
them was a complaint not against being governed per se but against

how they were being governed. Some of them deduced from their economic conditions and prognoses that they were perhaps seeking political leadership from an unworthy "master." In their concerted deliberations about the country to which they should relinquish their political voice, their slaves' desire for freedom rarely constituted a subject for systematic reflection. The reformists felt trapped in a situation in which they could neither eliminate their dependency on slave labor nor prevent Madrid from imposing this dependency. Because slavery boosted their wealth at the same time that it became the principal obstacle to their dream of taking their place among the white, "civilized" nations of the world, the reformists could not treat the freedom of slaves as an abstract debate about human rights without questioning their future as a burgeoning class and political community.

Although the reformists' ability to challenge colonial rule by freeing their slaves was an option that the Creole bourgeoisie would not take until, as the legend goes, one of its members—Carlos Manuel de Céspedes—liberated his slaves and, in so doing, helped to ignite Cuba's first war of independence (1868–78), the ethical and geopolitical impasse that the reformists faced in the 1830s and '40s was not of their making alone. The idea of civilization that European nations exported to the rest of the world as a means of establishing and regulating world order cannot be considered a mere "emanation" from this continent that Cuba, for instance, simply failed to assimilate properly. According to Edward Keene, it is crucial to distinguish between the state-systems order that European nations developed among themselves in which they privileged a "common interest in mutual independence" and, most significantly, in mutual toleration and a second pattern of international order that was founded not on toleration, but on the promotion of "civilization" in the extra-European world.[46] Keene reports that the difference between these two patterns was clearly visible by the middle of the nineteenth century and that it is possible to note in legal texts from that period that there existed a "widely accepted distinction between the family of civilized nations and the backward uncivilized world beyond."[47] Citing John Stuart Mill's work as a point of departure, Keene states that the two main elements that informed the nineteenth-century understanding of civilization were material development (economic and technological progress) and a moral component that relied on the presence of an educated and refined population and good government based on just and effective political, judicial, and administrative systems.[48] Yet the material and moral aspects of the notion of civilization that European nations exported to its colonies underwrote imperial and colonial systems that divided sovereignty across borders and enforced individuals' rights to their "persons and property."[49] So long as "property" included slaves, as it did in Cuba at the time, the Creole bourgeoisie, and especially its reformist members, did not speculate openly about universal freedom because the colonial government forbade it and because they were unwilling to fathom this freedom if it meant that they would need to divest themselves of their rights to the ownership of human property. If, as Keene asserts, spreading the idea of civilization across the globe involved attaching individual rights to persons and property, then these economic rights rationalized the relationship between "civilization" and slavery in Cuba.

Cuba's reformist Creole bourgeoisie could not act against the colonial government to separate the simultaneously legal and immoral nature of a significant portion of its wealth from its bid to join "the family of civilized nations." Its "clipped wings," as Moreno Fraginals put it, can thus be seen as the result of a self-inflicted wound and colonial domination: these members of the local bourgeoisie refused to consider emancipating their slaves as a means of freeing themselves from Madrid's insistence on keeping the island supplied with slaves, and successive Spanish governments counted on this refusal in order to retain the colony. So long as American colonies were treated as spaces of exception from the legal and moral positions that European nations established for and among themselves on that continent, Cuba was necessarily subject, as all of the Americas were, to the *refraction*—not emanation—of bourgeois ideals that the imperial metropolis exported.

THE URGENCY OF LITERATURE

Literary writing for the members of del Monte's circle was not merely a reprieve from an oppressive colonial climate but an engagement with the difficulty of reconciling the Creole reformists' economic and philosophical aspirations in order to take their place within a broader transatlantic bourgeoisie. In the introduction, I briefly described how del Monte and his group of reformist "young liberals" planned and executed the separation of the Comisión Permanente de Literatura from the pro-Spanish and pro-slavery Sociedad Económica de Amigos del País and reconstituted it as the Academia Cubana de Literatura or Academia Literaria.[50] Thanks, in part, to lobbying strategies that took place behind the scenes in the royal court in Madrid in 1833, the queen regent, María Cristina de Borbón, decreed the establishment of the Instituto Filológico de María Cristina on December 25, and the Academy met for the first time on March 4, 1834. The news of the royal decree must have stunned the members of the Sociedad Económica: not only did the official founding of the Academy mean that the young liberals possessed a clandestine network that extended to the royal court in Madrid, it demonstrated how successful they had been at promoting their campaign, receiving approval for it at the highest legislative level, right under the noses of the Sociedad Económica and two of its most powerful Creole figures, Juan Bernardo O'Gavan, the Sociedad's director and Saco's personal enemy, and Claudio Martínez de Pinillos, the island's highest-ranking tax inspector. Needless to say, the august society immediately began machinating the Academy's demise.

For the Creole reformists, news of the royal decree represented the welcome prospect of their finally being able to write and discuss ideas in an environment in which the monarch's royal sanction would shield their literary activities from censorship. Until then, censorship had consistently obliged them to approach issues that deeply concerned them, such as slavery, in an oblique manner. Prior to this period, as Carlos Alonso has shown, avoiding the moral implications of slavery constituted a defining feature of Cuban antislavery writings.[51] Examples of this strategy abound. They include, for instance, the reformists' plan to translate and publish Comte's *Traité de legislation* in order to generate a "public" discussion of slavery. The treatise was eventually translated and published in Barcelona, but, perhaps because it contained five volumes of technical subject matter, the study went mostly unnoticed in Cuba, except for the mild attention that it received from a few law students.[52] A less indirect approach to slavery that did not escape readers' attention was a review article that Saco penned about a British travel book on Brazil, in which he condemned the slave trade in Cuba, calling attention to the increasing numbers of Africans and the relative decline in the size of the European population. Saco was the first Creole to attack the slave trade openly on the island, yet, as Murray observes, he still needed to resort to writing about "volcanoes erupting in other parts of the Caribbean," which was a metaphor that was regularly employed to allude to Haiti and, subsequently, to Jamaica.[53] Oblique approaches to issues of freedom were also frequent in writings that were more obviously literary. In her readings of the poetry of the free mulatto poet, Plácido (Gabriel de la Concepción Valdés), Sibylle Fischer demonstrates the extent to which compositions, such as his sonnets "To Poland" and "To Greece," negotiate complex reflections—articulated from within a censored colonial environment— on degrees of freedom beyond struggles for national independence and sovereignty.[54] With the possible exception of Saco's explicit denunciation of the contraband traffic in humans, these various references to other places in the world (to forcibly any place but Cuba) produce a cosmopolitan effect; but this kind of cosmopolitanism is less a cultivated sensibility than it is a testament to the extreme caution and creative effort that were required in order to allude to slavery and colonialism in Cuba.[55]

Creating an autonomous space for literature was fundamentally a strategy for expanding areas of social and intellectual discourse. What the young liberals considered "literary" undertakings thus involved the publication of critical texts from a variety of fields. A year before the Academy was officially established, and with the leadership and collaboration of Varela, Saco, José de la Luz y Caballero, del Monte, and others, they launched the *Revista Bimestre Cubana* from within the Sociedad Económica's education section. This journal was probably the most important of its kind to emerge on the island during the nineteenth century. Saco was its first director, and he gave the publication an encyclopedic format in keeping with the Creole reformists' interests and their taste for Enlightenment epistemologies. Luz y Caballero was responsible for articles on philosophy and education, del Monte for the journal's literary content, and Saco took charge of the sections on economics and sociology.[56] The journal was both universal in its sources and local in some of its content; its goals were to combat erroneous and superficial arguments, dogmas, vices, misleading views of reality, lethargy, and conservative thought.[57] Emboldened by their recent accomplishments and the faithfulness with which they modeled the *Revista* on similarly prestigious journals in England and the United States, Saco began tackling domestic issues directly, as if he were publishing his analyses in an uncensored environment. His review of the travel book on Brazil met with O'Gavan's and Martínez de Pinillos's irritation, and they tried (unsuccessfully, on this occasion) to have Saco ejected from the journal. The latter defended the directness of his critiques, warning against timidity and silence in the face of what he perceived as a people hurtling toward its ruin, and championed "writers' noble mission" to save their patria.[58] Two years later, after the Sociedad Económica secured a royal decree suspending the Academy's activities, Saco published a defense of the association to which Martínez de Pinillos and O'Gavan took offense and for which the outspoken reformist was sent into exile.

Although the reasons that motivated the young liberals to create the Academy in the first place are not fully known, it is suspected, as Ileana Rodríguez asserts, that they were rooted in issues that had to do with but were broader than the liberation of thought and culture.[59] The personal enmities that led to such schisms, intrigues, and banishments represented the surface features of internal political, economic, and cultural crises that were further exacerbated by a volatile contingency of geopolitical circumstances that included British abolitionist activism in the area, the proximity of revolutionary Haiti, ambivalent attitudes toward the newly independent Spanish-American republics, the attractiveness of annexation to the United States, and Spain's hardline policy on sustaining the contraband traffic in slaves. This dangerous mix convinced Madrid to place almost unrestricted powers in the hands of Captain-General Tacón. It was no surprise, therefore, that the internal antagonisms and feuds that divided the Sociedad Económica were closely linked to a number of politically charged agendas that Rodríguez concisely lists as liberalism or liberalization; reformism, separatism, annexation, or independence.[60] In this intense environment, del Monte chose not to follow Saco's example, continued to tackle the slave trade and colonialism obliquely, and shied away from public controversies. The idea to create the Academy had been del Monte's, but he proved reluctant to go beyond this daring. His reticence may partly have been due to compromises that belonging to one of Cuba's wealthiest and most influential families entailed, but the public del Monte was a perpetual proponent of moderation—a politically diffident liberal reformist—in a period of crisis who left Havana whenever the colonial government clamped down on subversive activities and preferred to leave his publications unsigned or attributed to pseudonyms. According to Sophie Andioc Torres, there was a remarkable difference between the audaciousness that del Monte expressed in letters to close friends and the complete absence of this stance in his public writings.[61] Only del Monte's spirited defense of the Academy in an open letter to the public that was published in Matanza's *La Aurora* on April 29, 1834, lies outside Andioc's otherwise accurate observation. In this letter, del Monte responded by defending his honor and attacking specific members of the Sociedad Económica for its many intrigues and plots against the reformists' activities within the Sociedad and the Academy.[62]

When the mandate arrived in October of 1834 for the Academy to suspend its activities, a mere seven months after its first official meeting (behind closed doors, curiously enough), the young liberals retreated to the private sanctuary of del Monte's home, where they engaged in discussions about the European literature of the day, wrote poems and narrative compositions about their landscape and the sugar plantation's social environment, and began penning Cuba's first novels. This inward turn and "freedom" through withdrawal into collective thought and self-representation follows a stoic pattern that intensified as some of the reformists gradually disengaged from colonial politics and, especially, as the group lost political leverage and the chance to represent and debate their views in Madrid. Although liberal reforms found fertile ground in Spain in the 1830s—going so far as to eradicate what was left of slavery in the Peninsula in 1836—the government blocked the Cuban, Puerto Rican, and Philippine *diputados* (representatives) from attending the Cortes from 1834 to 1837 and added a constitutional measure stipulating that "special rules" would henceforth rule the colonies.[63] Saco, whom the young liberals managed to have selected as a Cuban delegate, defined the situation at that time as one in which Cuba had been converted from an overseas province into an enslaved colony.[64] Members of the Delmontine circle expressed a similar sense of being snared in circumstances that they did not create. After reading Anselmo Suárez y Romero's speech on Rousseau's "Social Contract," José Zacarías González del Valle wrote to his friend rhetorically inquiring, "What pact did we make to remain in society? None. We were born into it, when we entered we were not in a position to be able to choose, so that we are Spanish and Christian, not because we like it that way nor would want to consent to it, but because of an unavoidable occurrence."[65] This experience of colonialism as an inevitability produced stoic self-knowledge.

The literary circle's space and time away from the agitations of political life did not grant its members absolute creative freedom. As the group's host, del Monte had significant influence: in addition to introducing the circle to Victor Hugo, Walter Scott, and Goethe, he urged them to focus their creativity on bringing local issues to life, especially the horrors of slavery and the interconnected lives of masters and slaves.[66] Yet there also existed, as César Leante argues, a "subtle indoctrination" that pervaded the circle's activities.[67] Examining the correspondence between González del Valle and Suárez y Romero, Leante interrogates the concern that the latter expressed about criticism that he received from del Monte regarding aspects of *Francisco,* the novel on which Suárez y Romero had been working. Apparently, del Monte considered the slave-protagonist's speech "subversive."[68] In González's response to Suárez y Romero, who was around eighteen at the time, he reassures him that the members of the group who were circulating installments of the novel were reading them in order to learn how their own demeanors might be improved, which was one of the literary circle's principal goals. A letter that Suárez y Romero sent to del Monte provides more details about the novel's supposedly subversive content. In this correspondence, the young novelist recreates his thoughts, for the patrician's benefit, as he was working on the novel: "I said in my sorrow—white men, you, sirs, are tyrants with the slaves, so be ashamed to behold one of those wretches here, a better man than you. Herein lies the cause of my error."[69] In representing the speech of slave protagonists, the literary circle's members had already been working in an area that was rife with artistic and ideological traps. For Antonio Vera-León, when Suárez y Romero italicized the speech of blacks in order to differentiate it from "white" speech, the latter did not promulgate a democratization of Cuban voices but bowed, instead, to the "literary reformism" that characterized the circle's activities.[70] Such attempts to capture black speech in a literature that focused on a national identity and that was written by white Creoles meant that the young liberals had, like Manzano himself, ventured into what Julio Ramos refers to as "hybridity's least visible and administrable zone."[71]

Del Monte's directives, therefore, were less concerned with the slaves' desire for freedom than, as Leante puts it, with "the modification of the master's conduct toward the slave."[72] Despite the literary circle's stoic disengagement from open political conflicts during the mid-1830s, the patrician nudged the young writers to create a literature that would eradicate what he viewed as the moral decay and barbarism to which slavery had led the island's sugar-producing bourgeoisie. His essential aim, in other words, was to appeal to his political opponents and the Creole majority through literature and to persuade them of the need to eliminate the slave trade and, eventually, slavery. Given these "guidelines," it had been Suárez y Romero's "mistake" to imagine that a slave might be more sensitive and morally upright than his master. To suggest as much would have been appalling to a readership that lived among its slaves treating them as property. For del Monte, literature's loftiest value lay in its ability to instruct readers about the ways in which they could improve their moral conduct; but he refused to extend this idealism to slaves. Analogous to the way in which the Creole reformists contemplated freedom for whites alone, the road to moral perfection in del Monte's conception of literature would also need to be segregated. Suggesting that the slave was incapable of the kind of honor and propriety that Suárez y Romero's protagonist demonstrated revealed the paternalist ideology that informed del Monte's attitude toward the slaves around him.

The view that slaves were like children who voluntarily and innocently looked up to their masters for intellectual and moral guidance is a paternalist conception of slavery that seeks to justify the slave owners' practices. This paternalism is not grounded in an understanding of slaveholders as conscious exponents of and believers in a perverse moral position; nor does it imply that the master's actions are unconscious but not evil. According to McGary, the first view is historically inaccurate because there is little evidence to support the claim that slave-holders thought that by owning slaves they were acting in the latter's best interests, and the second rationalizes the slaveholders' behavior by jeopardizing "what it means to describe behavior as bad or evil."[73] The paternalism that del Monte displays in frowning on the protago-nist's characterization and speech in *Francisco* is both an ideology and a broad set of practices that are underwritten by a consistent body of legal codes and that link plantation life to political configurations such as the slave-owning nation-state and/or empire. This perverse enforcement of "morality" in the service of immorality promotes and conserves an unequal power relationship that del Monte reiterates in his critique of the novel's character.

The patrician's penchant for didactic literature also extended to poetry. According to Salvador Bueno, del Monte believed that poetry should render a service as well as foment the improvement of the hu-man species and the advancement of society; he felt that the work of art should rest on solid moral foundations.[74] For the critic, at the same time that del Monte's utilitarian notion of poetry drew from an Enlighten-ment tradition, the patrician's conception of the poet strayed more to-ward Romanticism: he thought that poets were born with innate facul-ties for perception, creativity, and expression, which could be polished and improved, but that a natural talent must first be present.[75] Bueno's del Monte seems to straddle the fence between two eras of Western literary history, which implies that the patrician irrevocably belonged to his tur-bulent times. However, neither was didactic literary writing limited to the Enlightenment nor was the idea of the poet's "natural talent" unique to Romanticism. Another of Bueno's observations about del Monte's atti-tude toward Romanticism is more useful. The young liberals were clearly interested in European Romanticisms and debated them heatedly; it was del Monte's opinion, though, that Romanticism's excesses needed to be kept in check.[76] Lisandro Otero goes as far as to assert that del Monte was a "declared enemy of romanticism" because its nationalist and revo-lutionary spirit threatened the notion of the "national" community that del Monte imagined.[77]

At the very least, what can be said about del Monte's cautious ap-proach to the European Romantics is that this attitude remained consis-

tent with the moderation that he espoused in public. The fact that there
was such consistency in the positions that he assumed inside and outside
the circle makes it possible to claim that this foundational space of Cuban literature was not free of coercive practices, as subtle as these might
have been. Del Monte encouraged the members of his literary circle
to cultivate a literary sensibility around the subject of Cuban slavery
that would interpellate and be instructive for the island's broader Creole
bourgeoisie; however, his unwillingness to attack colonial rule directly
made revolutionary Romanticism too iconoclastic and, hence, risky for
his literary agenda. Nonetheless, del Monte still found effective ways
to combat the slave trade surreptitiously. In December of 1836, when
Cuban delegates were still being prevented from attending the Cortes
in Madrid, del Monte returned to the Sociedad Económica to head its
literary section. It was working from within the Sociedad this time that
he furnished the Irish abolitionist Richard Robert Madden with interviews, reports, Manzano's autobiography and some of his poetry, Suárez
y Romero's *Francisco,* and other literary pieces as evidence for the report
on the contraband slave trade in Cuba that the Anti-Slavery Society was
preparing for the British government in London. Even though I have
not found clear evidence that del Monte made the decision to return to
the Sociedad Económica because the island's political representatives
had lost their voice in the Spanish government and in order to engage
in undercover work for the reformists, I read del Monte's willingness to
supply Richard Robert Madden with economic data, additional empirical information, and literature as a sign of growing frustration that he
and his fellow reformists experienced as of 1834. Andioc Torres marks
1838 as the year that del Monte began to rethink his position as hopefulness changed to fear and fear to rage.[78] In this literal sense, literary writings from del Monte's circle secretly transcended its colonial confines
to become resources for the abolitionists' cosmopolitan philanthropic
humanitarianism.

A SONNET'S "UNIVERSAL" APPEAL

One evening in 1836—the exact date remains unknown—del Monte introduced the autodidact slave and poet Juan Francisco Manzano to the

literary circle that met regularly at his neoclassical *palacete* in Havana. Amid the sumptuous surroundings of the newly built Aldama mansion, in an ample upstairs salon that displayed a large map of Cuba on one wall and drawings and bookshelves replete with some of the latest European literature on others, Manzano was invited to read his sonnet "Mis treinta años" (My thirty years). The poem begins as a moment of self-reflection, mingled with astonishment, as the poet takes stock of the span of time that has transpired since his infancy. In attempting to fathom his life experiences over this period, he intimates that it is with fear and trembling, rather than with due attention, that he hails the hardships that have characterized his existence. At the fore of this reflection is his amazement that he was able to sustain a struggle against "so god-forsaken a fate" (*suerte tan impía*), if that is what one might call, he proffers, "the relentlessness / of my wretched being to evil born" (*de mi infelice ser al mal nacido*). The poet then declares that he has lived in this sorrowful state for thirty years, assaulted at every turn by grim misfortunes. He ends the sonnet resigned to the knowledge that the cruel war that he has endured in vain amounts to nothing compared to what lies ahead.[79]

Judging from what we know of him from letters that he wrote to del Monte and, especially, from his autobiography, Manzano would probably have invoked the solemn tone that his sonnet required. Because he spent his childhood as a page and house slave for members of the Cuban sugar-producing bourgeoisie, he would surely have been familiar with drawing rooms, such as del Monte's, and the decorum that he encountered there. Other factors in his background also suggest why Manzano might have been fairly at ease reading his poem before del Monte's literary circle that evening. As a child, he relished performing in public. Because of his obvious gift of gab, he had been nicknamed "golden beak" (*pico de oro*); honing his prodigious memory by recalling the short plays (*loas*), speeches, sermons, and poems to which he had been exposed in this milieu, he would recite them by heart for his mistress's guests, who, in turn, usually rewarded his parents. In his first mistress's home, he thus grew up associating his performances with favorable treatment and special compensation. With his precocious verbal skills, it was not long before he began to improvise rhymes and compose verses. By the time he read his sonnet for the literary circle, Manzano was already a published poet and a public figure in Havana. He undoubtedly possessed the "natural" talent that del Monte applauded in a poet.

Yet, with its pervasive melancholy and stoic finale, "Mis treinta años" does not smack of childlike innocence. Even though Manzano would have been around thirty-nine years old when he read his sonnet at the Aldama mansion, his verses convey more solemnity than a mere lament about the passage of time. If we continue to read Manzano's poem as a reflection on his life, it is apparent that what led him to compose these somber verses were his personal experience of slavery and the analysis of enslavement that hindsight afforded him. Now, it seems logical to assume that chattel slavery was so singularly traumatic an experience that it would be nearly impossible for a slave to articulate his or her understanding of this experience to anyone, even more so to a room of slave owners. Dwight McBride notes that British abolitionists occasionally called upon slaves, like the Bermuda-born Mary Prince, to help them convince listeners and readers who had no firsthand knowledge of bondage that slavery was evil and that it had to be abolished. For such an audience, it was as if slavery gave rise to "an experience gap that only a slave [could] fill."[80] Manzano's sonnet deeply affected the gathering in del Monte's salon. According to the critic José Luciano Franco, the recitation aroused "so profound an emotion" at the gathering that del Monte and others immediately spearheaded an initiative to buy the poet his freedom.[81] The sonnet also came to be considered one of the best of its time in Cuba and was translated into three languages soon afterward.[82]

Later in 1836, del Monte and his cohorts collected the required eight hundred pesos to manumit the slave-poet in a humanitarian and "civilizing" act that was at the same time inseparable from finance capital.[83] Did the decision to buy Manzano his freedom result from the "expansive and self-sacrificing" faculty of the "distanced imagination" that Lee attributes to some of Britain's most important Romantic poets?[84] Arguably, the experiential "distances" that these poets' imagination would have had to cover in order to articulate the slaves' sufferings would have been greater than those of the young liberals, whose contact with their slaves required different engagements with the daily practices of disavowal that were essential for the proper functioning of plantations. The day-to-day empirical knowledge that the Creole reformists possessed of chattel slavery meant that whereas they might have resembled what Baucom identifies as the sympathetic observers who pursued humanitarian justice disinterestedly through British abolitionism, the reformist members of del Monte's literary circle were certainly not vicarious but actual witnesses to the torments and distressed lives of *their* slaves and, in particular, knowledgeable evaluators of the appropriateness of Manzano's manumission price.

What was there about Manzano's poem that appealed to the circle's members and spurred them to work toward freeing the poet? At some point during the recitation, they must have considered the sonnet an autobiographical composition: they could hardly ignore that the poet who stood before them was also a slave. (Whom, one might ask, would del Monte have contacted in order to arrange for the poet to be there that evening? Would Manzano have carried a *cartilla*, or permit, that authorized him to be on the street at night? Or was he obliged to accompany one of the circle's members in order to go to and from del Monte's home?) Because masters disavowed their slaves' humanity in order to assure the daily functioning of forced labor on their plantations, intellectual exchanges between masters and slaves about the nature of slavery were understandably rare. In plumbing the depths of the communication that took place between Manzano and his listeners, what needs to be considered is the fact that the audience for whom he read his verses differed from those that he might have created in abolitionist circles in, say, London or Boston in the degree of abstraction and disinterestedness with which both groups would have apprehended his complaint. Given the local circumstances in which the poet made his humanitarian appeal, it is worth exploring the basis upon which these Creole reform-minded slave owners might have identified with the sentiments in Manzano's sonnet.

The most evident common ground for the enslaved poet and these reformists is the lyrical voice's articulation of a stoic disposition in the face of insurmountable difficulties. Despite the poem's brevity, it contains ample allusions to adversities (godforsaken destiny, grim misfortunes, cruel war, sorrowful state) that are sufficiently abstract in the sonnet to appeal to an audience beyond those who would have suffered actual bondage. A culminating summary of the experience of being subjugated to such adversities is to be found toward the center of the poem, when, in the process of describing itself, the poetic voice defines its essence as an unhappy existence that is further downtrodden by its having been destined to come into and remain in an evil world (*al mal nacido*).[85] Arguably, one of the more "universal" readings of "evil" for Manzano's listeners may have been the state of being born, according to Catholicism, with original sin (that is, with Adam's and Eve's sinful partaking of forbidden fruit in the Garden of Eden that all men are said to inherit). Even though the members of the literary circle would have grasped this possible interpretation, they might also have insisted, for the sake of consistency, on the path to redemption from original sin that Church doctrine describes and that is nowhere to be found in the sonnet. Attaining redemption means recognizing that one has sinned in the first place, but the poetic voice makes no reference to the knowledge of having committed any transgressions. In claiming innocence, therefore, it is possible that the lyrical voice may be surreptitiously criticizing how slave owners dared to consider themselves Christians since they were responsible for submitting their slaves to a godless destiny (*suerte tan impía*). In any case, this declaration of innocence still ends up as a straightforward appeal for justice, be it human or divine.

A more likely source of empathy for the del Monte circle would have been to identify the stoicism that the poet articulates in "Mis treinta años" with aspects of European Romanticism that its members explored in their literary gatherings at the Aldama mansion. The Creole reformists would have appreciated the Romanticism of the lyrical voice's heroic struggle against overwhelming odds. They would have grasped the depth and range of the emotions that the sonnet manages to articulate in a few lines: the fear and respect that are invoked in response to the sweeping panorama of a lifetime of suffering and the astonishment at somehow possessing the fortitude to bear such misery as the poetic voice looks back at the past and forward into the future. Nevertheless, as Bueno and Rodríguez have argued, it should not be assumed that del Monte and his circle merely absorbed European Romanticism in order to imitate it blindly.[86] Not only were they also readers of Balzac, whose realism contrasted sharply with the Romantic idealization of sensitivity, instinct, and the unbridled imagination, but they paid heed to their host's cautious Romanticism—what Bueno prefers to call del Monte's "literary Americanism."[87]

In light of the close attention that del Monte's circle paid to their colonial environment, it requires no stretch of the imagination to appreciate the degree to which slavery would have been understood as the evil to which the poetic voice refers in the sonnet. This allusion, it should be noted, does not mean that the lyrical voice abandons the universal dimensions of its self-reflection. It would have been unthinkable for Manzano to promote a less than universal reading of his poem and employ a more open and accusatory voice in this period of heightened censorship. It is evident, nonetheless, that slavery so thoroughly pervaded the physical world of the island into which Manzano was born that it can be said to have constituted the most significant feature of his "universe." More specifically, the first three actions through which the poetic voice situates itself in the poem—"I look," "I shudder," "I greet my fortune"— invoke incremental stages of self-reflection, from an initial awareness of the world, through the consciousness-producing experience of fear, and ending with the recognition of an "unhappy consciousness" as the poetic voice hails (and, in so doing, submits to) its own predicament. For Hegel, the fear of death and of transience is an incipient, defining moment of self-consciousness. When the poetic voice declares that it shudders, stirred by terror, as it contemplates the fleeting nature of everything that surrounds it—in particular, the years of suffering that have unaccountably flown by—this emotion corroborates the philosopher's proposition that such fear causes consciousness to quake "in every fibre of its being" as "everything solid and stable has been shaken to its foundations."[88] When the lyrical voice bows, before the overwhelming power of its unhappy existence, to the premonition, as the sonnet precisely states, that the future portends at least as much misery as the past, the poetic voice arrives at this resignation after having withdrawn into the private world of introspection. This kind of withdrawal accurately defines both the Hegelian notion of the stoic self-consciousness and the Romantic impulse to subordinate social dilemmas to the unrestrained imagination.

Interpreting "to evil born" in Manzano's sonnet as a reference to slavery opens up additional inflections of the broad exegesis above. Adding the slave's experience of bondage to the poem's incremental stages of self-reflection makes it possible to supplement a modern theory of consciousness, such as Hegel's, with information about a struggle for agency under some of the most trying conditions that men have ever imposed on other men. For example, in the master-slave dialectic, work in a phylogenetic reading possesses the duality of oppressing the slave and an affirmative value because it leads the slave to become "conscious of what he truly is."[89] As opposed to the master, who vicariously enjoys the objects of labor that the slave produces, the slave begins to perceive his independence of mind because he creates objects that appear to have a life of their own. It is in this manner that the development of his consciousness outstrips his master's. Hegel avers that "through this discovery of himself by himself the bondsman realizes that it is precisely in his work wherein he seemed to have only an alienated existence that he acquires a mind of his own."[90] In a phylogenetic reading, the experience of forced labor does not imply that slaves were invariably more likely to attain self-consciousness than their masters. For the philosopher, what is also crucial about the discipline of work is that in keeping desire in check, producing "independent" objects from his labor, and, consequently, becoming self-aware, the slave staves off the transience or "fleetingness" of these objects that so terrifies him.[91] However, even though the violent expropriation of the objects of the slave's labor certainly reinforces their transience in a profound way, the forced labor of chattel slavery leads to consequences that are far more frightening for the slave than the fleetingness of the objects he produces—consequences that are as crucial to the subject as the affirmative value of gaining self-consciousness through work. Because, as Lawson reminds us, slaves were legally considered property with "no private existence," chattel slavery turned them into fleeting objects like the ones that they produced for their masters in the marketplace.[92] In Hegel's view, work helps to eradicate the slave's fear of transience and death; in being owned as human property, however, the slave labors at the same time that transience suffuses his or her very existence.

Manzano's status of being born subject to the evil of slavery draws a boundary between his experience of enslavement and the reformists' reflections on their uncomfortable position in Cuba's colonial society. Certainly, Manzano's sonnet and his reading of it could not have produced a more concretely advantageous outcome for him: in essence, he made an indirect appeal for compassion before a gathering of slave owners who were interested in promoting social reforms on the island, and they ultimately responded by securing his manumission. Yet the episode, I have been suggesting, is more complex. There are deeper considerations that need to be explored both in the invitation to have him read his poem for the circle in the first place and in the latter's motivations for facilitating his freedom from bondage.

Demonstrating compassion was central to the identity of the "man of feeling," and he "needed to objectify his virtue by relieving the sufferings of innocent victims."[93] As far as the young liberals in del Monte's circle were concerned, philanthropic compassion was precisely what separated them from the proslavery Creole bourgeoisie and certainly from the rest of the Cuban bourgeoisie. Liberating Manzano was a socially progressive and civilized act, not so much because he was enslaved —had it been solely for this reason, they would have favored emancipation for all the slaves on the island—but because he was an enslaved poet. As "men of feeling," the circle's members appreciated Manzano's stoic disposition because it captured something of theirs under colonial rule: analogous to the lyrical voice's apprehension in the sonnet's final lines that the future portended at least as much oppression as the past, the young liberals felt trapped by their ambiguous relationship with colonial rule and could not envision a simple way out of their dilemma. Manzano's sonnet ends not with a cry for freedom but with a reassertion of fortitude and of a stoic willingness to face the future. Even though these lines suggest the possibility of a shared sensibility between the poet and the circle's young liberals, the abased social position from which Manzano knowingly delivers these lines should also be taken into consideration. Rather than give rise to the sensibility of equals, this stoic finale comforts the reformists by corroborating how, as Davis argues, the "key to progress lay in the controlled emancipation of innocent nature as found both in the objective slave and in the subjective affections of the reformer."[94] It served Manzano well to articulate his awareness of enslavement in terms that applied to the young liberals as well as to him.

How, then, is the "universal" appeal of Manzano's sonnet to be assessed? If, as Alonso argues, a way of measuring the distance to be traveled in order to be modern entailed the "obsessive readings of the latest books, the scrupulously documented travels to the metropolitan countries, the incisive, painstaking, and pained studies of local reality," then Manzano's sonnet provided the literary circle with an additional means of measuring its relation to the modern.[95] The poem "traveled" beyond the island's shores: an English translation of it was included in a portfolio that the British Anti-Slavery Society gathered in order to denounce slavery, and France's most important abolitionist translated it into French and published it in one of France's most widely read antislavery books. In this very literal sense, "Treinta años" had probably traveled further and faster than any single poem from Cuba until then. A transatlantic antislavery propaganda network, which began with del Monte's literary circle and fanned out to the United States, England, France, Germany, and Spain, furnished its "transport" beyond the crisis-ridden colonial environment. Yet this cosmopolitan geography would not have come into being, had there not been an equally significant movement of the poem from Manzano's private reflection on his experience of slavery to its reception by men whose legal status was free but whose collective thinking about freedom and enslavement obeyed an array of self-conscious attitudes that included stoicism, empathy, benevolence, compassion, pity, and paternalism. The appeal for understanding to others outside one's experience of the world does not transport that experience wholesale as if it were an object or commodity. If Manzano's sonnet is to be judged as a composition that possessed universal appeal, then a particular aspect of the context in which he composed it must be taken into account.

As I have already indicated, when Manzano wrote his poem, he could not afford to have it read as an open and direct denunciation of slavery in the rigorously censored environment of colonial Cuba. As a recognized poet in Havana, he undoubtedly would have been well versed in communicating his ideas through "indirection and suggestion," which, for Alonso, was a standard procedure that the young liberals practiced in their antislavery writings.[96] In a public reading of "Treinta años," Manzano's most effective protection in the face of this coercion was to posit the poem's self-reflection in a universal register through which he might generate an appeal for an empathetic understanding of his enslavement. The universal, in this sense, camouflages but delivers a local complaint. The poem, I want to argue, is not reducible to Manzano's capacity for imitating the poetry that he heard around him; the meaning and function of poetry for him, which I examine in the following chapter, clarifies this point. Rather, the uniqueness of the composition resides in the effectiveness with which it articulated liberationist stances and causes apart from his. Nevertheless, the sonnet's "universal" appeal still possesses an important definable limit: even though the stoicism with which the sonnet ends serves to animate and satisfy the sense of virtue and self-sacrifice of the bourgeois "man of feeling," the same cannot be said for the enslaved subject who is obliged to toil with no hope of reward, dignity, and honor.

A final point needs to be broached concerning the impact that the poem might have had on del Monte and the literary circle. The sonnet undoubtedly stirred the young liberals into purchasing the slave-poet's freedom, and their actions eventually led to this concrete outcome. Yet, there is something more to be said about the circumstances of their receptivity to Manzano's predicament and composition. Except for Franco's report that the poem's recitation had deeply moved listeners, there is little empirical evidence to go by in order to ascertain its affective impact. Therefore, I have explored the meanings and resonances that the verses probably generated and have tried to imagine the poet's overall delivery. But, precisely because of this dearth of information, what can we say about the openness of Manzano's listeners to what they heard? Even though I provide more details in chapters 3 and 4 about the sentiments, rationalizations, and motives (both conscious and unconscious) that characterized the abolitionists' and Creole reformists' literary interests and writings, I would like to introduce what is perhaps the main theoretical difficulty in exploring how the young liberals understood their role as reformist slaveholders on a daily basis.

Did these members of the Cuban bourgeoisie obtain Manzano's freedom because he had declaimed his sonnet before them? Not entirely. It
is reasonable to assume that in purposefully arranging for Manzano to
recite his verses at del Monte's mansion, the young liberals had expected
to acquire new knowledge about the relationship between poetry and
the lived experience of bondage. From a psychological perspective, they
conceded an enslaved poet the rare opportunity to summon a sense
of themselves as the "men of feeling" that they had been cultivating in
their efforts to foster conditions for the birth of a local literature and
community. Yet this license also involved certain risks: it allowed Manzano, through the recitation of "Treinta años," to cast innuendos on the
routine ways in which the young liberals consistently avoided thinking
ethically about their roles as slaveholders and to cause them to reflect on
his enslavement. The conscious avoidance of the moral issues surrounding slavery was patent, as the reformists' antislavery writings indicate.
The fact that Varela and Gener reacted to the call for the freedom and
equality of all men by supplanting what should have been their reaction
to this appeal with the claim that Spanish imperialism also enslaved
them furnishes only one of several examples that punctuate the reformists' agenda. I am, however, also interested in introducing the idea of an
avoidance of slavery's moral questions that is so mundane as to be lodged
in the slaveholder's unconscious but perpetrated through perverse intimacy. Interrogating this avoidance permits us to understand how the
reformists could own slaves, indefinitely suspend the moral quandary
of this proprietorship, and advocate ending the slave trade at the same
time. It is crucial to emphasize that this attention to behavior patterns
that were so conventional that the reformists routinely elided slavery's
moral issues—at least until their discussion of them in del Monte's literary circle—is not meant to diminish their moral responsibility as slaveholders but to examine how they represented the limits of their ability
to act against the slave trade.

Now, to suggest that the reformists' desire to learn more about Manzano's experience of bondage arose out of their belief that such an experience was beyond their comprehension partly subscribes to what
Thomas Haskell notes as the interpretive paradigm of "self-deception"
that historians such as Davis and others have employed to explain the

simultaneity of and relationship between humanitarianism and capitalism during the period of greatest abolitionist activism in Britain. The self-deception hypothesis asserts that even though the abolitionists were moral subjects who were swayed by consciously engaged ethical considerations, they were also, according to Haskell's reading of Davis, "unwitting agents of class interests" who responded to social needs of which they were barely conscious.[97] Haskell argues that the self-deception hypothesis warrants attention because it succeeds in circumventing deterministic approaches to the abolitionists' humanitarianism, but he also claims that it leaves the historian with the unwieldy problem of how to approach the moral ambiguities of self-deception, such as the "degree of ethical responsibility a person bears for acts the consequences of which he has deceptively concealed from himself."[98] Haskell cogently argues his point, yet this final articulation of the hypothesis is misleading: to claim that there is something that a person has "deceptively concealed from himself" is tautological and, more significantly, provides this person with more conscious agency than the notion of self-deception need invoke.

However, if we took the "self-deception" of reformist slaveholders to mean their routine or mundane suppression of the knowledge that they were responsible for enslaving human beings, then we would come closer to comprehending the naturalness with which the young liberals believed themselves incapable of understanding the enslaved subject's experience of bondage from his or her point of view. It was not that the reformists could will this self-deception into being. The suppression of the knowledge that they might be able to fathom the experience of being enslaved provided a "moral shelter," as Haskell might put it,[99] or a "necessary fiction," in Basterra's terms, that allowed them to act and acquire agency in other areas, such as in the advocacy of a worldview in which they were the powerless victims of Madrid's prolongation of the contraband slave trade, rather than the potential emancipators of their own slaves. Manzano's recitation, therefore, insinuated itself in this mundane disavowal of the slave's humanity and *temporarily* compelled these "men of feeling" to be moved by the slave-poet's predicament, suffering, and stoicism. No recitation, however, would have radically transformed the literary circle's members into full-fledged abolitionists;

more than for the abolitionists living in London and Boston at the time, it would have meant assuming the enormous moral burden of having enslaved human beings with whom they shared practically every aspect of their social lives on the island. Consequently, the purpose of obtaining Manzano's freedom was not to transform him into the reformists' social equal; liberating the poet afforded the young liberals the opportunity to objectify their virtue as enlightened men of feeling, divorce themselves from the rest of the local and metropolitan bourgeoisies, and begin to burnish their reputation as the founders of a "civilized" local community.

TWO

In Spite of Himself

Unconscious Resistance and Melancholy
Attachments in Manzano's Autobiography

The vast majority of slaves in the Americas did not escape bondage but found diverse and reasonably successful ways of withstanding its daily physical and psychological grind. Even though slavery was a broader phenomenon than the autonomous and single-handed ability of slaveholders to subjugate slaves by force, imagining how environments and circumstances compelled slaves to act in ways that seem counterproductive for their struggles to transcend bondage continues to require careful analysis and reflection. To suggest that masters wielded absolute power over slaves and, by implication, that slaves were entirely objectified beings does not allow us to perceive the necessarily subtle ways in which slaves resisted total subjugation on a daily basis. Although slavery demanded submission on the part of slaves, submissiveness cannot be considered an inherent character trait of enslaved subjects, not only because this view would constitute a disservice to those who strove to survive slavery, but principally because such an assertion would mean accepting masochism as the sole and permanent explanation for the slaves' actions or inability to act. In order to substantiate my argument against the notion that slaves could be subjugated into psychological states of absolute compliance, I want to explore the mundane, complex, and ambiguous psychic space between subjugation and submission that does not require us to characterize slaves in any particular way but affords us opportunities to appreciate how submissive acts, for example, can also constitute strategies, if not for outwitting masters, at least for alleviating the slaves' oppression. Even so, imagining how some of these strategies were consciously wrought is a far easier task than asserting that others were not. I would like to propose unconscious resistance as a psychological resource that emerges in the experience of being sub-jugated and is activated before the subject ever arrives at the threshold of absolute submission, if such a state exists. By demonstrating how Juan Francisco Manzano acted "in spite of himself," I examine instances of unconscious resistance that the poet narrates in his autobiography for what they can tell us about the routine psychological resources that al-lowed him to withstand and survive his enslavement.[1]

By describing an enslaved subject's act of resistance to oppression as unconscious, I am not attempting to establish an alternative essentialist characterization of the slave. Responding to the fallacy of the inherently submissive slave by positing a counter model that is equally essentialist is of limited strategic value, especially in a historical sense. For in a pa-ternalist regime of forced labor that held the upper hand by oppressing the enslaved subject at every level, even the most rebellious traits that were imputed to slaves on the plantation, such as unruliness or disobe-dience, were easily subsumed in moral alibis that advocated slavery as a means of providing slaves with discipline and the benefits of Western civilization. According to Kelly Oliver, the unconscious must be taken into consideration in order to understand the relationship between op-pression and affect. In doing otherwise, she asserts, "we become com-plicit with those who would blame the victims, so to speak, for their own negative affects."[2] In its widest sense, unconscious resistance can readily be identified with the survival instinct. However, I am interested in examining unconscious resistance as a psychological resource in order to ascertain how the enslaved subject, such as in Manzano's depiction of himself as a child, grows into an awareness of his enslavement and grapples continuously with this knowledge. The poet's autobiographical writing provides him and his readers with summaries and assessments of his life that are rendered from an external perspective, and the vulner-abilities that the account reveals—some of which recall the tender point to which Douglass refers in his autobiography as a counterweight in his bid for freedom—are continuously subject to interpretation. In other words, to claim that, in addition to the limited opportunities for open defiance that were available to him, Manzano unconsciously resisted enslavement "in spite of himself" constitutes a powerful act of interpretation, the ethical limits of which should also be stated.

First, it is essential to recall that the idea of writing an account of his life originated not with Manzano but with his mentor and future employer, Domingo del Monte, who requested the autobiography while the poet was still enslaved. The patrician's interest in Manzano's narration of intimate details about his life must also be considered in light of the demand for such narratives that a transatlantic Anglo-American abolitionist bourgeoisie required for its cause. Even though this demand, which at times instrumentalized the voices of the enslaved, emerged from the abolitionists' sincere attempts to speak out against slavery and on behalf of slaves, acquiring Manzano's autobiography specifically offered del Monte and the young liberals the opportunity to aspire to joining the ranks of the "men of feeling" who belonged to the same burgeoning international bourgeoisie as the abolitionists. Given his enslavement, Manzano was not in a position to deny del Monte's request. Second, although my interpretation of incidents in the poet's life also derives critical authority from a privileged external view of the events that he describes, my argument that Manzano acted in spite of himself does not describe a character flaw but emphasizes aspects of subjectivity that assume particular characteristics under the duress of enslavement. Acting in spite of the self engages the unconscious because this activity signals a compulsive or automatic response to coercion that may appear to contradict a subject's struggle for freedom but is in fact fundamental for his or her self-representation. The poet's account of his life provides examples of these paradoxes of subjectivity or what Basterra calls the "necessary fiction" that describes the subject's imagined relations to power.[3] In my approach to Manzano's writings, I argue that slavery deprives slaves in very precise ways of opportunities for gaining visibility as moral subjects in the societies that oppress them. Although his texts provide clear descriptions of and references to this deprivation, I do not claim that the poet's account of his life should be read as emblematic of all legally enslaved subjects, especially if this symbolism should mean downplaying the self-contradictions that inform his very humanity.

What image do we hold of ourselves as we negotiate the coercive forces to which we are continuously subject in our institutions and soci-

eties? How do we engage with or disavow these pressures in the course
of a day, or in that of a lifetime? These questions readily surface for modern readers of Manzano's autobiography. However, far from equating
the blatant and subtle oppression to which slaves were submitted with
the stressful situations of the modern workplace, my premise in posing
these questions is that a close examination of chattel slavery and the
ways in which legally enslaved subjects reflected on, articulated, and
strove for freedom can tell us a great deal about the complexity of the
will to survive under some of the most brutal conditions that modern
societies have imposed on human beings. The autobiography details
Manzano's life as a house slave and demonstrates the author's awareness of his self-representation in spite of the perverse intimacy to which
his autobiographical writing was submitted under the purview of the
Creole reformists who eventually became his liberators. Yet there is
more to Manzano's text than the surreptitious and limited negotiation
of an autobiographical writing space for himself within a slave-owning,
colonial society. The analysis to which he submits his character includes
descriptions of coerced attachment to certain aspects of his enslavement
and the peculiar melancholy that he identified as his personal trait.

In examining these two aspects of Manzano's self-representation,
which I consider forms of resistance to his enslavement, I have been
mindful of the politics of representation that surrounds the figure of the
so-called submissive slave. In *Between Slavery and Freedom,* McGary and
Lawson observe that in the history of the criticism on slave narratives
that began in the 1970s, Stanley Elkins's provocative claim that slavery
in the United States was responsible for producing a Sambo personality
launched an intense debate about the politics of research on slave narratives. His controversial hypothesis, which defines the Sambo figure
as lazy, loyal, and childlike, stimulated a host of arguments against the
perpetuation of negative stereotypes that included the myth that slaves
are to blame for their own enslavement, the notion that they prolonged
slavery by not offering resistance to it, and, in the contemporary period,
the devastating effect that the Sambo figure would have for those who
experience racial discrimination.[4] Refuting the notion that such a personality type could emerge from contexts of slavery, what McGary and
Lawson appreciate about the hypothesis that Elkins proposed was that

it led scholars to think about the nature of resistance to and from within bondage.

Given that absolute personal freedom from coercion has never existed in any society, the analysis of Manzano's life story that I present throws light on the daily psychic work of finding alleviation from slavery's oppressive practices. By claiming that alleviation from these practices is one of the most common measurements of freedom from coercion that can be ascertained within slavery, it becomes possible to fathom and assess the challenges that the majority of enslaved subjects faced in their efforts to survive oppression. I am thinking specifically of those who did not "make history" because their routine forms of resistance had never attained the status of the "heroic." Pointing out the difference between the heroic and the mundane struggle against slavery, William L. Andrews draws a distinction between the Romantic and realist stages in African American slave narratives. According to him, the antebellum slave narrative developed its "classic" form in the hands of fugitive slaves between 1840 and 1860, the heyday of American Romanticism when, for example, Douglass's narrative found many admirers. By contrast, he asserts, the postbellum slave narrator rarely appeals to the ideals and religious and ethical debates of the earlier period but looks, instead, to "evaluate slavery according to its practical consequences in the real world of human action."[5] In his study of what slaves in the southern United States wrote about their living conditions, Paul D. Escott employs the term "the boundaries of reasonable resistance" to describe the multiple ways in which slaves resisted slavery on a daily basis. He argues that because the vast majority of slaves were unable to deliver themselves from bondage they sought measures to weaken its impact. He further claims that "this decision should not be confused with the idea of accepting one's situation. The slaves did not accept their bondage, but external power left them few options. Knowing that they could not make themselves free, the vast majority of slaves struggled, instead, to lessen the extent of their enslavement."[6] For Escott, the greater part of the slaves' repertoire of resistance took place within the day-to-day concerns of plantation life.[7] Similarly, Moreno Fraginals underscores that slaves often practiced a feigned obedience—a strategy that he considers a form of passive rebellion—that allowed them to resist oppression and channel the trauma of slavery.[8] In a view that takes us closer to conceiving how the routine struggle against oppression need not emerge from conscious action, McGary reminds us that in order to evaluate what constitutes an act of resistance, analysts "should not always give primacy to an agent's intentions" but might concentrate, instead, on "the conditions that the agent faced when he or she acted or failed to act and the avenues available for reducing oppression."[9] For slaves, there was no personal or social space that remained untouched by slavery, so that drawing attention to their thinking while they were embedded in slavery allows us to make more precise observations about the subjectivity and agency of legally enslaved subjects.

In the last chapter, I indicated that paternalism was a false ideology through which slave owners attempted to convince themselves and others that slavery was in the slaves' best interest. This moral alibi permitted them to participate in a brutalizing regime of forced labor without having to question the economic necessity of owning slaves. According to their reasoning, the slaves needed and should be grateful for their masters' enlightenment, civilizing customs, and care. This perverse championing of moral conduct in the service of a broader immorality structures the relations of power between master and slave in distorted and self-contradictory ways. In what follows, I examine the ordinary attempts of an enslaved subject to weather, resist, negotiate, and write about paternalistic practices and forms of perverse intimacy that compelled him to be fond of his enslavers at specific moments in the account of his life. This analysis, especially of what Manzano describes as his melancholy, allows me to forward the claim that if slavery systematically constrains the enslaved subject's ability to develop a self-consciousness capable of openly assuming an ethical stance vis-à-vis his or her enslavers, then it is the enslaved subject's compulsive propensity for creativity beyond the strict assignments of forced labor that facilitates the greatest degree of routine psychological resistance to oppression and that seeks to compensate for the negation of the moral development of enslaved subjects. The fact that Manzano should represent himself through diverse if not conflicting traits reveals the complexity of his character—a complexity that may strike us as contradictory because of the ways, for example, in which he oscillates between resistance to slavery and attachment to other forms of servitude in the text. Because his humanity is more complex than any two-dimensional representation of him in which he might come across as possessing or even incarnating uncomplicated, wholly conscious, or relentlessly utopian motives and tendencies, the apparent paradoxes that Manzano imputes to his character are not surprising. The issue thus becomes how to make sense of these paradoxes so that we can afford ourselves a more comprehensive understanding of his subjectivity; needless to say, it is also crucial to arrive at this understanding in light of the enslaved poet's awareness that members of del Monte's literary circle would eventually be scrutinizing and editing his writing. For just as Manzano protected himself from being accused of publicly speaking out against slavery by composing "Treinta años" in a universal register, so too would he have wanted to be certain that denouncing his second mistress's cruelty in writing would not lead to punishment. Following the next section, which describes and interrogates the circumstances in which Manzano taught himself to write, I analyze these instances of self-representation for what they tell us about his subjectivity within bondage. In the section where I examine his references to melancholy, I also argue that Manzano's impulses to exercise his creative imagination became an effective, albeit compulsive, resource for resisting the full psychological onslaught and internalization of slavery's laws and practices.

MANZANO'S ACCESS TO WRITING

According to Manzano's account, it was shortly after he had been sent to Havana, in order to recuperate from injuries and a depression that took hold of him following a particularly traumatic series of incidents, that he began to take interest in writing. As the events unfolded, Manzano had been wrongly accused of having sold one of the capon chickens that had been delivered to the home of his second mistress, the Marchioness de Prado Ameno, and he was to be taken to the sugar mill at El Molino, where he would be whipped until he confessed his purported crime. The overseer was duly summoned, and upon his arrival he quickly bound the slave's hands with rope, mounted his horse, and forced Manzano to run ahead of him using the length of the rope like a leash. At the time,

Manzano would have been somewhere between fourteen and seventeen years old. On the road to the sugar mill, he tripped, fell, and was immediately set upon by two vicious dogs. One of them bit into his left cheek, sinking its fang all the way to one of his molars, while the other made short work of his left calf and thigh so that the entire leg, bleeding profusely, eventually went numb. The startled overseer leapt from his horse and succeeded in chasing the dogs away. However, when he finally managed to turn his attention to Manzano, he hurled abuses at him and pulled on the binding rope so violently that he ended up dislocating the youth's right arm. Manzano's account does not indicate how much time transpired before these wounds adequately healed, but there was no doubt that his punishment remained pending.

For nine consecutive nights, Manzano was ordered to drop to the ground, where he was pinned down by five blacks and, in the presence of the overseer and his assistant, administered twenty-five lashes. As is frequently the case with torture victims, he found himself in the desperate situation of not being able to deliver the "right" truth: "I said a thousand different things because they were demanding I tell the truth and I did not know which truth they wanted. . . . I said nine thousand different things as they shouted at me, 'Tell the truth!' and whipped me. I no longer had anything left to say, anything that it seemed might end their punishing me."[10] Every morning, the marchioness would receive a note with the details of what Manzano had revealed the night before. On the tenth day, the "truth" finally surfaced that even though the missing capon mysteriously made its way around the compound, it eventually showed up in the kitchen and was subsequently eaten by the steward. In any case, Manzano's punishment came to an abrupt end, and he was assigned to loosen *bagasse* and transport sugarloaf cones to the filtering house until further notice.[11] One day, soon afterward, Manzano had put down one of the sugarloaves in the filtering house when the roof suddenly came crashing down. The impact sent him through an opening under the filtering house, but he managed to escape serious injury. Andrés, a Creole slave who was also at work in the filtering house, was not so fortunate: falling beams crushed his skull, scraped the skin off his head, and left him with bulging eyes. Needless to say, the gravely injured man died shortly afterward. Accidental or not, this string of violent episodes and brushes with death must have shattered Manzano's nerves and pushed him to the brink of despair: "I sank into such a depression that I did not emerge from my sorrowful despondency, even when I saw all the children engrossed in games or when they called to me. I ate very little and was almost always in tears."[12]

It is no surprise, therefore, that Manzano should consider his being taken to Havana and left in the service of Don Nicolás, the Marchioness de Prado Ameno's second son, a welcome reprieve from the whims and volatility of his mistress and the brutality of the whip. Manzano was not much older than his master, and he clearly recalled and appreciated the two occasions, prior to the incidents at El Molino, when Don Nicolás and his brothers introduced a bit of sweet bread through a crack in the door of the coal cellar where Manzano would be locked up overnight in retribution for any childish prank. Now, a few years later, and in his young master's service at a comfortable distance from the plantation, Manzano's affection for his master was boundless.[13] In fact, such was his attachment to Don Nicolás that Manzano, writing about this period of his life some twenty years after he eventually escaped from the marchioness's home, glosses over the curious paradox, in his own words, that his young master loved him "not as a slave, but as a son, notwithstanding his young age."[14] Paternalism, as a common practice and false ideology, rationalized relations between masters and slaves so that these relations might take on the appearance of being necessary and natural. That there was absolutely no possibility for Manzano to imagine that his master might consider him like a brother, despite their closeness in age and the life that they had shared within the same household, throws light on both the early socialization of masters to assume power over their slaves and Manzano's induced acceptance of this subjugation.

However, reducing Manzano's stated attachment to Don Nicolás to a personality trait, to the compliance of the so-called submissive slave, does little to facilitate our comprehension of his predicament and ends up victimizing him. What lies at fault in any reductionism of this kind is the temptation to uphold a specific, universally recognizable struggle for freedom to which Manzano should have aspired. The risk of assuming this stance not only lies in the manner in which we measure the particularities of Manzano's desire for freedom against a universal and abstract struggle for freedom; if we are incapable of granting that no absolutely universal definition of freedom exists, because the potential for and limits on freedom are directly proportional to the specific contexts in which they emerge, then we, Manzano's readers, can easily fall into the trap of holding him fully accountable for not trying harder to free himself from bondage during his adolescence. Because of his youth and most recent encounters with death, Manzano reacted rationally to his more humane treatment by attaching himself to the person that he held responsible for the improvement in and stability of his daily existence. This claim does not exonerate his enslavers: on the contrary, by considering his attachment a rational albeit induced response to the obvious reduction of his oppression, we can begin to perceive how his "affection" for his master might result not from some masochistic tendency on Manzano's part, but from one of slavery's most terrifying psychological tools. Next to punishment and death, nothing struck greater fear into the hearts of enslaved subjects than the cruel arbitrariness with which they or their loved ones might be sold or handed over to a new master. Given circumstances in which, as human property, he was permanently subject to transactions beyond his control, Manzano appreciated that he had been suddenly delivered from an unbearable situation; deprived of self-determination, he was placed in a position that obliged him to identify this substantially less stressful stability with his young master. Under these conditions, this coerced affection for his master takes on the appearance of being natural and sincere. Writing about when he ended up as Don Nicolás's personal slave so soon after the violence that he suffered because of the missing capon, he states: "That sadness, rooted so deeply in my soul, began to dissipate."[15]

Manzano's desire to learn to write emerges in the context of his subservience and coerced attachment to Don Nicolás. In preparing his young master's desk, chair, and books for studying every morning, he writes, "I began identifying with his habits so thoroughly that I, too, began my own study regimen."[16] This issue of imitation and, in particular, the critical attitude that Manzano began to develop about its significance for his self-education figure prominently in his decision to devote himself to learning to write. As a child, his prodigious memory facilitated an aptitude for imitation, which in turn provided him and his family with some earnings: "When I was already ten years old and knowledgeable in all that a woman could teach me about religion, I would recite not only the entire catechism by heart but also almost all of Fray Luis de Granada's sermons. I also knew many lengthy passages, short plays and interludes, dramatic theory, and stage sets. They took me to see French operas, and I was good at imitating some of them, for which my parents used to receive the allotment of gifts from me that I would collect in the parlor, although it was always more from the sermons."[17] Because his ability to remember and imitate such lengthy passages outpaced his capacity to assimilate the meaning of what he recited, his "words" would sometimes land him in trouble. When the marchioness discovered him innocently reciting *décimas* that "were neither spiritual nor amorous" before the old domestic servants who had gathered to listen to him, she strictly forbade them to speak with him.[18] The meaning of the words that he pronounced on those occasions remained a mystery forever: first, because nobody, including the child that Manzano was, could explain what they meant and, second, because the two thorough beatings that he received as a consequence dissuaded him from ever reciting them again.

Looking back on his youth, Manzano purports that knowing how to write at that early stage of his life would have rescued him from a predicament in which his mistress sought to control when and to whom he recited his words as well as from a frustration due to which it was impossible for him to study the verses that he composed. Although he had composed several *décimas* by memory by the time he was twelve years old, learning to write was an activity from which Manzano was purposefully barred. Confined in this manner to listening to his own voice—to employing his memory, voice, and hearing in place of the written word's capacity for stimulating reflection—he recalls that his "facility for expression was such that just to talk, I would talk with the table, with the painting, with the wall."[19] Being kept from learning to write in his early youth undoubtedly allowed him to perfect certain verbal skills; in his autobiography, however, he views the inability to write as a missed opportunity for thought and analysis.

Manzano reiterates this conviction when he recalls the way in which his desire to learn to write emerged. According to him, it was poetry that best suited how he articulated particular moments in his life: "Through-

out all the stages of my life, poetry—sometimes happy, sometimes sorrowful—afforded me verses in harmony with my situation."[20] By contrast, he grew frustrated that even with access to his master's rhetoric
books his learning progressed no further than what he could memorize.
What this statement means, of course, is that Manzano had taught himself to read at some basic level. Furthermore, it was this irritating awareness that unlike his experience with poetry, which gradually shifted from
mimicry to improvisation and creativity, approaching his master's books
with no tools except for his prodigious memory produced only sense-
less imitation. Once he had made up his mind to learn to write, he also
faced a series of practical problems: "I did not know how to cut quills
and refrained from taking any from my master. I, nevertheless, bought
myself a penknife, quills, and very fine paper, which I placed over a discarded sheet written in my master's hand in order to accustom myself to
the feel of fashioning letters. I worked along tracing the shapes on the
paper below. With this method, in less than a month I could already write
lines that imitated my master's handwriting. For that reason there are
certain similarities between his penmanship and mine."[21] Don Nicolás,
who found out about these activities from those who witnessed them,
initially ordered him to abandon this pastime, arguing that it was not
appropriate to his station.[22] In one of the only passages in his autobiography that brings to light an ongoing act of defiance, Manzano reveals that
he would indulge himself learning to write by the light of a candle stump
when everyone else in the household had retired for the night. So long
as this clandestine disobedience did not interfere with his daily tasks,
it remained a part of his routine activities while he was Don Nicolás's
page. This ongoing resistance corroborates Sylvia Molloy's claim that
Manzano identified not with his master per se but with the writing skills
that the latter inadvertently provided.[23]

Curiously, Manzano places far greater significance on writing than on
learning to read. His motives for wanting to write and the way in which
he learned to do so partly explain the relationship that he establishes between both activities. His approach to the written word differs markedly
from those of other authors who had been enslaved, such as Gustavus
Vassa (more familiarly known as Olaudah Equiano) and Douglass. Unlike Manzano, who spoke to the objects around him in order to find some

way to study his words, Equiano became interested in reading at an early age because he felt an urge to talk to and listen to books: "I have often taken up a book, and have talked to it, and then put my ears to it, when alone, in hopes that it would answer me; and I have been very much concerned when I found it remained silent."[24] Douglass learned the alphabet when he was around eight years old under the tutelage of Mrs. Auld, one of his mistresses, and against the wishes of her husband. It was when the latter vehemently warned his wife against continuing this instruction that Douglass began to suspect that the "white man's power to enslave the black man" was contained in books and reading.[25] This suspicion inspired him to build upon the basic reading skills that he acquired in his master's home. Equiano attended school in England, and Douglass became an autodidact after he acquired the fundamentals of reading. However, even though both began learning to read with the conviction that books contained important knowledge and that the written word provided access to that knowledge, Manzano was initially more proficient at writing than at reading and associated the written word not only with the letters on the leaves of paper that Don Nicolás discarded and with those that appeared in the books that lay within his reach, but, most of all, with the desire to write down the numerous verses that he felt compelled to compose because they taxed his ability to remember them all. Prohibited from learning to read and write, the only book that Manzano seemed to have handled with any consistency contained verses by the neoclassical Spanish poet Juan Bautista Arriaza y Spervilla. Even so, he employed Arriaza's verses as models for learning how to write poetry.

Writing autobiographical prose, Molloy argues, was a more difficult enterprise for Manzano than poetry.[26] From the perspective of Orlando Patterson's assertion that slavery for the slave was the equivalent of social death, it is extraordinary to find Manzano's brief but eloquent reflection on what it meant to be writing about himself from circumstances of social nonexistence in a letter that he wrote to del Monte on June 25, 1835. Penned some twenty years after he escaped from the Marchioness de Prado Ameno's home, and while he was still hiring himself out as a slave in Havana, Manzano reports on the difficult progress that he was making in completing the autobiography that the patrician had requested and that he began writing earlier that year. Given the patrician's social status and Manzano's enslavement until 1836, the latter must have considered this request nothing less than fully binding. Responding to del Monte's apparent haste to obtain the narrative, Manzano informs him that even though he was restricting himself to the "most interesting events," he still had not gone beyond 1820 but expected to finish the autobiography soon.[27]

Turning his attention to the difficulty of writing about a life in bondage, Manzano admits that he had been tempted to discontinue his writing on at least four occasions, mostly because an account of so many calamities might read like "a bloated chronicle of lies."[28] This initial concern about credibility stems from an anxiety about self-exposure. On the one hand, Manzano feels urged to communicate that cruel beatings at a tender age had brought on the early knowledge of what he refers to as his humble condition; on the other, he states that he is ashamed to expose this condition and finds himself at a loss about how he should demonstrate "the facts" while "leaving the most terrible part in the inkwell."[29] Dilemmas of this kind are frequent in slave narratives. According to Dwight McBride, slaves who wrote about their enslavement faced rhetorical problems such as having to describe bondage and physical punishment to a readership that was removed from these experiences of slavery in almost every sense. These slaves thus found themselves in the paradoxical position of attempting to articulate this experience as subjects who were struggling to transcend slavery while they also "understood themselves to be agentless" vis-à-vis white abolitionists who owned the means of publication.[30] In Manzano's case, he sets out to reconcile a negative view of himself in which he associates his enslavement with public spectacles of personal punishment and humiliation with the decorum that he sought to maintain in his duties and that he attempts to cultivate in his autobiographical writing and correspondence. For him, complying with del Monte's request meant that he was obliged to revisit these violent spectacles and, to a certain degree, participate through his own narrative self-construction in abasing himself in the eyes of readers. It is thus with the intention of maintaining his dignity that he wishes that he could separate the "facts" from their "most terrible part."[31]

Unlike the poetry that Manzano wrote and published while he was still enslaved, the prospect of exposing himself through autobiographi-

cal writing produces the discomfort of "double-consciousness." Even
though the reformist sympathies that characterized del Monte and his
circle differ appreciatively from the context to which W. E. B. Du Bois
refers, Manzano's concern about how his readers will perceive him exemplifies the African American intellectual's observations about the
unsettling threat of self-denigration that results from the internalization
of an extraneous, collective, and prejudicial white gaze. Even though
Manzano does not claim to have resolved how he should come to terms
with a mode of writing that obliges him to set a personal account of subjugation against his desire to construct a dignified self, he alerts del
Monte and his circle about what they should expect to find in his life
story. Given the inevitability of returning to scenes of punishment that
he admits to having abbreviated or censored, Manzano forewarns the
patrician that he should be prepared to behold a feeble creature stumbling along (*rodando*) amid the gravest torments, turned over to various
overseers, and being the target of disgrace without the slightest consideration.[32] Worried that he might lower himself too much in del Monte's
estimation, Manzano writes in a letter to the patrician: "Remember
when you read that I am a slave and that *the slave is a dead being before
his master,* and do not underestimate what I have gained: consider me a
martyr and you will find that the endless whippings that mutilated my
immature flesh, will never corrupt your dearest servant, who, trusting
the prudence that characterizes you, dares to sputter a word on this
subject, and more so when the one who has given me reason to moan
is still alive."[33] Manzano's paradoxical statement in which he identifies
himself as a slave and then addresses del Monte from this purported
site of what Orlando Patterson calls "social death" illustrates a deep
awareness not only of his status in colonial society but also of the limits
of social mobility for an enslaved subject. In shifting from the particularity of declaring his social identity to the abstraction of the slave as a
dead being in the presence of his master, Manzano is clearly interested
in informing his literary mentor that even though slavery functions by
dehumanizing the slave, he remains uncorrupted. Although Manzano
had never been del Monte's slave, he acknowledges the patrician's power
and influence and is fully aware of the coercive pressures that assail
the position from which he writes. The fact that the poet rose to fame

in Havana through his published compositions exacerbated an enig-
matic personal situation. On the one hand, he received praise for his
literary sensibility: from the perspective of their common paternalist
ideology, del Monte and Madden, Manzano's first translator, would have
concurred that the combination of Manzano's "natural" talent and his
coerced predisposition to please his would-be liberators exemplified
literature's "humanizing" effects on the enslaved subject. On the other
hand, the poet remained enslaved while he wrote his autobiography so
that his self-conception straddled a social antagonism that extended
from his being human property and an object of disavowal to his valued
but limited agency as a writing subject.

In the final analysis, the act of writing and the struggle to secure
his freedom were closely related in Manzano's mind. The association
that he made between them gave precedence to poetry not only because writing his verses allowed him to elude his mistress's scrutiny
and proscriptions. Because he was adept at composing his own poetry,
Manzano could also enjoy the feeling of having mastered his own poetic
expression. (Ironically, it was probably the resounding success of his
sonnet, "Treinta años," that persuaded del Monte to ask him to write
his life story.) Prose proved to be a challenge of a different sort since
the prohibition against his learning to read effectively deprived him
of more books and models for writing. Not surprisingly, his writing
was phonetic, which does not present a problem of intelligibility in
Spanish if his texts are read aloud, and it also lacked punctuation and
paragraphing. Moreover, as his correspondence with del Monte clearly
shows, writing a narrative about his life presented a series of intellectual
difficulties for which there was no precedent on the island, including
questions about the criteria for selecting episodes from his experience
as a slave; his image as an oppressed and downtrodden slave, which he
consistently associates with personal weakness rather than with the
brutal system that subjugated him; and the fear of committing himself to inscribing episodes of his life while the Marchioness de Prado
Ameno, his volatile second mistress, was still alive. There was also the
unstated but ever present circumstance of writing his life story for a
group of "enlightened" slave owners. These dilemmas did not surface
in the satisfying compulsion with which he composed and wrote down

his poems, even as some of these compositions, like the unpublished "Desesperación" (Desperation) and "La visión del poeta," (The poet's vision) eloquently condemned his enslavement.[34]

PERVERSE MOTHERING

Manzano's candid representations of his emotional state bestow a psychological complexity to his writing that exceeds and complicates the abolitionist expectation that the slave narrative genre should enumerate reasons to denounce slave owners but not intimate how slaves might express an attachment to their masters. How, then, is it possible to account for Manzano's stated affection for his two mistresses and young master? Two unsatisfactory responses come to mind. The first is that life in bondage pleased him. Born on a sugar plantation, raised as a house slave and page, and having no experience of what it meant to live emancipated from slavery, Manzano describes a childhood of induced affection for his first mistress, the Marchioness Justiz de Santa Ana, and a period of deep sadness and consternation that began with adolescence in the home of his second mistress, the Marchioness de Prado Ameno. Despite the difference in attitude toward both periods of his life, he constantly sought ways to alleviate his bondage and, with adulthood, to save the amount of money required to buy his freedom. In fact, Manzano pursued all the privileges that were available to him (marriage, the right to request a new owner, and manumission) under the Cuban slave code of 1789, and, when the opportunity eventually arose, he escaped to Havana.[35] These actions are inconsistent with those of a contented slave. The second unsatisfactory response is that slavery was so overwhelmingly pervasive that it left him with no psychic space from which he could marshal resistance. Even the most cursory reading of the autobiography reveals the consistency with which Manzano reflected on his enslavement and sought the psychological means to withstand it. In light of the circumstances that gave rise to his decision to learn to write, the most obvious answer to this question is that his bondage and a sequence of horrible events obliged him to overvalue his young master's "benevolence." The facts would lead us to conclude as much, but this statement requires further inflection if we are to avoid subscribing to the second unsatisfactory response, that is, to the proposition that Manzano was entirely powerless to resist the practices of perverse intimacy through which his enslavers might foment his voluntary compliance.

Between these two unsatisfactory extremes—a putative masochistic desire to remain enslaved, on one hand, and an absolute psychological subjugation, on the other—there lies a psychic middle ground that permits Manzano to exercise varying degrees of agency from within his legally enslaved condition, as paradoxically self-defeating as this agency might occasionally seem. In order to explore this middle ground, it is essential to view Manzano first and foremost as a human subject, who, from infancy to early adulthood, attained greater self-consciousness and, with this knowledge, developed precise attitudes toward the limits that his enslaved condition placed on his ability to act. Although Manzano's path to greater albeit aggrieved self-consciousness is consistent with the pattern of development that Hegel describes in his theory of consciousness, it is to the legal particularity of the condition into which he was born that reveals aspects of the extent and limits of his agency as a child and afterward. Manzano came into the world as a slave: his status was legally defined by the concept of *partus sequitur ventrum,* which stipulates that the child inherits the mother's condition and grants the child's owner the right to enslave or sell him or her. In the following analysis, it becomes evident that this legal provision, which appears outwardly to refer to a determined socioeconomic relation between the child and his or her biological mother, not only rationalizes how Manzano's mistresses drew domestic benefits from his bondage; through a common but pernicious twist of the slave owner's paternalist practices, *partus sequitur ventrum* permitted his mistresses to usurp his mother's place and thereby impose a "maternal" authority (with its accompanying affective peculiarities) that Manzano, as an infant, routinely experienced. How could this perverse mothering not assail his psychological resistance to bondage by encouraging him to think about its practitioners in sentimental terms? Yet the burning question that I propose to answer in this section is why, given what Manzano came to learn about slavery as an adult, he still insisted on idealizing his childhood.

Before proceeding, it will be necessary to touch briefly on the principal paradox of subjectivity. According to Butler, subjection is "the process of becoming subordinated by power as well as the process of becoming a subject."[36] In other words, because subjects always emerge already embedded in power structures—with childhood being a classic example—the attachment to a subjugating power is the means by which one "persists as oneself" in spite of subordination.[37] This attachment to power is fundamentally an issue about living under and with subordination. Nevertheless, if it is to avoid being thoroughly objectified by power—being reduced to a mere effect of power, as the second unsatisfactory response that I mentioned above implies—the subject must at the same time deny its relation to that subjugating power. As Butler states it: "No subject can emerge without this attachment, formed in dependency, but no subject, in the course of its formation, can ever afford to 'see' it."[38] Furthering this notion that the subject denies or blinds itself to its attachment to power, Basterra argues that the subject holds on to this denial as a "necessary fiction" not simply because this "fiction" helps the subject to constitute itself but also because the subject's worldview and place within the latter would collapse without this desired fabrication of the subject's relation to power.[39] To speak of a subject's attachment to the power that subjugates it does not mean that this subject *consciously* goes out into the world in search of a power before which it prostrates itself. This relation assumes the existence of power, not as an autonomous force that lies only somewhere outside the subject, but as one with which the subject grapples internally in a process of self-reflection that Hegel calls the "unhappy consciousness" and that Du Bois designates as the possession of "double-consciousness."

Manzano's autobiographical writing is mediated by his desire to preserve a special view of his childhood and, on this basis, to construct a dignified self for his readers from del Monte's literary circle. Rather than succumb entirely to perceiving himself as the powerless object of his enslavers' disavowal of his humanity—specifically, as "a form of entertainment" for his first mistress and as a "lapdog" for his second—he produces a romanticized account of his childhood in which he highlights his special status in the plantation household.[40] It is this preferred, imagined account of his relation to power that constitutes psychological resistance to the fact of his enslavement. In the autobiography's opening pages, he takes satisfaction in revealing his presumably privileged birth and childhood. He proudly recalls that his enslaved mother was one of the "maids of distinction" who had been raised according to her "class and station in society" to serve the Marchioness Justiz de Santa Ana.[41] His father, who was allowed to marry his mother, was the head house-servant, and he was a proud man who forbade his children to play with the black children on the plantation; Manzano also claimed that his family was not liked because his parents lived together.[42] The poet further enhances his social standing by asserting that his mother had been esteemed, *"singled out for training,"* treated like a daughter, and, moreover, that he himself had been held in the marchioness's arms more than in his mother's and was considered the child of his mistress's old age.[43] As if to dispel any notion that he had fabricated this account of his childhood, Manzano declares that there were still "some living witnesses to this fact."[44]

In his analyses of slave narratives, Lawson contends that regardless of the way slaveholders treated them, slaves understood that it was human ownership that constituted the most destructive form of oppression.[45] Yet, despite this systematic oppression, Manzano appears almost conceited about the way in which the marchioness usurps his parents' authority over him. A revealing incident illustrates the kinds of distortions that occur as a result of human ownership: "On one occasion my father shook me harshly for being quite unruly. My mistress found out, and that was enough for her to refuse to see my father for several days until she restored him to her good graces at the behest of her confessor, Father Moya, of the Order of San Francisco. She did so only after making clear to him which parental rights were his as a father and which were hers as a slaveholder who assumed the role of a mother."[46] As an infant, it would have been difficult for Manzano to remain unscathed by the ubiquitous and unnatural practice by which a slave owner's legal rights superseded those of parents who lived in the same household. Having been born into slavery and associating his welfare and purported privileges in the household with the Marchioness Justiz, Manzano describes a childhood in which the thought of life outside of slavery did not seem to cross his mind. He even goes as far as to exalt his childhood, associating it with "wandering through a garden of very beautiful flowers, *a series of joys.*"[47] Even so, this agreeable depiction of his childhood is not what it seems. In a moment of self-conscious writing, after deciding that he would restrict himself to invoking only pleasant memories, such as the day when his first mistress celebrated his baptism by establishing his parents' manumission price, Manzano suddenly interjects: "I should have been a bit happier; but let's go on."[48] Such traces of suppressed information typically punctuate slave narratives; ellipses, for example, permit authors to curtail thoughts that are too painful to recall or that incriminate them in some way. (In his English translation of the autobiography, Madden omits all the ellipses.) Manzano's intimation that he was not as contented as he should have been furnishes one of several glimpses at the fissures in a fanciful account of his childhood that he proffered for his readers and, most importantly, for himself.

A child who has known nothing else but domestic slavery would be able to recall happy moments, such as the games that he or she played or improvised with other children. But Manzano, penning his life story when he was around thirty-nine and aware that he was constructing a written recollection from the vantage of adulthood, obstinately holds on to an idealized image of his childhood. That he should fondly recall the Marchioness Justiz de Santa Ana requires little explanation: by the time he learned to identify himself as the "child of her old age," his mistress had already exposed him to living under her legally buttressed maternal authority and to the peculiar bonds of affection that arose with and through this relationship.[49] By contrast, when he writes regarding the Marchioness de Prado Ameno,"I loved her in spite of the harshness with which she treated me," his "affection" arises from circumstances in which his mistress's unpredictable and disconcerting shifts in attitude, permitting him to take delight in childhood pastimes on the one hand and severely punishing him as a slave on the other, psychologically buffet him into perceiving her maternal authority as a reliable source of both oppression and "motherly" sentiment.[50] Manzano openly admits this so-called affection for the marchioness in his autobiography. However, in keeping with Butler's and Basterra's claims regarding subjection, this admission exemplifies the unconscious fabrication of his relation to those who subjugate him. He shelters himself from the full brunt of the knowledge of his oppression by attributing a sense of "motherhood" to his second mistress:

> When my mistress' temper mellowed toward me, I unconsciously relin-
> quished a certain hardened heart that I had acquired since the last time she
> condemned me to chains and hard labor. As she persevered in not laying a
> hand on me or in ordering others to do so, I had forgotten all the past and
> loved her like a mother. I did not like to hear the servants call her names,
> and I would have told on several of them if it were not clear to me that he
> who tattled was the one who offended her, an idea I heard her repeat many
> times.[51]

Manzano's "affection" conforms to a recognizable pattern of coerced attachment. Analogous to the way in which his fondness for Don Nicolás
arose in response to his being delivered from scenes of death and physical torture, his claim to love the marchioness, as if she were "a mother,"
logically follows from her "not laying a hand on me or in ordering others
to do so." In essence, a substantial though temporary alleviation from
physical punishment and other forms of oppression almost always precedes such expressions of affection.

   Although both marchionesses abuse their respective forms of maternal authority over Manzano, he consistently draws sharp distinctions
between their attitudes toward him. In contrast to the happiness that
he associates with his first mistress's home, he repeatedly cites the Marchioness de Prado Ameno's harsh treatment of him as he grew into adolescence. For instance, he recalls when she rebuked him for requesting
papers to solicit a new master, which was well within his rights: "She
asked me if I remembered my mom, and I replied that I did. 'Well,' she
said to me, 'I have taken her place. Do you hear me?'"[52] What must have
been deceptive about and constitutive of Manzano's induced affection
for the Marchioness de Prado Ameno was the way in which she evidently
required his presence and he rationalized this reliance. He writes that
she refused to let him out of sight "even when she was sleeping" and
that although she would periodically send him away to be punished, she
could not do without him for more than ten consecutive days.[53] This
view of the marchioness, in which her authority derives from slavery's
legal practices as well as her dependency on slavery, illustrates the extent
to which slave owners and their slaves were inextricably and antagonis-
tically interlocked in mutually constitutive social and coercive affective relations. In Manzano's case, the idea that his mistress always came
around to needing his company (and, what he refrains from stating, his

servitude) was propitious for leading him to believe that he could occupy a special position in her home.

The hegemony of *partus sequitur ventrum* in the domestic spaces that Manzano inhabited also emerges in what Fionnghuala Sweeney calls "a distinctively feminine sphere of influence, whose framework provides him with social identity."[54] According to Sweeney, the extent of this influence includes Manzano's education and training in a domestic and cultural space that was clearly feminized; the decorative status that he often assumed as a page; the control over his economic capital that his biological mother and, after her death, the Marchioness de Prado Ameno possessed; and his habit of viewing the world through the "lens of feminine culture."[55] For Sweeney, this male subject, "created in the shadow of feminine power," contravenes the paradigms of masculine agency that informed the gender paradigms of the nineteenth-century heroic figure.[56] As she suggests, and as Douglass's and Equiano's accounts bear out, the struggle for freedom has been frequently articulated and appreciated as a masculine quest for deliverance from bondage; it is perhaps on this score that Manzano's autobiography seems to falter for a readership that associates emancipatory struggles with a certain romanticized paradigm of masculine heroism. That the poet's account of his life veers away from this gendered paradigm in his self-representations, however, does not make his desire for freedom less significant. Analogous to the way in which he emerges as a subject within and against slavery's coercive practices, Manzano's social identity is both hampered and enhanced in these domestic spaces: while the law permitted his mistresses to exercise power over him, so that he was obliged to acquire and excel at certain domestic skills, it was these very activities that provided him with his social identity as a privileged house slave who possessed trades that would secure a livelihood after he obtained his freedom.

Perhaps the most convincing proof of the inequality of the Marchioness de Prado Ameno's and Manzano's interdependent relation is that whereas the latter, from his experience of slavery, would end up referring to his affection for the former, his enslaver did not express similar feelings toward him and occasionally insisted on rules that discouraged sentimentality. For instance, his attempt to ingratiate himself to the marchioness by distancing his behavior from that of the other servants who mocked her is promptly thwarted by her clever rule that she would rather remain ignorant of insults directed at her. Deprived of this leverage and reminded of his place with the other slaves, Manzano experiences the limits of his efforts to transcend his station. Yet, it is precisely in such failed attempts to curry the marchioness's favor that we begin to get a sense of why he adamantly subscribes to the illusion of a "privileged" and happy childhood. This necessary fiction appeals to him because it harkens back to an age of innocence when he had been too young to perceive his bondage qua bondage, to a period in his life to which he assigned all notions of freedom and happiness and, logically, for which he subsequently yearned as an adult. Moreover, this account of his childhood allows him to uphold a self-image in which he repeatedly represents his position among the slaves as constantly undermined by the marchioness's unreasonable demands and conduct toward him as well as by the evil that pervades all the mansions whereby other slaves and servants endeavor to "destroy the self-esteem of the one whom the master favors."[57] The loss of privileges with maturity represents an insurmountable challenge to his status as a Creole slave in the Marchioness de Prado Ameno's home. In *The Punished Self,* Alex Bontemps defines "Creole status" in the context of slavery as both a personal and a cultural strategy for survival. According to him, this status "promised an alternative identity—the possibility of being other-than-Negro in a world where Negro symbolized a wretchedness that could only be survived. Creole status therefore offered an escape from the stigma of wretchedness, in the same sense that acculturation promised, if not freedom, then acceptance and a life less wretched than that of Negro slaves."[58] Indeed, the loss of status and its accompanying survival code explains why Manzano opens his autobiography idealizing an infancy that he leads the reader to believe was exceptionally favored and ends the account describing how, shortly before his escape, a servant reproached him, "a mulatto youth like you, with as many skills as you have," for allowing himself to be treated worse than "any African."[59]

We arrive, then, at the paradox of an enslaved subject who struggled against and blinds himself to the knowledge of his own enslavement by claiming superiority over other slaves in the execution of his tasks, the proficiency of his skills, and the status that proximity to his mistresses and, later, to the del Monte literary circle afforded him. His conviction that he deserved special treatment because of the trades and writing skills that he acquired during his childhood and adolescence is not the same as expressing a desire to be enslaved: to be free or enslaved was a choice that was foreclosed to him while he lived in his mistresses' homes because there was no place outside of slavery from which he could propose such an option for himself. Manzano's need to defend a superior idea of himself, that is, to resist the idea that his bondage was no different from that of other domestic slaves, was relentless. In his correspondence with del Monte, he complains about attacks on his character, and he also composed a brief poem on the subject of calumny. In the final analysis, what must have made it feasible for Manzano to employ his selective memory of a "privileged" childhood as a foundation for establishing his sense of superiority as an adult was the conviction that he had somehow been unjustly or mistakenly enslaved as he grew into adolescence; that his bondage, rather than being a way of life, was an aberration that interrupted his natural development into a good, noble, and conscientious man. In his correspondence with del Monte, Manzano's insistence that slavery had not corrupted his soul attempts to communicate this conviction.

There is no denying that Manzano's sense of superiority illustrates the degree to which slavery's practices alienate enslaved subjects from personal and collective allegiances based on shared experiences of bondage and encourage slaves to pursue their personal welfare first. From within his enslaved condition, Manzano's most routine strategy for personal advancement included the obeisance that slave owners tended to reward because it upheld their own paternalist, "necessary" fiction that their slaves required and were grateful for their owners' moral superiority and guidance. Manzano quickly learned to take advantage of a cultural and class-informed sensibility by gratifying del Monte's sense of his own social rank and "enlightened" paternalism. In a letter to the patrician (Havana, December 11, 1834) in which he expresses his elation that del Monte planned to send his "poor rhymes" to England—what he called the emporium of European enlightenment—Manzano intimates: "But now that you, sir, in the sea of life have taken hold of the rudder of this boat that remained afloat by chance, to your hands I entrust it for, since

I tire from rowing and never reaching port, I hope that you guide it to where its poor sailor may heap blessings upon you, seeing you peacefully breathe that gratification that compassionate souls enjoy, not to deliver myself to the pleasures that originate here but to make of myself a true lover of my duties."[60] Penned roughly two years before he recited "Treinta años" at del Monte's mansion, the letter anticipates the cruel and fatiguing arbitrariness of life in bondage that the sonnet captures, as well as Manzano's ostensible willingness to bow to del Monte's position and influence, which he cleverly identifies with the patrician's "compassionate" soul. In *Blacks in Bondage: Letters of American Slaves*, Robert Starobin cites numerous examples of the fondness that masters and slaves in the United States expressed to one another in writing. Several examples, many of them formulaic, demonstrated the masters' paternalist attitudes, while slaves who held positions of responsibility corresponded with their masters expressing an affection that was more often than not coerced. According to Starobin, this correspondence should not all be taken literally because "slaves were conscious of the need to deceive for purposes of survival, not only when they communicated with each other, but also—and especially—when they addressed their masters."[61] There is, therefore, more to this obeisance than first meets the eye.

Manzano's keenness to become a "true lover of his duties" plainly advertises a work ethic and employability through which he seeks to liberate himself from bondage by insinuating that he would commit to servitude of a different order where more technical domestic skills might be needed. This communication to del Monte demonstrates a classic case of sublimation with the sole purpose of attempting to move beyond oppression. In fact, the poet entered del Monte's employ as a cook shortly after obtaining his manumission.[62] Manzano's bid for an opportunity to be conscientious at his tasks—to be regarded as superior in talent and skills—appears to contradict any relation to a collective struggle for freedom because the enslaved subject in this case seeks to excel at what he has been obliged to do. This attempt to secure personal economic gain above all else is constitutive of a burgeoning class identity, so that even though his deference toward del Monte's wealth and power disqualifies his struggle for freedom from being considered heroic or rebellious, Manzano was attempting to join the growing ranks of free blacks who far outnumbered white artists and artisans on the island. In the late 1830s, the increasing numbers of free blacks became a source of concern for colonial authorities, who became wary of their growing socioeconomic influence and anxious about their potential for establishing political allegiances with abolitionist and independence movements within or near Cuba.[63] As I illustrate in chapter 4, it was not by chance that the colonial government rounded up, tortured, and executed many of the leaders from this class of free blacks during the so-called Escalera conspiracy of 1844. Even though he escaped the fate of the free mulatto poet Plácido, who accused Manzano of belonging to the conspiracy and who was executed for purportedly being one of the conspiracy's leaders, Manzano was jailed for a year, no doubt due to his relationship with the young liberals and their literary circle.

Manzano's road to freedom was neither romantically heroic nor rebellious. Yet his belonging to a class of free blacks and mulattoes whose socioeconomic progress began to be perceived as a threat to the colonial order was achievable through the daily grind not only of efficient labor but—and always at the same time—of strategically acquiring relief from oppression within a system that relentlessly dehumanized him. He was not willfully servile. Rather, he deftly employed obeisance in order to gain his freedom: despite the Marchioness de Prado Ameno's efforts to impede his manumission and finding himself obliged to hire himself out as a slave indefinitely in Havana after he had escaped her home, Manzano successfully maneuvered himself out of bondage by creatively appealing to the sympathy of influential "men of feeling" from the Creole reformist bourgeoisie. Creativity beyond the exigencies of precise forms of labor constituted one of the poet's most crucial forms of resistance to bondage.

MELANCHOLY ATTACHMENTS

Manzano's self-characterization and frequent references to melancholy provide opportunities for examining how power functions within slavery. Proceeding in light of the premise that subjects achieve self-consciousness while already embedded in societies and institutions that coerce them to act in or react against certain regulated ways, I closely examine the process by which Manzano grapples with the master's laws, codes, and other such injunctions and describes forms of aggrieved self-consciousness such as melancholy. In her phylogenetic analysis of his self-representation, Susana Draper asserts that Manzano creates a subjectivity that resists being subsumed within the Hegelian dialectic of the master and slave.[64] Even though my intention is also to address what I perceive as an underdeveloped aspect of this dialectic with respect to historical slavery, I am more concerned with an ontogenetic approach to Manzano's subjectivity in which the struggle between master and slave is already lodged within his self-representation. My argument is that there is something necessarily amiss about the melancholia that Manzano describes in his autobiography; on the basis of these observations, I propose that an explanation for the apparent incompleteness of Manzano's melancholy may be found in the way that power—in particular, the false ideology of paternalism—is exercised within slavery. I say "apparent incompleteness" because I do not want to suggest that the enslaved subject is inherently handicapped in his or her ability to exhibit a melancholy self-reflection; rather, I would like to claim that enslavement produces unintended results that are supplementary to the objects and services that the enslaved subject produces. In the following discussion, what becomes obvious is that melancholy denotes not a pathetic and passive capitulation in the face of adversity but a life-seeking confrontation through which the subject encounters and creatively engages with the limits of its power.

Certain aspects of Butler's analysis of the "bind of agency" are useful for approaching Manzano's assessments of his melancholy. This concept is not entirely new to our discussion. What Butler refers to as this bind is perhaps best explained in her account of the subject's simultaneous subjugation by and response to power. She writes that as "power *exerted on* a subject, subjection is nevertheless a power *assumed by* the subject, an assumption that constitutes the instrument of that subject's becoming."[65] This statement describes how the subject emerges as a subject already embedded in coercive circumstances, only now the focus is on relations of power in which there is a qualitative difference between the power that is exerted on a subject and the one that the subject assumes:

"Power considered as a condition of the subject is necessarily not the same as power considered as what the subject is said to wield. The power that initiates the subject fails to remain continuous with the power that is the subject's agency."[66] In other words, something happens to power in the process of its internalization by the subject so that while this power contributes to the subject's agency, it is "necessarily not the same" power that the subject experiences through coercion. My phylogenetic analysis at the end of the last section corroborates Butler's proposition. In his oppressed condition, Manzano literally cannot wield against his owners the practices of slavery that are imposed on him; yet I also noted the skillfulness with which he deployed a discourse of class sensibility in order to obtain relief from his enslavement and, because he further cultivated this discourse in his writings, in order to make an appeal for his manumission.

Butler's earlier premise that no subject can ever afford to see its attachment to power—that is to say, some degree of self-disavowal works in tandem with the power that is exerted on the subject—underscores the functioning of power through psychic means. Subsequently, in a move to conjoin power and agency, she introduces an external element or contingency to her analysis of the bind of agency: "Agency exceeds the power by which it is enabled. One might say that the purposes of power are not always the purposes of agency. To the extent that the latter diverge from the former, agency is the assumption of a purpose *unintended* by power."[67] In my analysis of the melancholy that Manzano ascribes to himself, I will have reason to explore aspects of his agency that are external to the labor that is demanded of him as a house slave. In any case, this assumption that his agency can be evaluated in light of purposes unintended by slavery allows us to examine a little-explored aspect of Hegel's theory of the subject. In the philosopher's theory, the bondsman's consciousness supersedes the lord's because the discipline of work allows the former to create objects that appear independent of him; as opposed to the lord's vicarious enjoyment of the products of the bondsman's labor, the bondsman begins to identify with these independent objects, thus keeping the disconcerting transience of these objects at bay. For Hegel, the creative acts that generate the bondsman's growing self-consciousness occur within the process of labor. The following analysis of Manzano's descriptions of melancholy discerns and assesses the role of creativity as a byproduct of power within a regime of forced labor.

Manzano's autobiography furnishes details of what may be considered empirical albeit unsystematically gathered evidence of melancholy. He describes two features of his condition that corroborate some of Freud's findings in "Mourning and Melancholia." The first focuses on physical symptoms: "I have attributed my short stature and weak constitution to the bitter life I have led since the age of thirteen or fourteen. I was always thin, weak, and emaciated, and my face constantly betrayed the paleness of a convalescent, with enormous rings under my eyes."[68] More than the meticulously described accounts of the injuries that he received at the hands of overseers and slaves whose tasks included punishing other slaves, this description emphasizes long-term effects brought about by a "bitter life." Distinguishing physical scars from psychological ones, Manzano associates certain signs on his body with the stress of daily life in the Marchioness de Prado Ameno's home and eventually concludes that melancholy "took root in my soul and had physically become part of my existence."[69] More germane to Freud's observations about the melancholic's behavior, however, is Manzano's unusual refusal to eat. Recalling his narrow escape from serious injury while he was being punished with hard labor in the plantation's filtering house, Manzano writes:

> My heart was so troubled that I could not even stand the sight of food, which was for me the most sacred and essential kindness. . . .
> I sank into such a depression that I did not emerge from my sorrowful despondency, even when I saw all the children engrossed in games or when they called me. I ate very little and was almost always in tears. That is why I was ordered to clean the mahogany furniture, so I would not be crying or sleeping. All my liveliness disappeared . . .
> Everyone pestered me, trying to make me play, but I did not shrug off my melancholy state.[70]

In these excerpts, Manzano finds various ways to communicate the extent to which he had been engaged in a struggle with his sense of powerlessness. For Freud, to refuse nourishment under these circumstances is instructive because it reveals an "overcoming of the instinct which compels every living thing to life."[71] Later, in *The Ego and the Id*, he associates melancholia with the death drive, going as far as to claim that it would be difficult to separate this drive from the conscience that emerges through melancholia. I return to this issue of conscience shortly.

The second feature of Freud's analysis of melancholia that sheds light on Manzano's self-observations points to the melancholic's almost compulsive desire to speak about his or her suffering. According to Freud, the melancholic differs from a person who might succumb to remorse because the former is not affected in the same way by feelings of shame in front of others: "One might emphasize the presence in him of an almost opposite trait of insistent communicativeness which finds satisfaction in self-exposure."[72] However, the relationship that Manzano draws between melancholy and the *content* of his "insistent communicativeness" suggests that his notion of melancholy differs from Freud's in a crucial area. The following account begins to illustrate this distinction: "From the age of thirteen to fourteen, the joy and vivacity of my character and the eloquence of my lips, dubbed the 'golden beak,' all changed completely into a certain kind of melancholy that, with time, became a personal trait of mine. Music enchanted me, but, without knowing why, I would cry, and enjoyed that relief, so that when I found an opportunity I sought solitude in order to allow my grief free rein. I would cry rather than sob, but I was not faint of heart except during certain states of depression, incurable to this day."[73] In this passage, Manzano juxtaposes two kinds of satisfaction: a "joy and vivacity," whose disappearance he laments, and another that finds release in solitude. The first readily corroborates Freud's identification of melancholia with the loss of a loved object or ideal, namely, the purportedly happy and privileged childhood that Manzano enjoyed when he lived in his first mistress's home. His relief through solitude, the second form of satisfaction, contradicts Freud's claim that the melancholic finds pleasure in denigrating himself in front of others. That an enslaved subject should habitually seek privacy for personal reflection and release is immensely valuable for abolitionists as they challenged the slave owners' disavowal of their slaves' humanity. But the compulsion to communicate that Manzano reveals for public scrutiny has almost nothing to do with shame, remorse, and a delight in communicating them. His "insistent communicativeness" differs from

Freud's notion of it in a way that allows for an analysis of the peculiarities of melancholy for an enslaved subject.

In "Mourning and Melancholia," Freud argues that because of the inability to mourn the loss of a loved or idealized object, "dissatisfaction with the ego on moral grounds is the most outstanding feature" of melancholia from a clinical perspective.[74] According to him, the melancholic's pathology lies in the self-denigration or the turning against the self, as Butler puts it, that he or she performs in front of others.[75] Freud, though, is less concerned with the issue of whether or not the melancholic's self-effacement is accurate "on moral grounds" than with the acts of self-reproach themselves. His clinical observations allow him to postulate that in these acts a critical agency splits off from the ego and, in turning to pass judgment on it, forms what is "commonly called 'conscience'" in most cases and, one may deduce, melancholia in more pathological ones.[76] Freud also asserts that the key to the clinical understanding of melancholia is to be found in the observation that the attacks under which the melancholic places his or her ego are in fact directed at a loved object or ideal for which mourning has not been possible, but they have been shifted away from it and redirected on to the ego.[77] What Freud eventually concludes about this open self-disparagement is that a "mental constellation of revolt" has "by a certain process, passed over into the crushed state of melancholia."[78] The melancholic's "insistent communicativeness" thus facilitates proof of this pathological turn against the self.

In light of Freud's initial approach to melancholia, it might seem reasonable to suggest that Manzano's melancholy stems from a failure to reproach the Marchioness de Prado Ameno openly and that this thwarted rebellion has somehow been internalized. This view, however, would not be entirely accurate for Manzano according to Freud's clinical observations. Setting aside the foolhardiness of rebelling in this manner while enslaved, the fondness that he expressed toward the marchioness was coerced in ways that disqualify her as a propitious object of love. Manzano, moreover, does not indulge in berating himself in front of others; on the contrary, he consistently seeks occasions to exhibit and take pride in his verbal and manual skills. Almost every example of melancholy to which Manzano refers is accompanied by an allusion to some form of compulsive communication that is not self-denigrating but private, frequently lyrical, sometimes subversive, and mostly liberating. For example, at the same time that he acknowledges that melancholy had taken root in his soul, Manzano writes that he found pleasure in composing sad verses under the *guásima* tree.[79] On another occasion, he associates his impulses to tell the children magical tales and recite poems that he composed by memory with the "distressing state" of his heart.[80] Finally, the following account of one of his performances intimates a subversive content that Manzano, unwittingly or not, communicates: "My mistress, who did not let me out of her sight even when she was sleeping, because she even dreamed about me, must have fathomed what was going on. One winter night, surrounded by children and servants, they made me repeat a story. My mistress hid in another room behind some shades or curtains. The next day, for no good reason at all, as they say, they immediately gave me a thrashing, gagged me, and sat me on a stool in the middle of the parlor with signs I cannot recall, in back and front of me."[81] Manzano's understanding of melancholy emphasizes the frequency with which he experiences the limits of his power. Nevertheless, his penchant for telling imaginative tales in public and composing sorrowful verses in private does not substantiate Freud's observations about the melancholic's development of an internal critical agency that publicly disparages the ego as a form of release. What does Manzano's compulsive verbal creativity say about his melancholy? How, in other words, is this partial fulfillment of melancholia's features to be understood?

As an enslaved subject in slavery, Manzano's life may be considered an unending series of encounters with the fact of his oppression. Nevertheless, his account provides no indication that the tasks, regulations, and codes that are imposed on him and constrain his freedom produce the turn against the self that Freud identified as the development of "conscience," which is not to imply that the enslaved subject in slavery is conscienceless. McGary and Lawson remind us that "given the brutality of slavery and the assault on the humanity of those held as slaves, it is remarkable that so many slaves were able to emerge from this brutal institution as moral agents."[82] As I already mentioned, Freud, in his first analysis of the subject, is more interested in melancholia's clinical symptoms than in evaluating the "moral grounds," that is, the content of the ethical injunction, that obliges the melancholic to indulge in public self-denigration. But, as an enslaved subject, on what "moral grounds" would Manzano be expected to stand in order to disparage himself? The warning to avoid punishment that Manzano received from an overseer on one occasion was, as he states it, "etched" in his heart;[83] however, rather than oblige him to conduct himself in accordance with an internalization of the power that is exerted on him, such as in the self-reproach frequently associated with the conscience, what the overseer's warning produces is an experience of fear that coerces from the outside and remains focused on the threat of physical pain. Moreover, his inability to internalize the overseer's warning as anything more transcendent than the fear of physical punishment is further exacerbated by the number of occasions that the overseer exonerated him from the marchioness's unreasonable demands that Manzano be severely punished for what a doctor who treated him on one occasion recognized as "childish pranks" and a "mischievous imagination, as typical of that age."[84] In short, inconsistent attitudes and behavior toward him on the part of some members of the slave-owning class and its overseers reveal fissures within slavery's hegemony. For the enslaved subject, these inconsistencies disturb the formulation and assimilation of imperatives that originate in slavery's codes and practices and that its agents fail or refuse to enforce.

In the context of Manzano's autobiographical self-representation, the idea that power should give rise to an unintended outcome describes an agency that emerges through the creativity of performance, that is, through the production of values beyond the demands and specific products of slave labor. Manzano's tasks were made clear to him from very early on: "From the time when I could first do anything, my destiny was to be a page."[85] All the same, the skills that he acquired beyond what was demanded of him as a house slave and page illustrate an assumption of agency that sometimes bordered on transgression. He learned to draw by observing and following the instructions of an art teacher who had been hired to tutor the children in the Marchioness de Prado Ameno's family. Such was Manzano's talent that the art teacher complimented him for his portraits, and he was subsequently permitted to assist another artist and designer who had been engaged to paint a glass display in honor of the visit of the governor's wife to the marchioness's home.

The servant who urged Manzano to escape alluded to these particular skills when the former chided him for being blind to the opportunities that fleeing to Havana offered. Even so, more than any other skill that he acquired beyond his forced labor, learning to write on his own was clearly the most defiant and consequential for his future.

The "insistent communicativeness" to which Freud refers does not function for Manzano as a vehicle for turning on himself or giving in to remorse. Rather, his penchant for verbal performance partakes of the life-seeking part of a melancholic confrontation with his enslavement. Even before acquiring the ability to write, as I illustrated earlier, Manzano compulsively sought ways to express himself. What occurs under a forced regime of labor, then, is the expansion of areas of creativity outside the demands of work that produces unintended results: "So as not to interfere with my productivity, I was prohibited from writing; but it was in vain. . . . Once they got hold of some scraps of papers full of *décimas*, and Don Coronado was the first to predict that I would be a poet, even though everyone was against it. He found out how I learned to write and why, and confirmed that most had begun that way."[86] Manzano's consistent association of his melancholy with creative impulses that manifest themselves outside of slavery's intended purposes provides a point of entry into the pending issue of what seems to be missing from his melancholia according to Freud's theorization.

Manzano discloses the existence within him of a melancholy condition removed from any accompanying sense of remorse or self-reproach because, as I will now contend, slavery forecloses the internalization and assumption of some of its own injunctions. In his explanation of the reasons why he selected particular episodes for his autobiography, Manzano is keenly aware that he is a priori deprived of the moral grounds from which he could be heard: "I realize that, no matter how much I try to speak the truth, I will never take my place as a perfect or even honorable man. But at least, in the eyes of the prudent judgment of impartial men, one will see to what extremes the prejudice of the majority touches the unfortunate being who has become the victim of some weakness."[87] He does not identify his inability to assume an ethical stance with some essential flaw in his character. Rather, his statement underscores that even though he can discern and appreciate the social value of "truth"—that is to say, even though he is intellectually and morally capable of assuming an ethical stance—he is summarily excluded from its pursuit in colonial society. Julio Ramos argues as much when he asserts that Manzano's was a "truth" that could not be "grasped . . . interpreted and judged" by the juridical apparatus in Cuba at the time especially because the slave's written testimony would have pushed against and reinscribed "the limits of the legal order."[88] In appealing to the "prudent judgment of impartial men," Manzano nonetheless envisions a more universal extension of "truth" than that which chattel slavery imposes as morally defendable. However, while this vision is his to enjoy, the ability of the enslaved subject in bondage to act ethically is not only proscribed within slavery (as del Monte's critique of the protagonist's speech in Suárez y Romero's novel demonstrated) but, as opposed to the turn against the self that marks the very foundation of the "unhappy unconsciousness," this stance risks being considered an act of defiance.

Manzano's realization that his enslavement forecloses his ability to confer honor on himself through the pursuit of "truth" and that such a pursuit presumably belongs to "prudent" and "impartial" others reveals why his melancholy elides the assumption of slavery's imperatives. Slavery not only attempts, by definition, to deprive the slave of agency; the legally sanctioned practices that buttress its official moral hypocrisy require the slave-owning class's constant scrutiny and control. It makes sense, therefore, that Manzano's "truth," as Ramos illustrates, emerges pressing against two juridical orders: one that is shaped by the judgment of a large number of men who might discern and reject the slave's "weakness" and another that looks toward "impartial" and enlightened others for justice.[89] A basic tenet in Hegel's master-slave dialectic is pertinent to this discussion. As I stated in the introduction, the philosopher's notion of the "unhappy consciousness" is predicated on the aftermath of the life-and-death struggle between two rival self-consciousnesses whereby the independent or dominant consciousness disappears only to emerge as an injunction or imperative that the dependent or subservient consciousness internalizes at the same time that it struggles to attain greater self-consciousness. What slavery accomplishes, however, is quite the opposite: it ensures that the master does not disappear, which means that the constant reiteration of the slave-owner's omnipotence through legal codes and infantilizing practices, such as the socialization of *partus sequitur ventrum,* creates obstacles for the internalization of those codes and practices through which the turn against the ego in conscience, self-reproach, and melancholy functions. At the same time that the legally enslaved subject is deprived of opportunities to assume ethical stances vis-à-vis the master, the slave-owning classes in the Americas historically had access to the discourses and practices of a paternalism that they considered morally defendable and that they employed to justify their possession and treatment of slaves.

ON WRITING ABOUT "FACTS"

Manzano's intimation in a letter to del Monte that he had almost given up writing his life story on four occasions provides insight into the relationship between the poet's uneasy assumption of an autobiographical writing subjectivity and the idiosyncratic melancholy that I described above. We know that Manzano profited from cultivating a universal appeal for justice through his most personal poetry: the appeal surreptitiously allowed him to reflect on his enslaved condition before an influential audience, helped to facilitate the road to manumission, and eventually provided his compositions with a cosmopolitan, antislavery reading public. In his autobiography, however, the appeal for justice that implicitly emerges from his descriptions of the cruel treatment that he received in the Marchioness de Prado Ameno's home did not reach audiences as wide as Equiano's and Douglass's. A number of practical reasons account for this limited readership, including the obvious impediment that no Spanish-language edition of the text appeared until 1937, the mysterious loss of the autobiography's second part, which would have supplied more information about Manzano's life after he escaped from the marchioness's home, and the fact that Manzano's figure and writings had not been disseminated in advance for the British reading public as had the writings of Equiano, Wheatley, and Douglass. In Phillis Wheatley's case, for instance, Kristin Wilcox argues that her poetic achievement was also "an account of the clergymen, merchants, political figures, gentry, and nobility in both Britain and America who helped to bring her poetry into prominence."[90] Moreover, Manzano's account of his life exhibits next to nothing of the evangelical traditions that characterized British and American abolitionist discourses. For Sweeney, the autobiography's lack of closure truncates any sense of heroic struggle since it provides "no catharsis for the reader, and therefore nothing to assure him or her of the existence, legitimacy or potential of western freedom, in either its European or its American modes."[91] Similarly, Draper asserts that the autobiography remained dormant in the archives for several reasons: first, the text did not provide an "ideal" representation of the slave as a writing subject; second, it failed to give rise to a subject who could be easily assimilated into an incipient national discourse; and, finally, it could not produce a writing worthy of being incorporated into either the Spanish literary canon or the future canon of the Creole bourgeoisie.[92] These claims return us to the scene of Manzano's autobiographical writing and to the complex circumstances in which he wrote his life story. Undoubtedly, del Monte's haste to have the autobiography in hand could in part explain the text's uneven writing style and abrupt ending, but the unremitting presence of del Monte and the young liberals during the writing process would clearly have been one of the most complicated challenges that Manzano faced.

It is likely that no fuller rendition of his life story would have aided the international abolitionist cause that the autobiography, unbeknown to its author, had been commandeered to promote. Although the absence of literary models offered Manzano the unique opportunity to have his voice heard beyond Cuban shores, the assumption of an autobiographical writing subjectivity cajoled into existence at del Monte's behest was simply unprecedented. Given this context, who were his readers meant to be? Not fully cognizant of the risks involved in disseminating his verses beyond the colony, Manzano delighted in the knowledge that his poetry, as he put it, might be read and appreciated in Europe, and he would have been inclined to think that the interest in his poetic compositions on the other side of the Atlantic was principally aesthetic. However, there is no indication in his correspondence with the patrician that they had discussed the autobiography's readership beyond the literary circle. Before the arrival of Madden, Manzano's would-be abolitionist translator, the poet's life story served specifically local purposes. Undeniably moved by a sonnet that condensed a lifetime of personal anguish, the members of the del Monte circle acquired more precise details about this suffering and evaluated them for their own literary writing. Manzano's account interested them not only for its focus on local life and affairs, which was a minimum requirement for the *costumbrista* literature that national bourgeoisies were beginning to cultivate throughout the Americas at that time, but especially for the descriptions of the miseries of bondage from the perspective of the enslaved. Unlike most abolitionists, the young liberals could sympathize with these depictions not only because they could verify them empirically but also because they could appropriate and inflect them to express their own aggrieved socioeconomic and political positions in the late 1830s. This proximity to their slaves and the perverse intimacy through which they rendered Manzano's stoic self-representations appropriable for their class and colonial struggles differentiated their cause and reader reception from those of geographically distant abolitionists.

This difference in readership arose from distinguishable moral positions. Slave narratives, with their attempts, as Sweeney asserts, to "fashion and write a self from a presupposed and legally enforced position of otherness," offered abolitionists the opportunity to observe the lives of slaves sympathetically from a physical distance and abstraction that they found conducive for developing their moral stance against slavery and in the pursuit of disinterested justice.[93] The Atlantic slave trade, as Baucom argues, gave rise to the "figure of the interested historical witness," a figure traceable from abolitionism to contemporary human rights discourses, who "bears witness" not only by observing, holding to, and subsisting beyond the crimes of chattel slavery but also by transmitting to others the sentimental "property of observing, holding, surviving."[94] Even though most abolitionists could not be considered survivors of bondage per se, their ability to acquire this sentimental property through readership permitted them to "bear witness" to injustices that took place far away and still claim the moral status of liberators. By contrast, and as I show in the chapter 4, the Creole reformists were unable to conform to the role of the "interested historical witness," even as they attempted to acquire the sentimental property that circulated among the abolitionists in the literature that they read and wrote in del Monte's circle. As colonial subjects, not only was their public ability to pass judgment on aspects of colonial life and to act accordingly precisely regulated; as slave owners, their empirical observations invariably turned them into self-incriminating witnesses. That is to say, although they routinely witnessed the cruelties of chattel slavery (either suppressing knowledge of their direct involvement or attributing the latter to colonial oppression), the reformists' physical proximity to, yet alienation from, slavery impeded their ability to assume the abstract stance from which they could disinterestedly view the cruelties that they witnessed. They were, first and foremost, committed to their political self-liberation and avoided any stance that would have led them to passing judgment on their own attachments to slavery.

When Manzano commented that in response to the difficult challenges of his autobiographical writing he had chosen to separate the "facts" from their "most terrible part," he was engaged in an undertaking that went against the grain of the abolitionists' desire to "bear witness," in slave narratives and Romantic literature that depicted slavery, to that "most terrible part." The impossible split that Manzano insisted on creating between the facts and horrors of bondage corresponded not only to the trauma of surviving and reflecting on his own suffering but also to the anguish in the writing process of adjudicating the actions that he took in order to survive—an anguish compounded by del Monte's "request" that he write the account while he was still enslaved. The slave-poet's admission that he attempted to separate facts from experience also manifests the extent to which his life writing might be considered a way, as Paul de Man provocatively suggests regarding autobiography, to "produce and determine" life.[95] In spite of the constraints on his writing, Manzano worked through the challenges of autobiographical subjectivity, so that between the time when he first wrote to del Monte about these difficulties and three months later, when he resolved some of them in the writing process, Manzano's notion of the "most interesting" events of his life changed, as Molloy asserts, to an appreciation of a "*something else* in himself besides the story of his misfortunes."[96]

Even though the young liberals considered themselves enlightened slave owners, they failed to acknowledge the pressure or, in Ramos's words, the "intense schism" that they imposed on Manzano as they induced him to occupy the position of "suffering body" and "observer."[97]

For him, the separation of facts from their terrible part represented a desire to construct a dignified subjectivity against formidable odds; in minimal fulfillment of this desire, he asserts that he would never be considered "honorable" in that slave-owning society, despite his knowledge of the "truth," thereby exercising the power to pass judgment on his enslaved condition and the society responsible for it. Yet, in a statement that illustrates the incompleteness of this ethical stance and of his melancholy, Manzano discloses that his stoic disposition is not just the result of personal self-reflection but will some day be looked upon favorably by "the prudent judgment of impartial men." The enslaved poet was fully cognizant of his reliance on the Creole reformists for his immediate well-being, but, in assigning the emergence of "impartial men" to the future, his words intimate the reformists' fundamental failure to assume impartiality on the issue of slavery as well as the absence of men capable of acknowledging his human dignity. Written in the context of a bondage with which the young liberals ambivalently identified themselves, Manzano's autobiography is thus also a critical account of the political and moral weaknesses of his "liberators."

THREE

Being Adequate to the Task

An Abolitionist Translates the Desire to Be Free

One of the most significant transformations in the study of British abolitionism began with the publication of Eric Williams's seminal *Capitalism and Slavery* in 1944. The late historian and first prime minister of Trinidad and Tobago argued against the widely held view, when he undertook research for his doctoral thesis at Oxford University, that philanthropic humanitarianism was the principal motivating factor in the movement to end the slave trade and emancipate slaves throughout the British Empire. Instead, he proposed that the rise of industrial capitalism and a transatlantic bourgeoisie that advocated free trade and wage labor and worked in tandem with abolitionist philanthropic humanitarianism rendered mercantilism and the slave-based sugar plantation that it supported an increasingly obsolete mode of production by the late eighteenth and early nineteenth centuries. Even though Williams's book was initially greeted as highly polemical—to the extent that there would be no British edition of the book for almost two decades after its publication in the United States—it would be fair to say that the study's influence has been such that most scholars of abolitionism today would concur that economic data or analyses should be taken into account in assessing the movement. Stated differently, it would be as if, in the historical evaluations of abolitionism before Williams's book, the abolitionists' quest to gain sympathy for the plight of slaves had overshadowed the role of economics. For some readers and critics, *Capitalism and Slavery* served as a useful reminder to scholars that the abolitionist was also an "economic man"; for others, the historian had swung too far in the opposite direction because he seemed to overstate the case for the decline of the slave-based production of sugar in the British colonies. Williams's substantiated claim that this decline occurred was central to his argument, but it would fuel criticism asserting that the book created the specter of a conspiratorial international bourgeoisie or, relatedly, that the historian's claims about abolitionism relied on a Marxist explanation that overdetermined the importance of the economic base. Nonetheless, more contemporary scholars who credit Williams for insisting on an economic explanation for the abolitionists' philanthropic humanitarianism have sought to temper some of his claims by retaining notions of humanitarian sentiment and sensibility in their socioeconomic debates and analyses.[1]

Richard Robert Madden's work as an abolitionist agent in Jamaica and Cuba and, in particular, as the translator of Manzano's autobiography and poetry into English for the British Anti-Slavery Society affords an unusually privileged view of the unstable, and at times contradictory, relationship between economics and humanitarianism in abolitionist activism in the field. A conscientious abolitionist whose family belonged to the Irish bourgeoisie, Madden also possessed substantial claims to a property in Jamaica, where he had been sent in 1833 to administer the newly legislated law that abolished slavery throughout the British West Indian colonies. Straddling what might appear to be a socioeconomic and political divide between slaveholding plantation owners and an abolitionist bourgeoisie was not a rare occurrence. In *Moral Capital*, Christopher L. Brown illustrates how propagandistic efforts to isolate such proprietors as a class whose depravity was unique to the Americas camouflaged complex entanglements between a British abolitionist bourgeoisie and an empire that had accumulated vast wealth on the basis of slave labor. At one level, Madden easily reconciled the contradiction by remaining true to his conviction that slavery was an abomination and by undertaking important missions for the abolitionist cause. In addition to his service as magistrate in Jamaica shortly after slavery was abolished, he provided the British Anti-Slavery Society with important reports and documents that he gathered in secret while he was stationed in Havana; by traveling to the United States expressly to testify that the captives on board the *Amistad* were not Cuban slaves, as the ship's owners had claimed, his deposition facilitated the U.S. Supreme Court's decision to free the ship's African captives; and, in a mission that he undertook after completing his assignment as the superintendent of liberated Africans in Havana, he produced a valuable detailed report that denounced illegal slave trafficking off the coast of Sierra Leone. As an abolitionist activist, Madden's credentials were impeccable. Yet, at another level, the shift from unwavering abolitionist at home to someone who enjoyed the privileges of his class in the colonies at the same time that he pursued his cause occasioned a temporary setback in his mission that he would ascribe in his memoirs to unconscious influences. The empirical and experiential knowledge of slavery that Madden acquired through his activism reduced the distance between the humanitarian and the objects of his humanitarian efforts in ways that the abolitionists at home could not fathom except through the persuasiveness of testimonies, other legally admissible documents, and literary compositions. Nevertheless, Madden's close observations of and proximity to Cuban slavery still did not eliminate important internal and external challenges to his appreciation of the slaves' conditions and, in particular, of the constraints under which Manzano expressed the struggle to free himself from bondage.

Conveying the horrors of slavery to readers across the ocean was a difficult task. The problem resided in how to produce the effect of verisimilitude for the communication of sentiment between writer and reader or, more specifically, between the (once) legally enslaved autobiographical subject and a reader who might be predisposed toward assuming the role of a sympathetic, imaginative witness. Since most abolitionist readers did not witness the kinds of brutalities to which slaves were submitted, they consistently attempted to acquire oral and written accounts of these abuses in order to substantiate their cause. For example, in the case of Mary Prince, who did not write but dictated her life story, the radical Birmingham Ladies' Society for Relief of Negro Slaves requested evidence of the whip marks on the body of the Bermuda-born slave and received signed testimony that the marks existed.[2] The astonishment of the Society's members was such that even though they had become familiar with Prince's life story, they still sought and acquired confirmation of the scars after not one but two inspections. The signed document was intended to reduce the physical distance between the indelible marks on Prince's body and abolitionists who were willing to bear testimony to the cruelty of slavery on her behalf. As Julio Ramos has shown with respect to an enslaved woman of Mandinga origin who demanded her freedom before colonial courts in Cuba in 1815, the assumption in Prince's case would also have been that the legally enslaved subject did not possess an autonomous voice in the eyes of the law and, consequently, that the "truth" to which he or she had access could not be represented without the aid of others, such as the abolitionists, whose authority and citizenship the courts acknowledged.[3] Given the British abolitionist push in Parliament to contest the moral legitimacy of slavery, the reports and testimonies that the movement compiled relied on empirical data and possessed juridical weight. Facts that could be enumerated, such as the birth and mortality rates of slaves, the number of lashes that they could legally be dealt, or the frequency of their uprisings, were readily recorded and presented in antislavery arguments. If influential moral arguments affecting the socioeconomic foundations of the British Empire in the Atlantic world were going to be made, and if the language that was needed was going to be considered truth bearing, then it was expected that that language would be transparent, unequivocal, and objective.

Yet something more was expected of the testimonial language through which slaves articulated their experiences of slavery. Over and beyond the enumeration of facts and figures, abolitionists regarded the adroit use of the language of sympathy and sentiment as the most effective way to stir "men of feeling" into action against slavery. Having clandestinely acquired Manzano's autobiography and some of his poetry, Madden would translate the formerly enslaved poet's writings and submit them, together with collected field data and interviews, as evidence of the cruelty of Cuban slavery at the World Anti-Slavery Convention in London in 1840. According to Baucom, this convention marked the first international human rights conference.[4] Delegates there debated how best sympathy could be generated in order to encourage the adoption of antislavery laws in the United States, and they consistently concluded that it should be done through sentimental literature. Madden did not translate Manzano's texts for a general reading public in Great Britain, but his rendition of them in English would be placed at the service of a political demand for sentiment that the most radical transatlantic move-ment at the time required. After the successful abolition of slavery in the British West Indian colonies in 1833, the Anti-Slavery Society turned its attention to internationalizing its movement and set out to investigate the reputation that Spanish slave codes had of being enlightened in order to undermine the assumption that slavery was more humane in Cuba than elsewhere.[5] Madden's translations contributed to this effort. In fact, one of his stated goals after returning to England was to correct Alexis de Tocqueville's report to the Chamber of Deputies (July 23, 1839) that slavery in Spain's New World colonies had been milder than in other European possessions.[6] However, his translations also demonstrate how he attempted to reconcile his intention, explicitly stated in his preface to the translations, to "vindicate in some degree the character of negro intellect" and a humanitarian effort that was not reducible to the noble expression of philanthropic sentiment but responded strategically to the abolitionists' geopolitical plans.[7]

In stark contrast to the concerns of the young liberals about translat-ing Charles Comte's studies for readers in a colony that censored the public discussion of slavery, Madden extended his and del Monte's com-mon belief in literature's "humanizing" role to his translations of Man-zano's writings and submitted them to a burgeoning transatlantic move-ment. Not only did the abolitionist approach his translations with the goal of enhancing their ability to rally sympathetic readers in the same way that literature could, but the treatment of the translations as evi-dence of the cruelty of Cuban slavery also required him to pay particular attention to those elements of the original texts that he considered sig-nificantly translatable for the abolitionists' goals. For Walter Benjamin, two conditions determine a text's translatability. He identifies the first of these as contingent on the response to the question of whether an "adequate" translator will ever be found from among all of the original text's readers.[8] The question is hypothetical, and the answer is no be-cause the translator, in Benjamin's view, can neither achieve the post-Babelian dream of reconciling languages within a realm of "pure lan-guage" nor attain what the original text accomplishes.[9] The translator, therefore, must simply settle for evoking the "echo of the original" in the target language.[10] In other words, Benjamin asserts, "the translatability of linguistic creations ought to be considered even if men should prove unable to translate them."[11] Does Madden's transatlantic abolitionist expertise and activism provide him with the necessary intellectual tools for deciphering Manzano's meanings? I begin this chapter by examining the abolitionist's preparation or adequacy as the translator of a slave's desire to transcend his bondage and oppression. Because, as Benjamin implies, even the most proficient translator can only aspire to be adequate to the tasks of translation, my goal is not to condemn Madden a priori to failed renditions of Manzano's struggles but to interrogate the abolitionist's attempts at highlighting the poet's intelligence and talent in the context of his cause.

Benjamin assigns greater importance to the second condition for determining a text's translatability, which is whether the work naturally lends itself to translation or even calls for it.[12] The idea that Manzano's writings should call for translation has to do not with the fame and afterlife of the original texts but with an agenda that sought to disseminate his autobiography and poems as already worthy of a politically inspired acclaim. Nevertheless, in order to determine what calls for translation in the poet's texts, Madden engages with a fundamental notion of adequacy in the practice of translation or *adequatio,* which is a term that Benjamin signals throughout his seminal essay, "The Task of the Translator," but does not mention outright. *Adequatio,* or the distance from the meaning and style of the original that the translator negotiates and establishes in the target language, is the principle and practice according to which a translation may be considered faithful or free vis-à-vis the original. As I show, Madden makes decisions about whether his translations should be faithful or free according to the literary genre in which Manzano writes and to the kind of voice that the abolitionist wishes to ascribe to the poet and former slave. However, before examining these tactical decisions, I would like to linger for a moment on Benjamin's argument against the traditional distinction of fidelity and freedom (or license) as conflicting approaches to translation.

According to Benjamin, this distinction can no longer hold for a theory of translation that values things other than the sheer reproduction of meaning. He argues that fidelity to the word, or the practice of translating words literally, fails to reproduce the "sense" in the original text:

"For this sense, in its poetic significance for the original, is not limited to what is meant but rather wins such significance to the degree that what is meant is bound to the way of meaning of the individual word. People commonly convey this when they say that words have emotional connotations."[13] Consequently, he asserts that no case can be made for literalness as the means by which meaning can be retained and even claims that meaning would be "served far better—and literature and language far worse—by the unrestrained license of bad translators."[14] Similarly, freedom in translation implies a priori that the rendering of the original work's sense is not paramount. Benjamin argues that free translation, rather than dwell on the original work's meaning, should assume the challenges of rendering meaning in its own language; that is to say, that the translator should aim "to release in his own language that pure language which is exiled among alien tongues, to liberate the language imprisoned in a work in his re-creation of that work."[15] Now, the metaphors of imprisonment, release, and freedom that Benjamin employs to describe how free translation distances itself from a rendering of the "original sense" afford my discussion a familiar frame of reference. The late-twentieth-century debate over the ways in which Manzano's texts had been corrected, edited, and translated calls to mind the tasks that Benjamin sets for the free translator as he or she negotiates an appropriate distance from any univocal rendering of the sense in the original text. Critiquing the terms that were employed in the twentieth-century debate about how the young liberals treated Manzano's writings, Sylvia Molloy refutes the frequent assumption "that there is a clear narrative imprisoned, as it were, in Manzano's *Autobiografía*, waiting for the hand of the cultivated editor to free it from dross—this notion that the impure text must be replaced by a clear (white?) version for it to be readable—amounts to another, aggressive mutilation, that of denying the text readability in its own terms."[16] An analogous claim can be made about translating Manzano. Despite Madden's argument to the contrary, the former slave's autobiography and lyrical compositions do not inherently possess a unique, truth-bearing language that the translator merely works to liberate. In addition to the messy complexity of the autobiographical writing in particular, which attests to both the impossibility of pure, unequivocal meanings and the ideological cross-purposes of rival struggles for freedom, Madden's task as a translator was doubly challenging: not only would he be faced with negotiating the fidelity of his translations to Manzano's writings, but he would need to do so in light of his shifting proximities to human suffering as an abolitionist in Europe and, subsequently, as an eyewitness among slaveholders.

THE MAKINGS OF AN ABOLITIONIST TRANSLATOR

The year that Madden spent in Jamaica had been disastrous.[17] Thanks to the influence of Thomas Fowell Buxton and other colleagues from the Anti-Slavery Society in London, the British Colonial Office appointed Madden to the office of special magistrate in Jamaica shortly after the passage of the law for the abolition of slavery in 1833.[18] Charged with enforcing the recent legislation, Madden departed for the island in October of that year. According to his memoirs, he undertook this humanitarian cause "with the ardour of his nature, the leading characteristic of which was an intense love of justice and a hatred of oppression in whatever clime or on whatever race it might be exercised."[19] But very little could have prepared him—a medical doctor with no experience in the practice of law—for what awaited him in his encounters with Jamaican planters and slave owners, who were convinced that he would be unable to reconcile his vindication of the rights and liberties of the former slaves with the administration of impartial justice.[20]

Madden and the five other special magistrates who were assigned to Jamaica met with the planters' fury. The latter were so angered by what they perceived as the British government's abrogation of their most fundamental rights as proprietors and members of the planter class that they conspired to oppose and even to avenge the new legislation. One of the most effective forms of resistance that they employed against the magistrates emerged from the very seat of the Jamaican establishment. The planters were well represented in the island's House of Assembly and the Corporation of Kingston and controlled the police force and local militia, making it difficult, if not impossible, for the magistrates' decisions to be executed. Meanwhile, Madden was confident that the rule of law would win the day. In a letter that he wrote at the time, he declared with conviction that "the colour of a man's skin can no longer be the criterion of his capacity, though the difference of a shade may fit him for society or exclude him from it; but now it cannot put him beyond the pale of the British Constitution."[21] Nevertheless, he also expressed the well-warranted fear that because "complexional distinctions, probably for years to come, will continue to distract society," many years would be needed before the members of Jamaican society would be able to treat one another as "fellow-citizens and fellow-men."[22] Madden's experience in Jamaica afforded him the uncomfortable privilege of knowing, on the one hand, that the law for the abolition of slavery had the full weight of the British Constitution behind it and of realizing, on the other, that racism could be operative in local society beyond the constitution's reach. At any rate, what eventually led to Madden's resignation were the two occasions when he was assailed. "I found the protection of the ne-gro," he recalls, "incompatible with my own."[23] It served no purpose for him to look to the other special magistrates for support because, of the five who accompanied him to Jamaica, four had perished from disease. Madden left Jamaica on November 15, 1834.

On March 15, 1836, a little more than a year after returning to London, Madden left for Cuba in order to take up the position of superintendent of liberated Africans in Havana. In addition to outlawing Spanish sub-jects from engaging in the slave trade on the coasts of Africa north of the equator, the Anglo-Spanish treaty of 1817 created his office in Havana and another in Sierra Leone as one of the measures by which both Eu-ropean countries could liberate Africans who were taken off vessels that were captured while engaging in the slave trade in Cuban and African waters.[24] Madden's principal responsibility was to safeguard the freedom of these Africans after they disembarked in Havana, and it was expected that he would perform his duties even as the demand for slaves in Cuba was so enormous that abuses among officials were commonplace.[25] "Jus-tice is bought and sold in Cuba," he remarked, "with as much scandalous publicity as the Bozal slaves are bought and sold in the barricones [sic]."[26] Similar to his experience of attempting to uphold antislavery laws in Jamaica, Madden soon became aware of the incongruity between Span-ish legislation regarding slavery and, in the case of Cuba, the general disregard for such laws among Spanish officials and others who profited from the slave trade. Unlike the abolition question in Britain and Jamaica, however, Madden encountered a situation in which the Spanish monarchy had been strategically ambivalent with British diplomats on the same issue since the 1820s, for obvious geopolitical reasons.[27] The Spanish government, particularly after the independence of the mainland Spanish American colonies, was not willing to risk losing the loyalty of Cuban and Puerto Rican planters by abolishing slavery.

This scenario, in which ineffective and disingenuous treaties limited his powers, must have appeared bleak. Furthermore, the year before he arrived in Havana, British ships had begun to concentrate their search efforts on the African coast, which meant that by the time he got to Cuba, the Mixed Commission there was already handling fewer cases.[28] Nevertheless, during his three-year stay on the island, Madden still found effective ways to devote his energies to the abolitionist cause. Before he left for Havana, Thomas Buxton, who had been busy preparing a pamphlet on slavery for the British government, wrote Madden to inform him about a certain "business of very great importance."[29] The abolitionist member of Parliament and cofounder of the Anti-Slavery Society had received positive reactions from the cabinet on the material that he had already gathered, and, dividing his subject into two parts (the "extent and horrors of the Slave-Trade" and suggestions for its abolition), he requested Madden's help in the following terms:[30]

> I am under solemn promise to the Government not to divulge the suggestions, as this would be fatal to their success; and it is the less necessary to do so at this time, as the plan I propose is quite independent of any means now employed, but yet you may render me and the cause very great service.
>
> I send you the proof sheets of that part which applies to the extent and horrors, and my earnest request of you is that after reading it you will be good enough to furnish me with any new proofs and elucidation—in point of fact, anything bearing on the various points that you can collect.[31]

Cuban officials considered Madden a dangerous man even before he disembarked on the island. Buxton's letter hints at the degree to which Madden's surreptitious inspections of sugar plantations, as well as the contact that he made with del Monte, his literary circle, and other reformist Creole elites who helped him to gather the portfolio of antislavery material with which he returned to London, constituted part of a mission that the Irish abolitionist had undertaken for the antislavery cause. Madden would end up structuring much of the material for this portfolio around his translation of Manzano's autobiography and poems.

Presumably, the evidence of slavery's horrors that Buxton requested should not have been difficult for Madden to acquire, but, according to the latter, it became necessary for him to withstand slavery's mundane but powerful effects in order to obtain it: "I lived for a whole year at the Havana before I could so far disembarrass myself of that deadening influence of slavery which steals so imperceptibly over the feelings of strangers in the West Indies, as to form an opinion for myself, and trust my own senses alone for a knowledge of the condition of the praedial slaves."[32] But what kind of knowledge was he after that would derive from his senses alone? On an island that possessed, he estimated, some 400,000 slaves and that had become the world's foremost sugar producer, Madden certainly had ample opportunity to investigate, witness, and record atrocities. Yet, as he points out, it took him a full year to shed his initial blindness to the slaves' condition because he could not until then trust his own senses to counteract slavery's "deadening influence" over the "feelings of strangers." Despite the clarity and urgency of the instructions that Madden received from Buxton and, as his son phrased it in the abolitionist's memoirs, his intense "hatred of oppression in whatever clime or on whatever race it might be exercised," there was something about the numbing effect of slavery (stealing undetectably over his feelings) that not only induced him to falter in his mission as an abolitionist during his first year but threatened to compromise his moral outrage. No longer an imaginative witness of human bondage engaged in a movement on the other side of the Atlantic to liberate slaves, Madden had firsthand encounters with slavery in the islands that thrust him into complicated situations that measured his moral fiber against the temptation to be lulled into moral complacency.

If Madden had indeed succumbed to slavery's "deadening influence" during his first year in Havana, it may have been because he still had not reconciled his firm ethical stance as a sympathetic, imaginative witness with the socioeconomic benefits from slavery that his class and, in fact, his family enjoyed in the Caribbean. An excursion that Madden took while he was stationed in Jamaica suggests that expressing moral indignation against slavery in Britain and enjoying the socioeconomic

benefits of human bondage in the islands were not necessarily lived as
a conscious social contradiction. Soon after arriving in Jamaica, Madden set out on an expedition to find Marley, a property that belonged
to his granduncle for which he had inherited "a claim to a considerable
amount."[33] While there, he learned that an old African, who had been
his relative's "favourite servant," was still alive, and he enthusiastically
requested a meeting. The exchange between them is so intriguing that
it is worth quoting at length:

> I had prepared myself for a very sentimental scene with the old negro. I had
> pictured to myself the joy of the aged domestic at seeing a descendant of
> his revered master. . . . but never was there a gentleman of an ardent turn of
> mind more cruelly disappointed.
>
> The negro was brought before me: he was a hale, honest-looking, gray-
> haired old man, about eighty.
>
> "Did he remember the old doctor?"
>
> "He remembered him well."
>
> "Where did he come from?"
>
> "Massa brought him out of a Guinea ship when a picanini boy, him wait
> on massa—serve massa very well; him serve massa when young and 'trong;
> but what use talk of such things now?"
>
> "Did he see no resemblance between me and the old doctor?"
>
> "No! him want to see nutten at all of nobody."[34]

Penning it decades after the incident, Madden frames this oddly invoked
conversation in which the dialogue takes place between third-person
interlocutors—as though an intermediary figure such as a translator had
been involved—thereby demonstrating the abolitionist's awareness of
the ingenuousness of his expectations at that time. The old man's frank
refusal to recognize the continuity of his former master's lineage in Madden not only jolts the latter into reassessing what he thought might have
been a sentimental encounter but resounded so forcefully over the years
that the Irish abolitionist even made the effort to recall the conversation
with dialectological accuracy.

As the episode reveals, Madden's wish to secure his claim to a substantial fortune coincides with his expectation of a "sentimental scene"
between himself and the old man. According to Davis, one of the strands
of the benevolence and spiritual awakening that swept through Western
Europe in the 1770s and informed abolitionism contained "unresolved

tensions between sympathetic benevolence and individual enterprise."[35] Yet the sentiment to which Madden refers, and for which he eventually rebukes himself, is not simply that of the imaginative witness engaged in a humanitarian cause; the scene also smacks of a "sympathetic benevolence" that is both paternalist (in ways that recall the Creole reformists' attitude toward Manzano) and readily transmitted, as Madden intimates with respect to his granduncle, from one generation to another. After practically a lifetime in bondage, the old man refused to indulge the abolitionist's fanciful expectations, which led to a cruel disappointment for the latter's "ardent turn of mind." Furthermore, a certain ambiguity is also to be found in Madden's retrospective self-characterization: does his "ardent turn of mind" allude to a particular trait, which, if he viewed it positively, would refer to the romantic, heroic disposition of one who feverously championed the emancipation of slaves? Or, if considered critically (as the episode's frame of reference implies with hindsight), does his "ardent turn of mind" allude to the excesses of youthful inexperience and bewilderment in a land where his claim to an inheritance, generated through the possession of land and human beings, temporarily eclipsed his abolitionist fervor? Without stating it outright, Madden's recollection of this episode shows that not only did the elderly former slave, who had been or was on the verge of being emancipated by the time he was "brought before" the abolitionist, know enough about his imminent liberation to refuse the "sentimental scene"; Madden also remembers the incident as singularly instructive for the way in which the old man's refusal dashed his anticipated enjoyment of the paternalist "benevolence" that typified the plantation class's attitude toward its slaves.

In stark contrast to his year in Jamaica, where the emancipation of slaves had already been signed into law, and to his first year in Cuba, where he felt obliged to learn how to trust his senses once more, Madden managed to become an effective abolitionist activist in his position as Havana's superintendent of liberated Africans. The literary circle that began meeting, first as the autonomous but short-lived Academia Literaria and then privately at Domingo del Monte's home some two years before Madden's arrival, offered an ideal rendezvous for the Creole reformists' desire for a space where they could write about local life and slavery and Madden's wish to learn more about the slaves and slavery on the island. In his preface to Manzano's translated texts, Madden contrasts slavery's cruelty and the need for literary activities, stating that "literature, even at the Havana, has its humanizing influence."[36] Given a context in which the Cuban reformist bourgeoisie distanced itself from the rest of its class by identifying with the enterprising spirit and humanitarianism of its British abolitionist counterpart, del Monte's and Madden's class allegiances and sensibilities and, more specifically, their common front against the slave trade led them to concur that the antislavery cause would be well served by literature's ability to humanize its subjects.[37]

Even though no descriptions of the meetings between the patrician and the abolitionist have been found—due caution and secrecy being the most effective measures against an anxious colonial government that would surely have regarded consorting with a known abolitionist in private meetings about Cuban society, politics, and literature highly suspect—the effects of Madden's presence and time-sensitive mission among the reformists were perceivable in other ways. For instance, del Monte's haste to have Manzano's completed autobiography in hand in 1839, before Madden's departure for London, suggests several things: that an agreement had been reached between del Monte and Madden, whereby Manzano's writings were going to be offered up as formal evidence of the "extent and horrors" of the slave trade for Buxton and the British Cabinet; that del Monte's decision to assist Madden (for the bulk of the portfolio with which the abolitionist left the island could not have been gathered without the patrician's help) and thus assume a more subversive role most likely constituted the patrician's personal response to Madrid's demotion of Cuba from an overseas province with political representation in the Cortes to a colony directly ruled from the metropolis;[38] and, finally, that del Monte's sense of urgency also had to do with the practical problems of preparing the former slave's texts for translation. Manzano wrote Spanish phonetically, which would not have challenged native and proficient speakers of the language. However, the fact that del Monte and members of the literary circle, Suárez y Romero in particular, worked in earnest to provide Madden with a copy of Manzano's texts in academically correct Spanish indicates that Madden did not possess sufficient command of the language to be able to work with the poet's phonetic writing.[39] In fact, his linguistic preparation for translating these writings was, at best, ad hoc: he had studied Latin, knew French and Italian from his medical apprenticeships on the European continent, and learned what he could of Spanish during his three-year stay in Havana. Judging by his errors in Spanish—he tended to Italianize his vocabulary—and his need to have his translation queries checked by native speakers in Cuba and England, Madden had not perfected his grammatical and lexical knowledge of the language.

Madden's proficiency in Spanish is an essential but not overriding factor in my discussion because the critical issues that arise in the abolitionist's translations do not derive from problems of language comprehension. If contingency matters in questions of translatability, Madden's experiences and abolitionist advocacy in England, Jamaica, and Cuba prepared him to become an adequate translator of Manzano's writings. From an empirical perspective, his exposure to the transatlantic world of slavery and abolition from social, legal, and political perspectives and the knowledge that he acquired from his activism and work in Jamaica and Cuba geared him, as few abolitionists could have been at the time, to comprehend the circumstances in which Manzano and members of del Monte's literary circle wrote and the value for the antislavery cause that they respectively attached to sentiment and generating a sympathetic understanding of slavery. But before turning to analyze Madden's views on the translatability of Manzano's texts in the following section, I would like to provide an additional piece of evidence of the breadth and depth of knowledge about transatlantic slavery that the abolitionist brought to his translating tasks.

In 1839, Madden left his permanent appointment in Havana in order to undertake an investigation of the slave trade on the West African coast. Even though Britain had passed the law for the emancipation of slaves in British colonies and Spanish policy remained opportunistically ambivalent about abolitionism, he had accomplished more for the antislavery cause during his stay in Cuba than during his year in Jamaica. The difference cannot be reduced to the lengths of his assignments. Arguably, the political space and the intrigues that pullulated in Havana at the time seemed to have provided him with greater maneuverability as an abolitionist agent than when he attempted to execute laws in Jamaica that the British Parliament had passed. For example, he publicly accused Nicholas Trist, the United States' consul in Havana, of assisting American ships that were engaged in the slave trade.[40] More significant was Madden's role in the renowned *Amistad* affair in 1839.[41] Upon learning of the incident, he went to the United States and testified that the Africans on board this ship were not Cuban slaves. This deposition, backed by Madden's statistical knowledge of the slave trade in Cuba, strengthened the defense's case for the liberation of the Africans and helped to clarify Britain's view on the matter: Henry Fox, the British minister in Washington, contacted the secretary of state, John Forsyth, in order to express Queen Victoria's personal interest in the case.[42] Even though the case would continue in U.S. courts for another two years, Madden's intervention was important and timely, and probably brought a satisfactory sense of closure to his antislavery activism in Cuba.

Besides other evidence of the "extent and horrors" of the slave trade that he had gathered, returning to London with the first part of Manzano's life story and a collection of his unpublished poems was a mission that Madden successfully completed for Buxton, the British Cabinet, and the British Anti-Slavery Society. The Irish abolitionist could thus credibly claim, as he did in his address to the Anti-Slavery Convention on June 17, 1840, that he had not worked in the "peaceful closets of philanthropy" but had been a "mercenary" and "soldier" in the field of slavery for seven years.[43] Madden undertook the translation of the texts in an atmosphere in which abolitionist societies in London, Paris, and Philadelphia actively encouraged the translation of antislavery writings.[44] However, the tasks of translating Manzano's writings involved challenges of a different order in which the abolitionist, because of his eagerness to promote his cause, occasionally distorted the meaning in some of the former slave's writings. Needless to say, Madden's desire to communicate politically significant information through his translation supersedes the language-to-language concerns that Benjamin considers the translator's primary work and at times places the abolitionist's rendering of the texts closer to dogma than to poetry. In short, the ethical issues concerning Madden's decisions about the translatability of Manzano's texts do not entail only an interrogation of the reasonable limits of free translation, that is, the liminal space where the abolitionist at times gave free rein to his Romantic sensibility; this inquiry also requires an evaluation of how the abolitionist translator's license affects the poet's articulation of the struggle to be free.

THE FICTION OF A FAITHFUL TRANSLATION

As I stated earlier, Benjamin's use of the qualifier "adequate" to describe the contingent relationship between the translator and the translatability of an original text is not arbitrary. I want to claim that besides alluding to *adequatio,* or the translator's skill at negotiating a semantic and stylistic distance from the original, the adjective connotes the idea of distance from an original, which, given this study's focus, carries at least two additional meanings that hinge on literary interventions. As a reminder, the first refers to the distance from particular scenes and events that the abolitionists sought to transcend by imaginatively witnessing slavery's violence and that the Creole reformists psychologically invoked because they lived in relatively close proximity to their slaves. For the abolitionists, therefore, literary writing and readership were meant to reduce the gap between lapsed though still shocking examples of inhumanity and sympathetic, imaginative witnesses for whom this literature became a source of sociopolitical solidarity. By contrast, the value that del Monte's literary circle attached to producing antislavery literature involved articulating a distance from the immediacy of and even the responsibility for the brutality that they, inadvertently or not, caused or witnessed. The second understanding of distance from an original is pertinent to life writing and invokes *adequatio* not only as a crucial issue for translation but also, more broadly, as a philosophical problem about truth and life writing. In other words, even before attending to what Madden considered translatable about Manzano's texts, this larger conception of *adequatio* obliges us to inquire about the distance between a life that is original, that is to say, both unique and originating, and its inscription: Is the written account true or equivalent to the life lived? Since it can be argued that the autobiographer tends to approach his or her life through *adequatio,* writing about life as if it were an original object only to realize, as Paul de Man claims, that this writing might indeed "produce" life, it is essential to establish the meaning of "original" with respect to Manzano's autobiography before examining Madden's argument for translating the account literally.[45]

According to Suárez y Romero's foreword to *Francisco,* it was Madden who originated the request for literary compositions that would offer him insight into the slave trade and the island's slaves.[46] As if the abolitionist's personal observations were inadequate, and abiding by his accord with del Monte that literature should serve the antislavery cause, the bulk of the portfolio with which Madden returned to London was literary.[47] Nevertheless, the only literary texts from Cuba that the abolitionist eventually translated and published were the former slave's autobiography and poems and another patriotic poem, probably composed by Rafael Matamorros y Téllez, a member of del Monte's circle. Mindful of the danger on the island to which he exposed Manzano, del Monte, and members of the literary circle by publishing their works, Madden consistently used initials or referred to unnamed authors and sources of information. Manzano's writings thus appear in a book that the abolitionist published in 1840 under the title *Poems by a Slave in the Island of Cuba, Recently Liberated; translated from the Spanish by R. R. Madden,* M.D. *with the History of the Early Life of the Negro Poet, written by Himself to Which are prefixed Two Pieces Descriptive of Cuban Slavery and the Slave-Traffic.*[48] The book begins with two of Madden's poems and ends with Matamorros y Téllez's previously unpublished poem as well as appendices that include his interviews with an unnamed gentleman (del Monte), six reports that the abolitionist wrote, a glossary of terms used in Cuba, and Manzano's original poems in Spanish. Madden's integration of poetry and Manzano's autobiography in this portfolio of statistics, interviews, and essays reveals the naturalness with which he and other abolitionists considered literary compositions a valid medium for articulating certain truths and providing bona fide evidence for their cause.

Because the odds against publishing Manzano's autobiography were enormous, a certain air of mystery surrounds the circumstances in which the poet wrote about his life and had his texts delivered to what he thought would be the "Emporium of European enlightenment." As we know, this writing was unlikely, almost impossible in its conception of a reading public: even though the autobiography had not been his

idea, he nonetheless felt pressed into writing it; in light of his correspondence with del Monte, he was led to believe that his readers on the
other side of the Atlantic would be interested in his writing for aesthetic
reasons; the account of his life imperiled his chances at manumission
because local authorities prohibited antislavery writing, and the Marchioness de Prado Ameno, whose depiction was mostly unflattering,
still held claims on his freedom; the only way to publish the autobiography involved smuggling it out of Cuba; and, finally, the text would first
be published in a foreign language, so that a wider readership where it
mattered most for del Monte's literary circle, which would have been in
Cuba and Spain, was negligible. That the account made it into print at
all is testament to the work of a number of intermediaries whose covert
handling and shuttling of the original manuscript fomented the conspiracy that led to the autobiography's eventual publication.[49] Despite
the obstacles to its dissemination, versions of the original autobiography
in the nineteenth century alone include Suárez y Romero's corrected
copy of Manzano's handwritten original; Madden's translation of this
copy; fragments of the autobiography that Francisco Calcagno probably
reproduced from Suárez y Romero's text in 1878; and Nicolás Azcárate's
copy, which was most likely penned around 1852 from Suárez y Romero's
version and rediscovered by Lee Williams at Yale University's Sterling
Library in the 1980s.[50] The twentieth-century versions of the autobiography (Ivan Schulman's and Abdeslam Azougarh's) are taken from José
Luciano Franco's published transcription (1937) of Manzano's original.
This meticulous detective cum archaeological work of investigating, describing, and analyzing the original manuscript's whereabouts, movements, and versions can be illuminating, as William Luis demonstrates
in his thorough edition of Manzano's works. Yet the idea of Manzano's
autobiography as a conserved manuscript is not the sense of an original
to which I want to turn my attention.

Manzano reveals the extent to which, were his autobiography to be
considered true to life, it would not be because he convincingly managed to assume the fiction of an independent authorial voice; rather, as a
legally enslaved writing subject, he periodically calls attention to the an-
guished exaggerations and silences that he felt obliged to include in the
account. As I noted in the previous chapter regarding one of his missives

to del Monte, he critiques his autobiographical writing for the ways in which he thought that it failed to be true to the life that he had lived. The idea that his text reads to him like a "bloated chronicle of lies" may have been an indication of the subterranean effect that del Monte's request for the account had on his writing: the patrician's reformist agenda to bring the cruelties of slavery closer to the consciences of Cuba's slaveholding bourgeoisie meant obliging his class to countenance and recognize its own hand in slavery's dehumanizing practices as well as insisting that Manzano bear the burden of this bourgeoisie's self-depiction. From the openness of the correspondence that Manzano maintained with del Monte, it is evident that the latter permitted or perhaps even encouraged the former slave to voice complaints about his life in bondage. Manzano's negative assessment of his "bloated" writing could also have been a consequence of his self-conscious efforts to transmit experiences for which the written word proves inadequate; hence, the frequency with which he states that the Marchioness de Prado Ameno broke his nose corresponds less to accountable incidents than to the compulsion to communicate the depth of the oppression and anguish that he suffered in her home. Furthermore, his desire to separate the "facts" from their "most terrible part"—a separation that manifests an awareness of what de Man would call the "impossibility of closure and totalization" in autobiographical writing—reveals a will to compensate for the ways in which slavery dehumanizes him.[51] Rather than limit himself to searching for an adequate articulation of his obvious circumstances, Manzano insists on rescuing his humanity from social death and invisibility and highlighting instances of sentiment and dignity in his self-representation. Consequently, equating the original autobiographical text to the truth of his life in bondage entails writing against his social condition by continuously reiterating or even exaggerating certain facts and suppressing the "most terrible part" of others. Like Benjamin's view that translating should be considered a mode that vitally links a translation to its original and vice versa, these necessary overcompensations illustrate how Manzano's autobiographical writing is original not only because the text is a unique artifact but especially because it coheres as writing that is a priori engaged with discourses and practices that made light, or nothing, of his humanity. Stated differently, Manzano's self-conscious articulations of excesses and omissions are instrumental for facilitating the autobiography's truthfulness to his life.

Madden's particular application of the translator's *adequatio* to Manzano's account of his life reconfigures the slave poet's autobiographical *adequatio*. In order to ascertain the effect of the reconfiguration, let us examine how the abolitionist justifies his decision to provide a literal translation of the poet's narrative. In his brief preface to Manzano's writings, Madden unequivocally states that del Monte had in fact "induced" the poet to write his autobiography.[52] All the same, the abolitionist appears ignorant of or simply elides, first, the effect that Manzano's debt to the "gentleman who was mainly instrumental in obtaining his liberation from slavery" might have had on the autobiographical account and, second, the poet's concerns as he attempted to reconcile issues of truth, human dignity, and life writing.[53] According to Madden, Manzano accomplishes the task "in a manner alike creditable to his talents and his integrity."[54] Contrary to the former slave's critique of his failure to achieve *adequatio* in his autobiographical writing precisely because of the discrepancy between the fact of his enslavement and his quest for self-esteem, this statement allows the abolitionist to claim that Manzano's text is so truthful and effortlessly penned that it requires little or no mediation. Madden praises the prose for the perfection with which it captures slavery and asserts, in light of such accuracy, that the account calls for a literal translation: "I have no hesitation in saying, it is the most perfect picture of Cuban slavery that ever has been given to the world, and so full and faithful in its details, that it is difficult to imagine that the portion which has been suppressed, can throw any greater light on the evils of this system, than the first part has done. I have given a literal translation of it, and that translation, revised by a Spaniard, will be found at the end of these poems."[55] The claim that this accurate portrayal of Cuban slavery requires a literal translation generates two related views. First, the assertion establishes that the empirical authority of the legally enslaved writing subject, as this authority coheres in Manzano's ability to deliver a "most perfect picture," governs the original's translatability. In other words, Madden proposes that the basis of the autobiography's translatability resides in Manzano's competence at invoking the experience of slavery. Second, the coupling of empirical accuracy with the need for a literal translation generates a conceit by which the translator endeavors to disappear from the translating scene. Both goals are crucial for creating the effects of transparency and immediacy that appeal to a readership of imaginative witnesses.

Madden's decision to translate the autobiography literally is easily rationalized in light of the abolitionist agenda to foster such a community of readers and, in particular, of his mission to produce explicit evidence of the cruelty of slavery in Cuba. Nonetheless, I would like to submit his stated faithfulness to the account's language to Benjamin's contention that "no case for literalness can be based on an interest in retaining the meaning."[56] For this twentieth-century intellectual, excessive attention to rendering literalness, especially when it is conceived as the mere transmission of information or "inessential content," constitutes the "hallmark of bad translations."[57] Paradoxically, then, Madden's bid to render a literal translation of Manzano's life story risks limiting the text to juridical evidence. That is to say, by attempting to treat the autobiography as purely empirical knowledge about slavery ("so full and faithful in its details") that would be creditable as parliamentary evidence, Madden focuses on reproducing the language of the text literally rather than on highlighting the "emotional connotations" of words that, according to Benjamin, free translations to assume their condition as a literary mode. Had the abolitionist translator been able to consult Manzano about his autobiography, he might have appreciated how the former slave's frustrations with writing involved not only the difficulty of recalling and enumerating the significant facts and events of his life but mostly the struggle to produce meaning from his stance as a legally enslaved writing subject. Ironically, Madden's assumption that a literal rendition of Manzano's narrative suited parliamentary procedure presses the text's meanings more into the realm of truth as empirical proof and away from the literary cultivation of sentiment and sympathy that abolitionism considered vital to its international agenda.

Notwithstanding, Madden's substantial changes to the autobiography contradict his claim of fidelity to the original. His modifications of the text include minor abbreviations and turns of phrase, the elimination of ellipses when Manzano could no longer describe a violent or traumatic experience, and, for dramatic impact, the rearrangement of the order in which the former slave presents episodes of cruelty and punishment. More importantly, two specific omissions in the translation challenge the translator's claim. The first is the abolitionist's deletion of references to Manzano's hunger and appetite, such as the following excerpt: "Always hungry, it is not surprising that I ate everything I found, and for that reason was considered an awful glutton. So it was that, since I did not have a customary hour to eat, I would stuff myself and gobble the food down almost without chewing, so I frequently had indigestion. That made me have to take care of certain necessities often. All of this brought on other punishments."[58] More than a demure refusal to avoid representations of bad manners and hygiene, the decision to suppress this passage suggests that the image of a voracious black slave was counterproductive for the abolitionist cause because it provoked invented, stereotypical fears of Africans and black slaves as primitive savages. Proslavery planters in the Caribbean and elsewhere could deploy such images to remind communities of the recent Haitian Revolution or, in Cuba, to disseminate the notion of the *peligro negro* (black peril) that influenced attitudes toward abolition on the island throughout the nineteenth century. Most of all, however, Madden would have wanted to avoid giving his readers the impression that the emancipated slave could not be socially managed. According to David Brion Davis's explanation of the abolitionists' ethic of benevolence, "the key to progress lay in the controlled emancipation of innocent nature," which is precisely why Manzano's admission that he could not control his appetite and his bodily functions would not have been well received.[59] There would be no room for apparent excesses of this sort in Madden's promotion of literature's "humanizing" influences.

The abolitionist's second deletion is surprising because the omitted phrase seems emblematic of the sentimental exchanges between masters and slaves that should have interested his cause. Madden first modifies Manzano's reference to his sentiment for the enslaver and then suppresses a phrase in which the former slave reveals his affection for the Marchioness de Prado Ameno. After stating that his mistress could not be without him for ten days straight, Manzano writes: "I loved her in spite of the harshness with which she treated me."[60] In an example of what Davis might have termed "controlled emancipation," Madden translates the sentence to say, "I was still attached to her, and shall never forget the care that she had taken on my education."[61] Further explaining his affection toward the Marchioness, Manzano declares: "When my mistress's temper mellowed toward me, I unconsciously relinquished a certain hardened heart that I had acquired since the last time she condemned me to chains and hard labor. As she persevered in not laying a hand on me or in ordering others to do so, I had forgotten all the past and loved her like my mother."[62] Madden's rendition states: "As my mistress treated me with a little more kindness, I insensibly began to be more calm, my heart more composed, and to forget her late harsh behavior towards me."[63] In light of the abolitionist's optimistic view of the slave's post-emancipation potential to submit to loftier forms of servitude, such as civic virtue, the dictates of the conscience, or, in this case, sentiment, what might explain the translator's decision to omit Manzano's stated affection for his former mistress?

As I illustrated in the last chapter, Manzano's admission provides a revealing glimpse of the complexity of his subjugation. His stated affection conforms to a familiar paradigm of coerced attachment whereby the assertion that he loves his mistress as if she were his mother logically ensues from her decision to refrain from punishing him. The temporary alleviation from physical and psychological oppression precedes the former slave's references to affection for his enslavers throughout the autobiography. Yet Madden misses this point or simply modifies or suppresses these references to the advantage of his cause. His decision to translate Manzano's coerced affection as attachment and gratitude for his education invites a reading in which the formerly enslaved poet is thankful for his mistress's tutelage and the responsibilities of self-education (or, for abolitionists, the future of post-emancipation self-mastery) that he is expected to assume. Furthermore, rendering Manzano's allusion to loving the Marchioness de Prado Ameno as if she had been his mother as the unconscious emergence of calm, composure, and forgetting suggests that the former slave (and, by extension, the legally enslaved subject) is capable, if not of forgiveness, at least of refraining from vengeance against his former enslavers. When Madden deletes Manzano's descriptions of his eating habits and of his affection for the marchioness, he contradicts his claim to be a literal translator of the autobiography, discards the complex configurations and meanings of sentiment that Manzano invokes in his statements, and ultimately skews such insights into the relations between masters and slaves toward preparing readers for an idealized post-emancipation imaginary. I would also argue that Madden's deletion of Manzano's affection for his former mistress, in particular, intimates the translator's conviction that the former slave's sentiments for his enslaver had been misdirected; that is to say, given both Manzano's and Madden's efforts to rescue the former's dignity through autobiographical writing, literature, and translation— albeit in their respective approaches to *adequatio*—the abolitionist did not consider the marchioness a worthy object of Manzano's sentiment. Arguably, and as Brown illustrates in the case of a Virginian planter in England who was vilified there for his hand in slavery before the American War of Independence, the abolitionists partook of an ideological need to represent slave owners, slave merchants, and other proslavery advocates in the Americas as solely responsible for slavery's brutalities.[64]

POETRY AND ABOLITIONIST POLITICS

If Madden determined that the oppression that Manzano described in his autobiography required a literal translation, the abolitionist took greater license when it came to the former slave's poetry. Part of the explanation for the readiness with which he liberally translated the poems is to be found in the privileged status of poetry as a medium for communicating sentiment among the abolitionists. Before the publication of famous slave autobiographies in Britain and the United States, such as Equiano's and Douglass's, Phillis Wheatley's *Poems on Various Subjects, Religious and Moral* (1773) became a celebrated book among Anglo-American abolitionists. According to Helen Thomas, even though neoclassical style predominated in Wheatley's collection of mostly poems and letters, her book demonstrated a relationship with the Romantic poets in its focus on the imagination, liberation, subjectivity, and memory.[65] In the United States, while Thomas Jefferson acknowledged religion but not the art of poetry for inspiring Wheatley's compositions, the African-born poet, on the other side of the Atlantic, received influential visitors during her stay in London, where she was regarded as a celebrity and where her book received excellent reviews from the British press and renowned abolitionists such as Thomas Clarkson. More pertinently, the critic asserts that Wheatley's critique of colonial slavery and racial ideology (and its transformation of religious spiritual awakening into a "duplicitous discourse of protest and rebellion") provided a model for the discourse of liberation that would inform the work of British Romantics.[66]

Madden's abolitionist activism unfolded in an environment in which poetry and antislavery politics were frequently allied. The early years of abolitionism witnessed an increase in the composition of poems about and against slavery by Romantic British poets and their precursors, such as William Cowper, Mary Birkett, William Blake, Mary Robinson, Samuel Taylor Coleridge, and William Wordsworth. Women played a crucial role in British abolitionism, and poems by the educator Hannah More and the poets Anne Yearsley and Helen Maria Williams added to the antislavery sentiment that swept through Britain at the time. While Cowper's "The Negro's Complaint" (1788) and Birkett's "A Poem on the African Slave Trade" (1792) directly tackled the traffic in African slaves, Robinson's "The Negro Girl" (1800) and Blake's "The Little Back Boy" (1789) decried the trade respectively through a representation of sentimental love between slaves and an appeal to maternal affection. Without discounting the importance of pamphlets, lectures, and speeches, poetry was increasingly employed to rally the British population against the slave trade. Antislavery poems were also composed for an elite readership: Coleridge's "Ode on the Slave Trade," composed in Greek, earned the poet the Browne Gold Medal at Cambridge in 1791, and Wordsworth, between 1803 and 1807, penned the elegiac "To Toussaint L'Ouverture" and "To Thomas Clarkson, on the Final Passing of the Bill for the Abolition of Slavery." Recalling a black female passenger whom he met fleeing France after its government decreed the banishment of all blacks from the country, Wordsworth's "We Had a Fellow Passenger" (later titled, "September 1st, 1802") is perhaps the only poem in which the poet broached the subject of racial ideology. Notwithstanding, as Thomas argues, Coleridge and Wordsworth gradually "translated" the discourse of captivity and liberation that informed the discourse of spirituality among radical Protestant prophets of the day into "the power of poetry"

and associated this discourse with the "imagination's power to impregnate and thereby liberate the 'living soul.'"[67] Wordsworth's tribute to
the fallen Toussaint L'Ouverture, for instance, negates his demise by
celebrating the imagination ("Man's unconquerable mind") as one of the
formidable "powers" that the Haitian leader left behind.[68] Even in the
version of *Lecture on the Slave Trade* that Coleridge's published in 1796,
the faculty of the imagination overshadows the poet's critique of the
slave trade and slavery.[69]

Freely translating Manzano's poems offered Madden the opportunity
to create imaginative witnesses who could partake of the imagination's
liberating powers in order to sympathize with the plight of slaves on
the other side of the Atlantic. He took advantage of this license in order
to position himself as an eyewitness, a decoder of practices in Cuba's
slaveholding society, and a promulgator of abolitionist sentiment and
politics through literature. Madden provides the clearest statements
about translating Manzano's poetry in the preface to the portfolio that
he submitted to the Anti-Slavery Society. Alluding to his authority as an
abolitionist who witnessed slavery on the island, he avers that any fair
opinion of the poems would necessarily need to take into account the
context in which they were written, for "how are these circumstances
to be estimated by one ignorant of the nature of Cuban slavery?"[70] Thus
capable of deciphering how Manzano coded his poems in order not
only to avoid official censorship but also to refrain from breaking the
slave's personal golden rule that he or she should never be overheard
speaking ill of the master or of slavery, the abolitionist claims to offer a
"sense of the writer (sometimes purposefully obscured in the original)
as plainly as the spirit of the latter, and the circumstances under which
these pieces were written, would admit of."[71] Finally, apologizing that
his translation did not do justice to the poems, the abolitionist asserts,
nonetheless, that he believes that he has done enough to "vindicate in
some degree the character of negro intellect." Given the steady rise of
pseudo-scientific racism in Europe a decade later, this vindication seems
radical. However, as Joselyn Almeida argues, this redemption entails
"taking possession of Manzano through the translated text and Madden's appropriation of Manzano's cultural labor."[72] Moreover, in keeping
with the abolitionist (if not the British Empire's) paternalist ideology

of purportedly benevolent tutelage, Madden sustains that "the blessings of education and good government are only wanting to make the natives of Africa, intellectually and morally, equal to the people of any nation on the surface of the globe."[73]

Affirming his authority as an eyewitness whose tasks include describing the unimaginable, Madden contends that the distanced imagination cannot adequately capture the cruelty of the slave trade. In "Evils of the Cuban Slave-Trade," an appendix to the portfolio of materials that he submitted to the Anti-Slavery Society, he writes that even though the brutalities of the trade require "no exaggeration," they are "beyond the power of the imagination to picture to itself."[74] In order to resolve how he would communicate what could not be imagined, the abolitionist begins the portfolio contextualizing Cuba's colonial slaveholding society with two of his own poems, "The Slave-Trade Merchant" and "The Sugar Estate (A Poem, Illustrative of Life and Death in Cuban Slavery)." The compositions provide the portfolio's readers with the cultural and political framework for Manzano's writings that Madden would deem necessary to enable their imaginary witnessing of the poet's plight while he was enslaved. Fundamentally, the translator acclimatizes the reader with detailed descriptions of local types, places, and activities and employs some of the evidence that he gathered from interviews (with an unnamed del Monte) on the history and economics of slavery on the island as well as from the reports that he appended to the portfolio to compose his verses.

In his poems, Madden repeatedly exhorts the reader to visualize Cuba's slaveholding colonial society. For instance, "The Slave-Trade Merchant" concentrates on the figure of the local slave trader urging the reader to contemplate and then deconstruct the falseness of appearances that characterizes him (and that Madden learned to decipher as he combated the "deadening influence of slavery" during his first year in Havana). Vision is thematized throughout the poem. In the first stanza alone, the word "Behold" is consistently employed to call attention to the slave merchant, his traits, and his way of life in a gradual shift from a telescopic to microscopic analysis of this figure: "Behold, yon placid, plodding, staid old man" introduces a respected member of colonial society that the poetic voice incrementally denounces in the poem. "Behold,

his house" inaugurates a description of wealth, pomp, and grandeur that
ends with the warning that "What's gorgeous, cannot always be quite
chaste." "Behold, his heart!" initiates a look at the source of human sentiment only to find that "E'en in the calmest breast, the lust for gold /
May fix its fatal canker in the core, / Reach every feeling, taint it more
and more (Madden, "The Slave-Trade Merchant," stanza 1). "Behold, his
conscience!"—the poem's longest reflection on the merchant—focuses
on the enigma of a deep and deadly repose of the soul that the poetic
voice depicts as a "peace that's owned by him who feels / He does no
wrong, or outrage when he deals / In human flesh" (stanza 2). Yet the
most compelling means by which Cuban slavery is rendered tangible
for the portfolio's reader is the poetic voice's denunciation of the slave
trade's transatlantic commercial network and its financial, speculative
power. Evoking the "human hell" (stanza 4) of the middle passage and
the merchant's hypocrisy of calling himself a Christian who walks "in
reason's light" but wages "eternal war with human right" (stanza 5), the
poetic voice describes the merchant's influence, stating that

> The pen does all the business of the sword,
> On Congo's shore, the Cuban merchant's word
> Serves to send forth a thousand brigands bold,
> "To make prey," and fill another hold;
> To ravage distant nations at his ease,"
> (Madden, "The Slave-Trade Merchant," stanza 5)[75]

Apart from rallying a reading constituency to his cause, Madden's invocation reveals the merchant's lucrative and moral distance from acts
of enslavement, his belief that "in guilt's great chain, he's but the farthest
link" (stanza 6), and the fact that he "kills by proxy only in the fray"
(stanza 7). In this poem, Madden successfully captures the psychological
distancing that allows the merchant to act not only with impunity but
also with an apparently clean conscience.

Composed in two cantos, "The Sugar Estate" employs a traditional
opposition between city (Havana) and countryside (a Cuban sugar estate) in order to approach and refute the widely held myth in abolitionist circles that Cuban slavery was mild in character. Madden probably
composed this long poem just prior to or in tandem with his "Address
on Slavery in Cuba," which he delivered on June 17, 1840, at the Anti-

Slavery Convention in London. Thematizing distance in these verses, the poetic voice begins by situating itself at a physical and moral remove from a bustling, decadent, and ultimately abject city through recourse to a repeated "Far from . . ." in the opening five stanzas of the first canto. In these stanzas, Havana's cosmopolitanism consists in the dynamism of merchants, planters, slaves, strangers, Creoles, brokers, and nobles that the trade in slaves generates. The trope of the immoral city in occidental letters is traditionally articulated as repulsion for a way of life that a poetic voice or narrator experiences and subsequently shuns. Yet, presented early in the first canto, Madden's scathing criticism of life in Havana renders the city's urban bustle intelligible not only from the perspective of the abolitionist cause but also from the arguably anxious stance of one who had initially succumbed to the affluent bourgeoisie's urbane hospitality and manners and the temptation to moral complacency that they initially produced in him.

"The Sugar Estate" also articulates in verse Madden's sharpest condemnations of Cuban slavery from his address. Initially approaching the Cuban countryside as if it were a reified *locus amoenus,* the poetic voice gradually explodes the idyll of the tropical landscape that it begins by celebrating in some fifty verses. Reminiscent of the wandering pilgrim of Renaissance lyrical poetry (or its neoclassical recuperation), a traveler arrives at a house belonging not to a simple farmer as the literary commonplace might have it, but to a planter and count that the poetic voice portrays as a "youthful noble" with "grave signs of premature decay" (1.8). It is from this point on in the first canto that Madden interrogates the two principal elements that blind observers to the conditions of slaves on the island: the slave-holding bourgeoisie's beguiling hospitality and the ways in which the failure to provide Cuban slaves with protection under Spanish laws on slavery buttress the necessary fiction to which the master adheres that his slaves are happy. In "The Protection of Slaves in Cuba," another report that he appended to the portfolio, Madden notes that although visitors inquire about the treatment of slaves at the planters' tables, "where truth is drowned in hospitality," this understandable curiosity "is merged in a courteous acquiescence in the sentiments, or at least the statements of a liberal entertainer, and a gentlemanlike host."[76] The abolitionist eyewitness must place himself at a remove from the planter's hospitality and the transnational practices of bourgeois reciprocity that might allow him to recognize and savor it. This self-distancing, not on socioeconomic grounds but on the basis of a purportedly disinterested moral stance, serves as a prerequisite for viewing Cuban slavery "as it truly is" and acts as a counterpoint to the myriad rationalizations by which slave-owning planters distanced themselves from assuming responsibility for human bondage.

Madden reserves the poem's most biting irony for a fictitious dialogue between the traveling guest and the count in which the latter is pressed into defining his proslavery stance. To the planter's claim that he spends his time "making those poor negroes here, content" (1.9), the visitor responds, parodying the notion of mild enslavement, that since the slaves are "lightly worked," "fond of labour," and "so very grateful, Sir, for all you do" (1.11), they could be freed without injustice to them or grave harm to the planter class, even though the slaves, the traveler adds, "must be far too wise / To wish to break so good a master's ties" (1.11). This proposition unleashes the planter's antagonism as well as his principal arguments against abolition. First, although the count claims that he hates the "very name of slavery" (1.12), he asserts regarding human bondage that "Sir! in the abstract it must be condemned, / It is the practice only I defend; / For 'quo ad' morals, nothing can be worse, / But 'quo ad' sugar, 'tis the sole resource" (1.12).[77] Second, in response to a "vile" British government, whom he calls "a pack of wretches envious of our gains" (1.14), and to the abolitionists, whom he describes as "philanthropists who'd swear / That black is white, to bring their ends to bear" (1.14), the count appeals to an ideology of white supremacy—to "the sacred privilege and right / Which ev'ry law accords the skin that's white!" (1.14)—that has apparently failed to unite across the Atlantic on the basis of race. Third, the planter resorts to a traditional paternalist stance in which he claims that his only wish "is for the real welfare of the slave" (1.15) and that the slave's bondage in Cuba is a "paradise" where he might enjoy "title to a master's care" (1.15) in contrast to the life he would have had in Africa. Finally, taking aim at the feature of Cuban slavery that Madden reiterates most in his address, the planter argues that "the humblest slave's protected by the laws" (1.15) but decries the ineffectiveness and ambivalences in the colonial system of justice. In an appended report, the abolitionist writes that while the Spanish civil law on questions of slavery is excellent, "the law was never framed with any reasonable prospect of being enforced, it never has been enforced, and, what is more, it never can be enforced against the planters, who are the transgressors of it, because in fact, these are the men who are entrusted with the execution of it."[78] At the end of the first canto, the planter politely suggests that the traveler depart and distinguishes between the British abolitionist and Cuban creole bourgeoisies that the opposing stances on slavery in the poem represent: "Our ways, indeed, are not as smooth as yours, / But still they serve for us, we make them do, / We are not fond of anything that's new" (1.18). This consciously espoused social conservatism, conjoined as it was to the revolutionary economic liberalism of the time, represents one of the most salient self-characterizations of the slave-owning Creole bourgeoisie.

Because concealment, disavowal, and escapism are the planter's principal activities in "The Sugar Estate," it is not the count who succumbs to the internal struggles of conscience regarding slavery but the *mayoral* or overseer, whom Madden redeems in his poem's second canto. The argument in this canto is that economic oppression by the planters acquits some overseers of moral responsibility for human bondage. Nevertheless, redeeming the figure of the overseer as a vital source of the "truth" about Cuban slavery by invoking class antagonism, Madden fails to appreciate the extent to which the constant displacement of responsibility for slavery between the plantation owner and his manager helps to disavow the moral consequences of slavery on the estates. The overseer becomes blameless—"'Tis idle to remonstrate or resist, / Obey one must, or be at once dismissed" (2.13)—while the poetic voice, now in the role of investigator, takes the *mayoral*'s cue to demonize the planter class's turpitude, moral cowardice, and decadence, traits that the overseer and the lyrical voice in the first canto associate with the city. The poem's final verse, "God help the slave! and pity the opprest" (2.15), underscores this view by positing the slave-owning proprietor as solely responsible for the cruelties of slavery on the plantation. This moral isolation of the Cuban slave-owning planter is consistent with Madden's refusal to portray Manzano's second mistress as worthy of affection in the abolitionist's translation of the autobiography and illustrates the growing tendency

of the British abolitionists at the time to vilify slave owners and merchants on the other side of the ocean for the depravities of slavery as
if the metropolis had had nothing to do with the profits that human
bondage generated. Composed as portals of entry into the lucrative, immoral world of slavery, Madden's poems prepare readers to approach
and imaginatively witness Manzano's enslavement in exchange for the
literary creation of a moral distance and atonement that would absolve
him, his class, and his country from a long and recent history of chattel
slavery.

A TRANSLATOR'S LICENSE

Even though Madden underscores the importance of elucidating the
circumstances in which Manzano composed his poems, his translations
overtly call attention to the poet's enslavement, even when Manzano
does not allude to bondage at all.[79] The translator's bid to supplement the
poet's verses through free translation submits the poems to an abolitionist agenda in ways that run counter to Manzano's articulation of his desire for freedom. For example, in Manzano's "A la muerte" (To death) the
lyrical subject (a self-described common Christian) pleads with death
that it should not take its life when it commits excesses (lust, vanity, jeal-
ousy, rage, and arrogance) but, rather, when it fervently embraces God's
commandments. The universal register with which Manzano initiates
the poem's opening apostrophe—"Oh parca denegrida / del universo
azote" (Oh somber death / universal scourge) (stanza 1)—becomes, in
Madden's rendition, "Oh, thou dread scourge and terror of our race"
(stanza 1).[80] The abolitionist's translations typically lengthen the poet's
economical verses in order to maintain a uniformly consistent rhyme in
English as well as insert additional meanings. However, in his conscientious bid to supplement the original poem with religious tenets that
might convince abolitionist readers of the poet's spiritual devotion, the
translator attributes an unlikely if not sacrilegious expression of gratitude to the poet: when Madden supplements the poem with verses such
as "This gift of life, that God was pleased to give" (stanza 2) and "To
him who gave me life, nay more, revealed / The truths of life eternal and
of love" (stanza 5), he implies, perhaps counterproductively for aboli-

tionist thought, that slavery and, specifically, racial terror do not result from human actions but constitute part of a divine plan for which the formerly enslaved poet should be grateful.

Similarly, even though Manzano adapts the Greek myth of Daedalus and Icarus in "Un sueño" (A dream) to express a desire for flight and freedom from affliction, which the lyrical subject invokes without specifying its cause, the translator grounds his rendition in precise references to slavery that undermine the poet's practice of nuanced circumlocution. Madden thus renders the word *etíope* (Ethiopian) (stanza 11), which is a signifier that connotes free African within a familiar classical imaginary and that retains this sense in the poem, as simply "slave" (stanza 16) in his translation. In veering from the original composition, the translator also adds the lines "where our doom is to sigh / In hapless despair, and in bondage to toil" (stanza 18) and describes the air to which the lyrical subject ascends not as liberation from Minos's imprisonment of the father and son, which the poet incorporates in his adaptation, but as "the place where the slave from his master is free" (stanza 20). Yet, the most questionable supplement in Madden's liberal translation is the association of Icarus's demise in the myth with chastisement in Manzano's adaptation: "The fate of poor Icarus seemed now for me, / And my daring attempt its own punishment brought" (stanza 25). Ironically, the translator remains faithful to the idea in the myth that Icarus's disobedience resulted in his fall, even though Manzano's poem avoids all reference to responsibility for the lyrical subject's and its brother's suffering. The poet conserves the myth's reference to Icarus's pride in mastering flight, but, in representing flight as freedom without limits, he omits Daedalus's warning about flying too close to the sun. Corroborating my argument in chapter 2 that slavery forecloses ethical stances from which enslaved subjects might disparage themselves, the poem presents no occasion for transgressing "natural" and manmade laws and suffering the consequences. In Manzano's adaptation, a violent storm suddenly and inexplicably materializes, engulfs the lyrical subject and the brother whom he is transporting to freedom, and imperils their lives. The poem ends with the description of a terrible clap of thunder that awakens the lyrical subject from the dream. Madden's liberal translation not only fails to reproduce the original's *intentio* by which meaning often coheres in carefully wrought circumlocutions characteristic of a censored colonial society. In his eagerness to disclose the dire circumstances in which Cuban slaves live, he supplants evidence of Manzano's acquisition and adaptation of "universal" culture (what the abolitionist and his class would have considered his familiarity with Greek mythology) with reductive references to slavery.

When Madden tackles the translation of Manzano's most acclaimed poem, "Treinta años," he introduces words such as "bondage" (stanza 3) and "chains" (stanza 4) that, as I noted in chapter 1, the poet deliberately avoids. This pattern of semantically grounding the poems in slavery does not demonstrate the critical disinterest or "objectivity" of the geographically distant imaginary witness; nor does the translator's insistence on making meaning in this manner coincide with Benjamin's assertion that supplementing the original literary text beyond its simple reproduction in another language should attend to the attributes that make the original literary in the first place (the unfathomable, the mysterious, and the poetic).[81] Madden is evidently less interested in treating his translations of Manzano's poems as mere language-to-language concerns than in wanting to communicate something beyond a literal translation of the compositions. The abolitionist wisely acknowledges that the poet is "sometimes purposefully obscured in the original," but he supplements the original poems with information about slavery that often reveals more about his mission on the island than about the circumstances in which Manzano wrote his poems.[82] Hence, despite the authority that he assumes in Havana as superintendent, abolitionist agent, and witness, he still misses the opportunity in his translation of "Treinta años" to invoke the experience of bondage from the enslaved subject's perspective and create a compelling case for sympathy. For example, the brilliant allusion to the experience of bondage that Manzano captures in the poem's second quatrain,

> I am surprised by the struggle that I have been able to
> sustain against so godless a fate,
> If that is what one might call the challenge
> Of an unhappy being, to evil born. (stanza 2)[83]

is rendered in Madden's translation as

> I marvel at the struggles endured,
> With a destiny frightful as mine,
> At the strength for such efforts:—assured
> Tho' I am, 'tis in vain to repine. (stanza 2)

While Manzano refers to the powerful notion of a godless or unholy fate—a succinct though oblique denunciation of the power of men to enslave others—his translator's use of the word "frightful" elides intimation of any agent responsible for human bondage. More importantly, the last two verses of the translation fail to capture how the lyrical subject submits contingent possibilities for action and agency (struggle, challenge) to the relentlessly confining, existential rigors of enslavement (unholy, unhappy being, evil) as a concise summary of the experience of slavery. Despite the flexibility of employing *adequatio* to his advantage in a liberal translation, Madden's rendition falls short of the poem's sincere appeal for sympathy and justice.

Given such instances of reductionism, even though he liberally translates Manzano's poems, how does Madden set out to vindicate "negro intellect"? The abolitionist translates poems in order to demonstrate the quality of the former slave's thinking on a number of complex themes. He capably captures and translates "A la calumnia" (To calumny), Manzano's brief but witty reflection on the pitfalls of slander for its practitioners, and he comfortably translates the poet's "Oda a la religión" (Ode to religion) in order to display the latter's knowledge of religious doctrine and eloquent description of religious sentiment. This second composition would have been immensely useful for the abolitionists, whose familiarity and engagement with (and, in some cases, authorship of) narratives of spiritual awakening predisposed them to read Manzano's ode sympathetically; the poem could have given readers the chance to associate the former slave's writings with narratives such as Equiano's autobiography, the most acclaimed slave narrative to have preceded the publication of Manzano's texts, or with Wheatley's poems. Arguably, Madden's interest in translating this ode is also a function of the paucity of religious writings by Cubans in his antislavery portfolio.[84] Not only did the abolitionist's inquiries have little to show in this area, Manzano's account of his life reveals no recourse to or quest for spirituality, despite the religious education that he received.

Madden's translation of the ode, which is his most liberal rendition of all, offers a profile of Manzano's religiosity that a number of supplements and omissions helps to shape as evidence, according to Davis's summary of abolitionist thinking, of the slave's potential to be lifted from "unwilling to willing servitude" through a process of controlled tutelage. (It is worth recalling that Madden's condemnation of slave owners and merchants did not dissuade him from translating Manzano's stated affection for his mistress as an attachment to his enslaver for the education that she claimed to have bestowed on him.) As if to emphasize the value of self-education for spiritual awakening, the abolitionist supplements the translation with the verses, "Oh, how the grandeur of the theme doth seem / T'enlarge my thoughts, and to inflame my breast" (stanza 2). Yet, because he might have preferred to associate Manzano's religiosity with reason rather than with unbridled emotion, he omits the poet's mention of the "profound ecstasy" in which the soul travels from the body to "its Maker" (stanza 2)—a familiar description of religious experience among sixteenth-century Spanish mystics. In fact, while the poet describes the soul's journey before initiating the ode's praise of religion, Madden minimizes this journey in favor of an immediate disquisition on the poem's stated theme. The translator also leaves out a crucial question that the lyrical subject poses despairingly to God toward the end of the poem—"Why do you leave me where sin comes forth / and not take me onto you?" (stanza 11)—because even though the question might legitimately seek an answer from the purview of a legally enslaved subject who received religious instruction, abolitionist readers might have deemed the query an irreverent challenge to God's design. Toward the end of the poem, Madden introduces verses that do not appear in the poet's ode: he turns Manzano's praise of religion and religiosity from the perspective of a single voice's prayer into, first, an abolitionist plea that religion shed its light on Christian slaveholders, "on those whose deeds / Belie the doctrines of the church they claim" (stanza 7), and, second, a request to "hear the captive's cry" (stanza 8).

Finally, Manzano's failure to do justice to Manzano's brief but complex reflection on time in "Al reloj adelantado" (To the clock that runs fast) demonstrates the abolitionist's missed opportunity to appreciate

Manzano's ingenuity. Whereas Madden's translation detachedly describes the clock as an observed object, Manzano employs apostrophe to address the clock and distinguish between its capacity to measure time, even as it ran fast, and the perpetuated time of misfortune, "The hours that don't pass" (stanza 1). The abolitionist's short, aloof rendition of the poem does not capture, for instance, the metaphor through which the clock's toothed gears are likened to the poetic voice's aggrieved internalization of a time of suffering:

> But if injury within,
> Or from amongst your sundry wheels
> Sharpened teeth
> Should bite into your soul;
> Learn from my breast;
> Which in so terrible a misfortune,
> For being timely
> Is bathed in tears.[85]

Nor does the translation approach the reversal at the end of the poem whereby the poetic voice discovers that even though its pain may coincide with the clock's mistimed march (*discorde curso*), this perpetual (*con el largo tiempo*) misery invariably overtakes time. Analogous to Manzano's reflection on melancholy in "Treinta años," but more intellectually demanding than the latter in its adroit invocation of opposing conceptions of time, the poem's hyperbatons might have proved too challenging for Madden's linguistic capabilities. Even if this were not so, the translator's linguistically simpler rendition of the poem illustrates that what was most translatable about the formerly enslaved poet's verses, as far as Madden was concerned, did not reside in the meanings that he could free from the original text as he rendered them in English but, in contradistinction to Manzano's desire that his works be evaluated for their aesthetic value, in the doctrinal reduction of the poet to a slave and his sentiments to their political instrumentality. Nevertheless, as a testament to the composition's literary worth, José Lezama Lima—Cuba's most erudite and internationally acclaimed twentieth-century poet—would include "Al reloj adelantado" in his seminal *Antología de la poesía cubana* (1965).

ADEQUATE VERSUS APPROPRIATE TRANSLATIONS

Several factors prepared Madden to undertake the translation of Manzano's writings. Apart from his knowledge of Romance languages, his
strong abolitionist convictions over the long run, and the investigative
offices to which he had been appointed furnished him with some of the
tools that he required in order to appreciate the context in which the
original texts had been penned. His willingness to assume responsibilities as magistrate in a post-emancipation Jamaica, where planters sought
to undermine the new laws; as superintendent of liberated Africans in
Havana, where the island's slave-owning bourgeoisie identified him with
British abolitionism; as an expert on contraband slavery who voluntarily
traveled to the United States to testify in the *Amistad* case; and, finally,
as an investigator, who left his permanent position in Havana in order
to produce a report on the slave trade along the coast of Sierra Leone,
all provided him with abolitionist credentials beyond reproach. In light
of Benjamin's suggestion that a text's translatability partly relies on the
contingencies of finding a translator whose experiences could inform
the tasks of translation, Madden's curriculum vitae and activism geared
him, as few of his abolitionist colleagues could have been, to appreciate
the contexts for translating Manzano's writings. However, even though
his experiences in a transatlantic field of abolitionist activism enriched
his ability to translate material for the portfolio, their personal challenges also obliged him to search for new ways to assert the movement's
fundamental ideal of assuming moral stances and pursuing justice on
the basis of disinterested objectivity. As he was no longer enjoying the
physical remove from which such stances were typically sustained, the
temptation to partake of the local benefits and luxuries that accrued to
his class initially tested his moral outrage at slavery—until, that is, he returned to and successfully completed his mission of gathering evidence
on the cruelty of Cuban slavery for the Anti-Slavery Society. Hence,
even though British abolitionism drew on narratives of human bondage in order to transform the sufferings of enslaved others into intimate
abstractions akin to but morally distinguishable from the perverse intimacies that I examine in these chapters, becoming an eyewitness and in
situ investigator placed Madden under the pressure of ethical impera-

tives resembling those that challenged the Creole reformist bourgeoisie. The slave-holding Creole bourgeoisie sought moral shelter from the burgeoning discourse on the universal right of all men to freedom in the particularity of their *local* claims to being enslaved by slavery itself, and Madden's mission involved overcoming *local* obstacles, especially that of succumbing to moral complacency, to the universalizing claims of abolitionism.

For Benjamin, a text's translatability also means discerning what aspects of it call for translation. An assessment of translatability in this sense implies that the original text should have a certain fame or "afterlife" that Manzano's writings, with the possible exception of the sonnet "Treinta años," could not have enjoyed in a slave-owning colony where any hint of sympathy for abolition or reform was immediately censored and where access to an Anglo-American abolitionist readership was extremely limited. Despite Manzano's eagerness for his poems to be appreciated for their aesthetic value in Europe, Madden's decisions about the translatability of the poet's writings demonstrated how the demand for antislavery evidence that guided the abolitionist's mission in Cuba reduced his vindication of "the character of negro intellect" to politically instrumental symbols of bondage rather than elucidate the complexity of Manzano's self-representation. Given the missed opportunities to explore the depth of the slave's psychological oppression and anguish, it could be argued that the abolitionist was a mediocre translator at best, that his attempts at *adequatio* when he translated Manzano did not contribute to a more thorough understanding of the effects of slavery on those whom it subjugated; but it is also certain that his determination of what was translatable about the poet's writings had less to do with valorizing the slave's sentiments on their own terms than with the sympathy that he meant to extract from them. Stated differently, although the abolitionists strove to free slaves from their status as property, Madden's translations, first and foremost, rendered Manzano's life and sentiments appropriable for readers predisposed toward sympathy on the other side of the Atlantic. In a sense, this outcome resulted logically from Madden's and del Monte's conception of literature as a "humanizing" influence in which, for the latter, rehabilitating slave owners took precedence over "humanizing" slaves through literary representation.

It should not be concluded, however, that opting to privilege the re-habilitation of slaveholders over the elucidation of their slaves' personal and collective quests for freedom ever presented itself as a clearly defined dilemma. Madden subscribed to a concept of literature's "humanizing" influence in which he approached his representations of both slaveholder and slave with characteristic didacticism. In this light, his translations promote the abolitionists' conviction that, perhaps with the exception of a small minority of enlightened young liberals, not only did the Creole slaveholders' claim to bourgeois propriety lack humanitarianism, but, just barely below the surface of their deceptive urbane hospitality, they were fully prepared to espouse their proslavery stance. It is possible to see how Madden's secret mission to acquire evidence of the cruelty of Cuban slavery would have led to this marked distinction between rival transatlantic bourgeoisies. Yet the translator's inadequacy when it came to representing the slave's struggle for freedom on his or her own terms meant that as revolutionary as abolitionism might have been for its day, it still subscribed to paternalist ideologies that maintained the movement within the fold of imperialism.

FOUR

Freedom without Equality

Slave Protagonists, Free Blacks, and Their Bodies

In a letter concerning the Missouri Compromise that he wrote to the American politician John Holmes from Monticello on April 22, 1820, Thomas Jefferson famously described the dilemma of slavery in the United States in the following terms: "We have the wolf by the ear, and we can neither hold him nor safely let him go. Justice is in one scale, and self-preservation in the other."[1] Even though the country had won its independence from Britain forty-four years earlier, slavery loomed as an issue that threatened to tear the United States apart, had it not been for the stopgap measure of the compromise that maintained the number of slave and free states equal and, with hindsight, postponed the Civil War. Cuba was still a Spanish colony in the 1830s, and the island's Creole reformists found themselves in similar straits. As I illustrated in chapter 1, Félix Varela and Tomás Gener, writing to Domingo del Monte from their exile in Philadelphia, portrayed themselves as enslaved by slavery because they felt that they could not heed the humanitarian call to emancipate their slaves without compromising their own self-preservation as a class. Furthermore, the reformists, who prided themselves on being an enlightened minority within a larger local bourgeoisie, understood that it was not the fact of colonialism alone that shackled them to slavery: Madrid's economic policy of ensuring a consistent supply of slaves was also politically strategic because it frustrated the reformists' ambition to reduce the number of slaves and free blacks on the island, which was a goal that they considered essential for the social and political progress of their class and community.[2] Yet Jefferson's statement is also paradoxical in a way that is useful for my discussion below. At the same time that he describes the relationship between the United States and slavery as their having "the wolf by the ear," which implies that the nation was precariously in control of the institution, he admits that slavery could be neither maintained nor eliminated because the conflict that it generated between free and slave states threatened to split the Union. In other words, how was "the wolf" going to be manageable if it could be neither restrained nor released?

In my reading of the literary narratives that emerged in Cuba in the 1830s, I invoke Jefferson's paradoxical statement regarding the unmanageability of slavery because it permits insight into the Creole reformist bourgeoisie's constant anxiety over the contingent relationship between slavery and the island's colonial status. Félix Tanco y Bosmeniel's *Petrona y Rosalía*, Pedro José Morillas's *El ranchador* (The slave catcher), and Anselmo Suárez y Romero's *Francisco, el ingenio o las delicias del campo* (Francisco, the sugar mill or the delights of the countryside) are novels that were written, like Manzano's autobiography, under the guidance of Domingo del Monte and his literary circle between 1834 and 1839. The short *costumbrista* narrative that Cirilo Villaverde would eventually transform into Cuba's most famous nineteenth-century novel, *Cecilia Valdés* (New York, 1882), germinated in the circle, while Gertrudis Gómez de Avellaneda, who wrote *Sab* (Madrid, 1841) independently from the group, was familiar with the plight of the Creole bourgeoisie and the obstacles that the reformists faced in securing the freedom of literary expression. It would be erroneous to read these novels as full-fledged expressions of abolitionist sympathies or, equally misleading, as mere imitations of the literature that circulated in transatlantic abolitionist circles. The circle's members actively sought models for their writing and looked to Victor Hugo's *Bug-Jargal* (1826) for inspiration, but immensely popular proabolitionist writings, such as Douglass's narrative of his life (1845) and Harriet Beecher Stowe's *Uncle Tom's Cabin* (1852), had not yet been published when this group of young liberals began discussing how to write narratives about Cuba that would depict slavery in ways that represented their particular context. Moreover, while British abolitionists increasingly vilified slave owners in the Americas from the last third of the eighteenth century onward as the principal perpetrators of the brutalities of slavery, the Creole reformists' desire to reflect their experiences of slavery in the literature that they wrote constituted an indirect and arguably defensive response to abolitionist pressures and influence. Employing sentiment didactically in literature about slavery interested the abolitionists and reformists alike, but for different geopolitical, class, and ethical reasons. Although del Monte and Madden concurred that literature should exercise an enlightening influence on slave owners, the circle's experimental didacticism can also be seen as an effort to rescue the Creole bourgeoisie from abolitionist accusations of moral depravity and, at the same time, to facilitate their aspirations to join the international ranks of bourgeois "men of feeling." Reform was their attempt to manage slavery on the island until such time as the elimination of the illegal commerce in slaves and the introduction of white immigrants would safely allow them to abolish it.

How do these narratives engage with the contingent relationship between slavery and colonialism during the '30s in Cuba? I argue that this contingency appears in the ways in which the representations of slaves as protagonists in this literature negotiate the reformist bourgeoisie's critiques of the relationship between slavery and colonialism and imagine a status for slaves and free blacks that must have been considered daring for the Spanish colony not long after the Haitian Revolution and its ripple effects in the region. Concerted efforts by white bourgeois authors—most of whom were slave owners—to conceive of black or mulatto protagonists in a literature that they purposefully sought to render as Cuban had no precedent on the island. As they penned their narratives, the circle's writers enjoyed a unique vantage: in addition to having become acquainted with Bug-Jargal as protagonist, the circle's members must have been inclined to think that their dealings in and personal knowledge of slavery, the double-edged attachment of their class to forced labor, and, in particular, their personal introduction to Manzano and his writings afforded them the opportunity to describe the social consequences of human bondage in ways that European authors could not. Therefore, the consistent development of slave protagonists in their texts cannot be ascribed exclusively to the mimicry of antislavery Romantic literature that originated elsewhere. The circle's members were aware of the risks of having their protagonists give voice to and embody critiques of slavery and colonial society; not only would this literary daring have been subject to scrutiny and censorship from colonial authorities, but it also risked alienating the rest of the local bourgeoisie, to whom, more than any other sector of the local population, they wished to appeal through their narratives. According to Tanco y Bosmeniel, fear, scruples, and revulsion were chiefly responsible for the absence of black characters in the literature of the time.[3] The creation of slave protagonists could easily have been read as antislavery propaganda and would have further exacerbated the reformist bourgeoisie's social and political isolation. In spite of these risks, which must have seemed less overwhelming behind closed doors at the Aldama mansion, the circle's writers almost unanimously created and experimented with enslaved black or mulatto protagonists.

Despite the radicalism of giving voice to enslaved protagonists in this colonial environment, these narratives are also notable for the consistency with which their authors depict lead characters whose submissiveness or frustrated desires for freedom invariably lead to their self-destruction or demise. As Sibylle Fischer argues, the fantasy of the submissive slave in this literature allowed slaveholders to suppress the knowledge that their slaves were anything but submissive and sustain the moral alibi that their proslavery paternalism was philanthropic.[4] In other words, the slave owners' fantasy of absolute control over their slaves constituted a necessary fiction, for to think otherwise, especially after the Haitian Revolution and the isolated slave rebellions that surfaced throughout the region, would have been a source of relentless preoccupation. By contrast, the tragic endings to which protagonists succumbed can readily be interpreted as capitulation on the part of authors who, in sacrificing their lead characters to enslavement without recourse, or even metaphorically to the romanticized bondage of unrequited love, privileged their own pessimism or melancholy under colonial rule over their slaves' bids to transcend bondage in any way that they could. So long as the Creole reformists could find no painless way to overcome their dependencies on slavery and on the related capacity of Spain's military presence to prevent their island from becoming "another Haiti," these protagonists seemed destined to meet tragic ends. Nonetheless, this capitulation, in which enslaved protagonists are sacrificed in order to produce pathos and enlightenment for local bourgeois readers, can also be considered the literary representation of a moral shelter whereby the Creole reformists presented themselves as the helpless victims of Madrid's ability to shackle them to their dependency on slave labor. In all likelihood, colonial oppression and the reformists' moral alibis were simultaneously in play, but it would not be until Carlos Manuel de Céspedes's legendary freeing of his slaves, which symbolically ignited Cuba's first war of independence in 1868, that an act of liberating slaves would supply the reformist bourgeoisie with the means to eliminate its dependencies on slave labor and Spanish military presence on the island. Needless to say, this hypothesis cannot be entertained except through hindsight. My point is that the fantasy of the submissive slave and the moral alibi of inescapable surrender to the colonial imposition of chattel slavery capture opposing "truths" in the contingent relation between slavery and colonialism: either the slaveholders controlled their slaves or they did not. I consider these protagonists the experimental, imaginary means through which these authors attempted to critique the specific relation between slavery and colonialism in Cuba and, in order to rescue their class from accusations of turpitude, to effect remedial changes in the way that the local bourgeoisie viewed and treated its slaves. In contrast to Pedro Barreda's argument that the character of the slave represented a "receptacle in which all the inequities of the system are concentrated," I focus my attention on how these protagonists were instrumentalized to make the case for slavery as the principal source of the moral depravity that hindered the Creole bourgeoisie's economic and political aspirations.[5]

According to current documentation, Manzano had not expected the literary circle to read and discuss his autobiography, nor did he know that Suárez y Romero would transcribe it from phonetic to standard written Spanish in order to facilitate its translation into English for the internationalization of the abolitionist cause that was underway in London. At a time and in a context in which the notion of intellectual property was loosely defined, there was no discussion among the circle's members about the ethics of employing Manzano's autobiography without remuneration as a resource for creating a specifically Cuban literature. Even though the extent to which aspects of his life story and, in particular, his desire to excel at his tasks influenced how the circle's writers created their protagonists remains open to further examination and debate, there is an uncanny resemblance between the characterization of these protagonists and two observations that Manzano made—and that I examined in the second chapter—regarding the difficulty of autobiographical writing for the enslaved or formerly enslaved subject. The first is his statement that no matter how much he tries "to speak the truth," he will never be considered an "honorable man" in a slaveholding society. I have already argued how this comment demonstrates Manzano's lucid critique that such a society prevents slaves from assuming moral positions a priori that would allow them to pass judgment on slavery and its practitioners. The circle's writers wished to have their protagonists speak truth to power, but, because the issue is also a question of whose truth (and whose desire for freedom) these characters articulate, the protagonists' speech and language are crucial factors for understanding the distance that separated the reformists from the enslaved and the power relations that mediated their cohabitation. The second observation that Manzano made about his autobiographical writing that is germane to the literary representation of these protagonists concerns their bodies. The poet's intimation to del Monte that the slave is "a dead being before his master" and, in the same private correspondence, that the "infinite whippings" that mutilated his flesh never succeeded in corrupting him provides insight into the uses to which the literary circle's writers subjected their protagonists' bodies. Susana Draper argues that because Manzano, as an autobiographical writing subject, was obliged to objectify his body, he could on occasion strategically move from descriptions of "the shame and horror of the punished body" to a reiteration of these sentiments at the level of the writer's use of reason.[6] What she identifies as the frequent split between body and reason in Manzano's autobiographical writing assumes a different configuration in the uses to which the circle's writers put their protagonists' bodies. While still seeking to inspire sympathy for his condition, Manzano preferred to leave descriptions of the mutilation of his flesh in the inkpot, whereas the reformists, like the abolitionists, were inclined to pursue the same sentiment by bringing brutal, physical torments to light, sometimes to morbid, exhibitionist extremes.

In her analysis of the discursive ruptures in the antislavery narratives that del Monte's literary circle wrote, Ilia Casanova-Marengo examines an underlying paradox in the representation of protagonists in these texts. She asserts that even though these writers opted for symbolically idealizing black slaves in their writings at the same time that they excluded them from an emerging national imaginary, this idealization still did not prevent the texts' narrators from exercising the epistemic violence of the white gaze on the black or mulatto protagonists.[7] One of the consequences of this erratic combination of idealization and violence in the creation of these protagonists is the frequent, noticeable disjunction between their speech and voices, on the one hand, and their bodies on the other. What interests me about this disconnection between voice and body, which is most frequently articulated through a radical opposition of eloquence and abjection in the same protagonists, is not its purported failure from the perspective of character development; rather, I view this disjunction as the unintended consequence of a narcissistic ideology through which the reformists imposed their experience of colonial oppression over their slaves' experience of bondage. Unlike abolitionists, who valued sentiment and sympathy as the means to transcend the physical distances that separated them from the slaves on whose behalf they spoke, the literary circle's writers subscribed to the perverse intimacy of supplanting their protagonists' desire for freedom with their own frustrations as an "enlightened" and morally superior though politically isolated sector of the local bourgeoisie. Drawing from Orlando Patterson and David Brion Davis, I have thus far employed the term "perverse intimacy" to refer to the abolitionist or reformist strategy of coaxing and pressuring slaves and recently liberated slaves into assuming purportedly loftier forms of servitude (such as commitments to upward mobility, class aspirations, local community, faith, love, etc.) as a means of maintaining social control over them in an effort, to recall and extend Jefferson's metaphor, to keep holding "the wolf by the ear." In this chapter, I want to make the case for the disjunctions between voice and body in these protagonists and the role of their bodies in the narratives as evidence of how the reformists' concerns for the welfare of the Creole bourgeoisie at large supplanted their slaves' struggle for freedom. In the following section, I examine the protagonists' speech, voices, and bodies for what they tell us about these writers' practices of perverse intimacy. The slave's punished body often appears as an object of exaggerated violence in some of the literary circle's writings, yet its representation anticipates the brutal treatment that colonial authorities meted out to slaves and free blacks and mulattoes during the Escalera conspiracy, which, I argue in the last part of the chapter, laid bare the unsustainability of freedom without equality, especially for the free colored population and colonial authorities.

SPEECH, VOICE, BODY

The first and most evident observation that has been made regarding the protagonists' speech is that because their Spanish is indistinguishable from that of their masters, they do not speak like slaves. The Spanish spoken by the free inhabitants in the colony differed according to several factors, including customary markers, such as the speaker's origin (foreign, Creole, or from a specific region in Cuba or Spain, rural or urban), education, profession, class, and gender; race was not a determining factor in the kind of Spanish spoken, though there may have been strong tendencies among the free blacks and mulattoes, who typically sought their livelihood in the cities, to speak an urban, popular vernacular and propensities among the bourgeoisie and upper class toward speaking a standard closer to the kinds of Spanish spoken in the metropolis. Among the enslaved, a range of proficiencies in Spanish existed depending on origin (Creole; from Sierra Leone, the Gold Coast, the Bight of Benin, the Bight of Biafra, Angola, or other West African regions; from one of these regions but raised in Cuba; Haitian; or Jamaican), place where raised, and labor activity (field, sugar mill, and/or domestic). Skin color was a significant but not determining factor in the Spanish spoken as slaveholders tended to place Creole and mulatto slaves in their households and to assign recently arrived West Africans to the fields. *Ladinos* were those who spoke better Spanish or an Afro-Spanish Creole and tended to work in the fields. Theoretically, slaves who worked in the sugar mills and refineries needed to be more conversant in Spanish than the recently arrived Africans would have been. Finally, and because of colonial and linguistic hierarchies, many among the free and, to a lesser extent, among the domestic slaves may have employed two varieties of Spanish (*diglossia*) depending on the degree of formality that the context required. In their daily contact with slaves and free blacks, the circle's writers would have been very familiar with the island's linguistic complexity. Yet, despite their insistence on portraying the most characteristic features of Cuba's landscape and social life and despite their reading of at least one of Balzac's realist novels, as a letter from Suárez y Romero to del Monte indicates, they unanimously ignored this linguistic reality when they created their protagonists.[8] The protagonists' consistent use of language denoting educated speech cannot be considered another instance of faulty character development principally because the circle's idea of what literature should accomplish in Cuba did not include a place for the protagonists' use of local vernacular.[9] As far as the abolitionists and reformists were concerned, the tasks of literature were to move, educate, and uplift through eloquence and an appeal for upright moral conduct on the part of slaveholders, so that employing anything but the speech that their class held as worthy of bourgeois propriety and the nobility of their protagonists was not a literary goal. It was this attitude that motivated the literary circle's members to have Manzano's autobiography transcribed into a standard written Spanish. Moreover, in a colonial environment, in which "correct" language and speech were fetishized because of the legal and social power that they wielded, the interest in making speech conform to the circle's moralizing literary experiments was even greater.

If the reformists experienced prohibitions on their freedom to speak openly about colonialism and slavery in Cuba, then their slaves' speech was more thoroughly circumscribed and regulated in all walks of life. In Tomás Gutiérrez Alea's classic film, *La última cena* (The last supper) (1976), an aesthetically accomplished and ethnographically accurate portrait of life on an eighteenth-century sugar plantation in Cuba, the slaves' use of the third person instead of the first to refer to themselves indicates how the master's language defines them socially on the plantation. This linguistic phenomenon constitutes a distortion of standard grammar that emerged in tandem with other ubiquitous mechanisms of language control. Muzzles or *bozales* were so frequently fitted on newly arrived African slaves that the name of the barbaric contraption became a way of distinguishing these slaves from those who were raised on the island. Eventually, the term also began to be employed metaphorically to identify and ridicule slaves who spoke poor or very accented Spanish. So widespread was the control and regulation of speech on the plantation that to be muzzled (*abozalado*) assumed a wide variety of forms on the plantation, even for Creole slaves whose proficiency in Spanish was beyond question. As Marilyn Miller demonstrates, Manzano was occasionally the subject of metaphorical muzzling in the Marchioness de Prado Ameno's house when she forbade him to recite his verses and relate stories before the domestic slaves or, more analogous to being *abozalado*, when she had him gagged when he could not refrain from engaging in these performances.[10] Teaching himself to write, as I illustrated in chapter 2, allowed Manzano to circumvent some of these prohibitions. Arguably, these examples of linguistic regimentation could have provided the circle's writers with creative narrative possibilities for enslaved protagonists who would uncomfortably inhabit the social and political environment that they wished to foreground in their writings, but the urgency of giving voice to their own complaints and anxieties trumped these occasions for experimentation as the writers collectively employed their protagonists' speech and voices in order to ventriloquize their main grievances regarding colonialism.

In the circle's antislavery fiction, omniscient narrators heavy-handedly criticize the flawed moral education of a new generation of patricians, while protagonists echo or espouse similar reprobation in words and through bodies that are sacrificed on behalf of the reformists' pedagogy of bourgeois civility. For example, the narrator in Tanco y Bosmeniel's *Petrona y Rosalía* minces no words in its scrutiny of the behavior of the young slave master, who, following in his father's steps, wreaks havoc in the lives of his female slaves: "But where Don Fernando indeed stood out, for it was about time that proof be offered, was in the perversion of his habits."[11] Yet, despite her personal experience in a depraved system of forced labor that allowed her to be raped with impunity and give birth to Rosalía, the older patrician's mulatto daughter, Petrona rhetorically asks, believing that the girl's father also impregnated her: "Can it be possible? And that man calls himself a Christian, a gentleman, a white man? After he did to me what he did, he dares to commit a sin such as this?"[12] In a slaveholding society in which masters raped female slaves or coerced them into having sexual relations with them and, moreover, after being similarly violated by Don Antonio herself, Petrona's appeal for the latter's gendered and racialized sense of moral decency appears misplaced. Rather than express rage and frustration about the inability to escape a legacy of violence that had also been perpetrated on her daughter, Petrona exclaims, "How perverse these men are!" and advises her daughter to be patient and offer up her travails to the Lord.[13] This resignation, this fiction of the submissive slave who bows to Christian virtues at the very moment when she learns of her daughter's rape and subsequent mistreatment, is further reinforced by the overwhelming sense of futility that Petrona evinces as slavery and her proprietors' immoral conduct subject her and her daughter to cycles of inescapable violence and degradation, and, eventually, to death by "natural" causes. Revealing that Rosalía and her son died during childbirth, a mere three months after Petrona's death, the novel ends with a critique of the economic greed that transformed humans into property. Don Fernando, the young patrician whose degeneracy leads to Rosalía's early death, and his mother, Doña Concepción, who cruelly victimizes the women slaves in lieu of confronting her husband and son about what the latter consider mere sexual escapades, simultaneously utter the final words in the novel: "Patience . . . we're out of a thousand pesos!"[14] That patience should be posited as an attitude of psychological and spiritual deliverance from the violence of slavery for Petrona as well as the slave owners' callous attitude toward the recovery of an investment captures the polarized and uneven positions of masters and slaves in this novel. However, consciousness of oppression brings no effort at resistance for these enslaved protagonists whose inevitable decline and deaths are offered up to Creole bourgeois readers as a critique of behaviors that hinder the social and political advancement of their class.

Even though Gertrudis Gómez de Avellaneda did not belong to del Monte's literary circle, her novel, *Sab*, which was banned in Cuba almost immediately after its publication in Spain, rehearses concerns over the island's economic and political future that characterized the Creole bourgeoisie in the 1830s. In the novel's criticism, one of Avellaneda's most commented on, creative strokes has been the protagonist's precisely honed racial indeterminacy. The omniscient narrative voice introduces Sab in the first pages as follows: "The recently arrived young man was of tall stature and average build, but with arresting features. He did not appear to be a white Creole, nor was he black, neither could he be taken for a descendant of the Antilles' first inhabitants. His face offered a unique combination in which the mixing of two different races could be perceived, and in which there was an amalgamation, so to speak, of the features of the African and European, yet without his being a perfect mulatto."[15] Not only does Sab's body reflect the miscegenation that obtained from Cuba's socioeconomic history, but the constantly shifting indeterminacy of his features and social station also destabilizes a range of expectations, thresholds, and taboos regarding class, race, and the ability of slaves to assume moral positions that were superior to their masters' in a slaveholding colonial society. According to Doris Sommer, "racial hybridization" became a matter of political survival for projects of national consolidation among Latin American countries after the wars of independence.[16] During the period when Avellaneda wrote her novel, the Creole bourgeoisie was keenly aware that such hybridization also had political consequences for its class because choosing between remaining a Spanish colony directly administered from Madrid, being annexed to the United States, or pushing for special economic advantages while remaining under Spanish rule also meant that slave owners would need to continue holding "the wolf by the ear" until such time as immigration could whiten the island's racial amalgam. As Casanova-Marengo succinctly states it, Sab's "racial/civil uncertainty and the ambivalence of his rank embody Cuba's colonial situation."[17] In short, the indeterminacies that Avellaneda attributes to her novel's protagonist invoke the trepidation with which members of the Creole bourgeoisie subjected themselves to or disavowed the urgent task of political self-analysis.

Yet Sab's racial and socioeconomic elusiveness also conditions how he addresses two radically opposed local communities. On the one hand, his physical indefinability permits him to engage in dialogue with his young mistress's suitor, Enrique Otway, who, during the men's first encounter, would not have deigned to inquire after the solvency of his future father-in-law's plantation from a slave. Sab, surveying his master's possessions in a pose reminiscent of a plantation owner, informs Otway that at one time the sugar mill provided its owner with some 300,000 pounds of sugar per year using over a hundred slaves but that its current production is limited to 6,000 loaves of sugar with a workforce that is half of its previous size.[18] Sab reveals these precise business details to a stranger of English extraction who, in fact, is motivated by the unbridled economic liberalism of an emerging transnational class that is positioning itself to overtake the more traditional Creole planters in wealth and influence and whose interests and investments, as Moreno Fraginals might have put it, were technical rather than ethical.[19] Carlota's betrothal to Otway represents the promise of economic sustainability and growth for the local bourgeoisie at the risk of disregarding all other considerations. Though the young patrician is not indifferent to his fiancée's charms, the narrator intimates that he is deeply "indoctrinated in the mercantilist and speculative spirit of his father."[20] On the other hand, Sab's position as the Buenavista plantation's enslaved overseer also allows him to articulate the novel's first expression of antislavery sentiment almost immediately after having provided Otway with information about the property's value. Rather than allude to slaves and work crews, as an overseer might, Sab describes the grueling workday of what would appear to be the typical slave (but is in fact a summary of tasks during the most labor-intensive period of the year) in a tone of lyrical melancholy that appeals for the young patrician's and the reader's sympathy. He ends the description on a note ultimately fearing that his words might have revealed a transgression on his part: "Ah, yes! This panorama of human degradation, of men transformed into brutes that carry the mark of slavery on their brows and an infernal desperation in their souls, is a cruel spectacle."[21] After admitting to Otway that he is a slave and mulatto, Sab also states that he has the honor of being the plantation's overseer, which is a position that slaves rarely occupied.[22] Capturing the anxieties of reformist thinkers who were seeking to transcend the moral dilemmas of their class, his indeterminate body generates a discourse about economic viability, on the one hand, and then straddles the paradox between the proper functioning of the plantation and the threat that unbridled antislavery represents to Buenavista's future, on the other. The Creole reformist bourgeoisie's belief that slavery enslaved it coheres in Sab's protagonism. Not only does Sab consistently reject the road to freedom, but he also insists on blindly attaching himself to the "lofty" servitude of an unrequited love for Carlota, his mistress.[23]

The extent to which Manzano's critical descriptions of the irascible Marchioness de Prado Ameno might have inspired the circle's writers can be debated, but the crucial role of matriarchs in the moral education of young patricians is a common theme in both *Petrona y Rosalía* and Suárez y Romero's *Francisco*. Because the reformists subscribed to the widespread hypothesis that living among slaves ruined their class's chances of upholding or strengthening its moral fiber, and because they knew that the emancipation of their slaves, for the time being, remained out of the question, the circle focused its critical attention on the domestic front. They singled out the matriarchs' overindulgent attitudes toward their sons—that is, the inexcusable ignorance about or disavowal of their sons' capriciousness, dishonesty, and immorality—as a cause for general concern. Ostensibly, these novels' protagonists suffer and die because slavery subjugates them so completely as to deprive them of recourse or escape; however, the plots that usher them to their demise originate as the inability of these mothers to be rigorous in their sons' moral education. In *Francisco,* the narrator begins the novel by introducing Doña Dolores Mendizábal's son, Ricardo, who, in his quest for the sexual favors of his mother's mulatto slave, Dorotea, is bent on eliminating Francisco, an African-born slave and her lover.[24] In the novel, the protagonist emerges as an unwavering pinnacle of virtue under the most unbearable circumstances. He is hardworking, loyal, and free of vices and has learned to read and write. Not only does he possess the requisite physical beauty of a "lofty soul," but, in keeping with the Creole bourgeoisie's fantasy of the submissive slave, he also displays a "peaceful disposition" and a "Christian's resignation" that practically elevates him to the ranks of religious martyrs.[25] The narrative voice continuously oscillates between extolling the protagonist's stoicism and lyrically describing the slave's deep-rooted, and at times tearful, melancholy.[26] As I mentioned in chapter 1, responding to del Monte's criticism that Suárez y Romero had exaggerated Francisco's virtues beyond reasonable expectations, the twenty-year-old novelist admitted that in his dedication to shaming white "tyrants" into curbing their excesses, his "error" had probably been to reveal a slave who thoroughly excelled them in virtue. Even though the literary circle's apparent consensus on Suárez y Romero's transgression indicates that there were limits to the degree to which Creole slave owners should be vilified for a brutal system of forced labor over which they claimed to have little control, the criticism still corroborates Manzano's assertion that, regardless of the efforts expended, the slave would never be able to achieve the status of a speaker of truth and an honorable man.

Nonetheless, scant critical attention has been paid to the fact that it is precisely the morbidly perverse and tyrannical Ricardo who overwhelms and marginalizes the protagonist in this novel. His dynamism steals the show. In addition to lacking all moral principles, he displays contempt for employees and slaves alike, keeps company with perverted, libertine youths, and has dealings with ignorant and wayward *guajiros*.[27] Given the extent to which it was mundane for slave owners to disavow the humanity of their slaves in order to consider them property, the depth and complexity of the young patrician's hatred for Francisco—the degree to which this slave became a sadistic obsession for the young patrician—are a constant source of intrigue at the same time that they appear exaggerated. Ricardo ostensibly positions himself as the maximum figure of authority on the plantation when he insists on having Francisco punished for his amorous relationship with Dorotea and, in particular, for her pregnancy, but the driving force that he conceals from all except the victimized slaves and those who mete out the protagonist's punishment is the wrathful vengeance that he stokes for having been rebuffed by his mother's personal slave. Much ado about the sexual lives of two slaves, it may be tempting to conclude, but Ricardo's overreactions are revealing. At the novel's outset, the narrator rehearses one of the literary circle's mantras: "It seems that slavery has spread its venom throughout our atmosphere annihilating the most philanthropic thoughts and leaving only hatred and scorn for the miserable race of colored people in its wake," but the patrician carries this hatred further than what the circle's invocation of sympathy for the plight of slaves would seem to require.[28] Ricardo's reaction to Dorotea's refusal to submit to his sexual advances may be regarded as histrionic, but it can also be considered the unintended consequence of a demand that the literary romance form makes on this antislavery novel. On one occasion, Ricardo goes so far as to say to Dorotea that he wished he were black, so that he might have the opportunity to enjoy her.[29] In her seminal *Foundational Fictions*, Sommer examined the importance of romance for the representation of nineteenth-century nation-building projects in Latin American novels and, among other things from the perspective of that period's racist elite, for positing the subliminal threat of incest as a risky consequence of national projects of "racial hybridization." So too has Vera Kutzinski amply interrogated the emergence and development of the fantasy of the *mulata,* such as Dorotea, Rosalía, or, most famously, Cecelia Valdés, in what she calls the erotics of Cuban nationalism.[30] However, the principal creative and ideological problem that the romance form presents for Suárez y Romero's triangulation of Francisco, Dorotea, and Ricardo is the significance beyond enslavement that the patrician must attach to the enslaved protagonist so that the love triangle might credibly hold. Because Ricardo represents the typical and necessary object of disgrace in the reformists' fictions of moral remediation, his unrelenting hatred elevates Francisco to the status of being the patrician's rival within the framework of the triangulation. This symbolic rivalry tampers with the bourgeoisie's fiction of the compliant slave by obliging the reader to place the master and slave on par. At a time when an independent Haiti continued to remind slave owners that open rebellion had paved the way for black empowerment in the former French colony—that, in their imaginary, the vengeful, cutlass-wielding rebel had been the protagonist there—the antislavery "radicalism" of characters like Francisco and Sab for the Creole bourgeoisie lay in the suggestion that a slave might rival or transcend his or her master in moral conduct. Even so, empowering the protagonist within this realm of bourgeois values still did not extract him from fictions of the submissive slave that compensated for real and imagined slave rebellions that haunted this class's attitudes toward the emancipation of its slaves and the social control of free blacks and mulattoes.

The justifications, apologies, and excuses that Manzano and Suárez y Romero communicate to del Monte in order to explain the difficulty that they experienced as they wrote offer special insight into how they rationalized their respective motives, rhetorical strategies, and aesthetic decisions. Unlike Manzano, who aimed for discretion in his writing, especially when he described the physical torture to which he had been subjected, Suárez y Romero considered fiction writing a way to release his deepest emotions. In the same letter to del Monte in which the young novelist admonishes himself for the heady idealism with which he portrayed Francisco, he provides additional information about motives and sources of inspiration that end up informing the creation of his novel's protagonist:

> Afflicted as I am, Señor del Monte, by the miseries of slaves more than you can imagine, I was determined to write a novel in which I could release the feelings in my heart, in which I could demonstrate that if there are whites who are zealous enemies of the Ethiopian race, there is no lack of those who grieve for their calamities with tears of blood: forever a friend of all men, I wish for no sobbing, no sigh of pain to be heard around me, and for everyone's life to slip along as serenely and gently as the moon sails by there in Heaven, accompanied by brilliant stars: I wish for mutual love, charity, peace, laughter, Sir; and not bitter wailing.[31]

Unlike most abolitionists, who looked to an antislavery literature of sympathy to overcome the physical distances that separated them from the slaves on whose behalf they spoke, the remove that divided the Creole reformists from their slaves was mostly intellectual, moral, and psychological. For reasons that I clarify below, Suárez y Romero's claim to be afflicted by the suffering of slaves seems heartfelt. Moreover, he reinforces his assertion by declaring his moral stance against racial hatred and then waxes poetic about his desire for universal peace, love, and happiness. It would be erroneous, however, to downplay his empathy and utopianism as merely youthful candor and impressionability.

Suárez y Romero explains that the suffering of slaves distresses him to the extent that writing a novel about it would allow him to liberate the feelings in his heart and, thereby, relieve *his* affliction. This confession adds more to his motives for writing than the circle's concerted promotion of didactic literature. The novelist's identification with the slaves' condition appears resolute: he claims that his affliction is beyond del Monte's imagination and, more significantly, that it permits him to count himself among those men of feeling who, in their absolute identification with the slaves' suffering, cry tears of blood. In his missive, Suárez y Romero further explains that because he himself is prone to patient tolerance for "the misfortunes of this wretched Vale of tears," he decided to equip Francisco with Christian resignation and compliance.[32] Nevertheless, because the slaves' plight emerges in his initial statement as an effect (the novelist's affliction) without direct cause, it becomes necessary to scratch the surface of his confessions to del Monte a little more. Because of the penury that befell his family after legal proceedings in Spain obliged his father to return there in order to clear his name, Suárez y Romero moved with his mother and six siblings to the Surinam Sugar Estate in Güines, near Havana, in 1839. It was during the year that he spent there that he finished writing *Francisco.* Through his direct contact with the plantation's activities, which, Moreno Fraginals asserts, were not mere literary referents but a daily business and spectacle, the slaves' suffering began to afflict him.[33] In other words, it was not pure philanthropic sentiment that inspired his desire for "no sobbing," "sigh of pain," nor "bitter wailing" to be heard around him, but a quest for psychological relief from the cruelties that he witnessed but could not name except as an abstract "suffering of slaves." Suárez y Romero's economic position improved enough for him to own slaves years afterward, but the violence that he encountered during his year on the plantation seems to have been a revelation. However, to describe and treat the slaves' suffering as a private affliction exposes the narcissism of perverse intimacy through which he defines himself as the aggrieved victim of such violence in his letter and posits literary writing in daily contact with plantation life and slavery as therapeutic. In repeatedly drawing attention to his affliction in this and other pieces of correspondence, Suárez y Romero displays more of the classical symptoms of melancholy, according to Freud, than Manzano does. In a subsequent letter to del Monte, the novelist intimates that while reading the poet's autobiography, "I have often burst into tears. I'm not ashamed to cry for things like this!"[34]

Nonetheless, it is Francisco's body that ends up receiving the brunt of the novelist's identification with suffering slaves. In fact, I would argue that if Francisco displays any protagonism in the narrative it is precisely that which his punished body obtains. In the same letter to del Monte, Suárez y Romero informs the patrician that he had found time to transcribe and correct Manzano's autobiography for the portfolio of evidence of the cruelty of slavery in Cuba that Madden intended to take with him to England. Having had the opportunity to compare Manzano with his protagonist, the novelist writes regarding the poet: "what naturalness, what grace, what sadness, how many horrors, how evil a mistress, poor Manzano always beaten, suffering, crying! Oh, God, this is not my Francisco, this hasn't been invented, it's true."[35] However, as if the "truthfulness" of Manzano's account could not accomplish enough for his creative writing, Suárez y Romero dramatically exaggerates the accumulation of abuses on Francisco's body. In the novel's opening dialogue between Ricardo and the overseer, the former anxiously inquires: "Did you take care of it? Did he bleed a lot? Did you leave him half dead?"[36] More than a simple demonstration of the supreme stoicism that these antislavery narratives require of their protagonists, the young patrician's insistence introduces a series of sadistic scenes, both visible to and concealed from the reader, that punctuate the plot and betray a palpable complex of fears and tensions. According to the narrator, Ricardo's hatred could partly be explained as inherent in white men of his kind, who cannot bear the thought of encountering upright men of color and are consumed by an insatiable fury.[37] That Francisco's presence on the plantation thwarts the satisfaction of the patrician's desire to be desired by Dorotea, which is a prime example of the mimetic desire that the romance form sets in play, also sets the protagonist up for elimination. Yet the detailed litany of successive punishments under Ricardo's scrutiny—the uninterrupted whippings over several consecutive days, the frequent loss of blood, the stinging concoction of whisky, urine, salt, and tobacco that are applied to open wounds, the exhaustion induced afterward by still being forced to work in the fields wearing shackles, the painful inability to walk, the high fever that sent him to the infirmary—exceeds expectations of human endurance and renders the protagonist more meaningful than his status as mere property.[38] Also germane to my hypothesis that Francisco's punished body possesses its own narrative autonomy is the narrator's precise calculations of the number of lashes that the protagonist receives: eighty at the start of the novel, three hundred and five over the course of ten days on another occasion, and, toward the end of the novel: "They had given him, over a period of ten mornings, sixty lashes on the first and twenty-five on each of the others, which came to a sum of two hundred and eighty-five."[39] What purpose is served by this detailed accounting of the whippings inflicted on Francisco's body beyond the capacity of human endurance?

Two important reasons explain this obsession with details of the physical torture to which Ricardo submits Francisco. First, in addition to substantiating the depth of the patrician's sadistic hatred, Francisco's chastised body invokes slavery's most gruesome abuses in the most graphic manner possible. This technique permits the author to render these abuses morbidly visible, so that readers are obliged to imagine (and, perhaps, recall or recognize their relation to) the violence that slave owners typically command others to do while they distance themselves from these brutal spectacles. (As the young novelist readily admits, being within earshot of these scenes still heightens their horror and effect on the imagination.) This literary effort to recruit reformists from the broader Creole bourgeoisie entails a dismantling of the slave owners' disavowals by producing opportunities for a remedial introspection (and, more subliminally, Christian redemption) before the reader's eyes. Francisco's abject, tortured body serves this didactic purpose and, as such, may be considered sacrificial. Second, stoicism represents a point of connection, transference, and projection between the reformists' belief that slavery enslaved them and the fiction of the compliant but durable body of the slave in which the Creole bourgeoisie as a whole was psychologically invested. For the local bourgeoisie, economic progress meant laboring stoically under a colonial regime that regulated or prohibited its economic and political freedoms. From the perspective of this class's paternalist expectations, slaves were also expected to toil similarly predisposed toward stoicism in order to merit their owners' alleged protection and care. This fantasy of the slave's stoic, laboring body is present in Petrona's advice to her daughter that they should offer their trials and tribulations to God; in Sab's relentless desire to place himself at the service of an unrequited love; and in Francisco's willingness to bear the tortures to which he is submitted so long as Dorotea remains faithful to their love. The slave's body constitutes an economically essential but unwilling source of labor in the enslaver's dream of prosperity; yet the same body, which must be physically subjugated, regulated, and occasionally excoriated to conform to the enslaver's desire for compliance, does not participate in the stoic self-knowledge that informs the reformist bourgeoisie's idea of itself under colonial rule. Rather, that body becomes a way to measure, alleviate, and articulate someone else's oppression: in a period of fear and anxiety regarding the role of slavery in Cuba's political future, the slave's body exists to be disciplined in the

Creole bourgeoisie's fantasy of absolute control and to be abused and sacrificed in the reformists' fictions of class redemption. Analogously to how Hegel conceived the expropriation of the fruits of the bondsman's labor for the lord's benefit, the slave's body possesses a vicarious, sublimating function in the literary circle's articulation of the reformist bourgeoisie's critique of their economic and political plight and their dream of a civilized and whiter Cuba. Similarly, when Suárez y Romero foregrounds his affliction in light of the suffering of slaves, he overdetermines the process of identification so that whereas Manzano and Francisco might cry bitter tears, those who grieve for their condition produce "tears of blood." In other words, the protagonist's body must also be capable of bearing the most inhumane abuses so that it might provide the novelist with an opportunity to ventriloquize and sublimate the depths of an affliction. *Francisco,* with its ironic invocation of bucolic delights in its subtitle—to my knowledge, the first antislavery novel to be written in the Americas—proposes suicide as an appropriate end to the stoic existence of its protagonist. Yet, even in death, the protagonist's lifeless body is discovered in a state of advanced decay, thereby retaining its abject function in the narrative to the bitter end.

More than mere appropriations of the noble slave trope, these narratives seem to perceive and then foreclose that Hegelian moment when the master is superseded (because the vicarious enjoyment of the slave's labor proves inadequate for self-consciousness) and the slave transforms himself through modes of speculation that labor (and not revolutionary upheaval) provides. In other words, if these novels could be said to represent a struggle for the creation of the Creole bourgeoisie's awareness of itself as a community, the demise of slave protagonists and the expendability of their bodies appear as ideologically necessary for the reeducation of this community and, from a phylogenetic view, constitute a preemptory corrective to the idea that a community of free blacks and mulattoes and former slaves might some day stake competing claims on national consciousness. In this sense, these narratives eerily foreshadow the Escalera conspiracy of 1844, with its brutal assault on this burgeoning community, at the same time that they sustain the reformist Creole bourgeoisie's "necessary" fiction that its community is a helpless victim of slavery's barbarism and, by inference, of the latter's institutionaliza-

tion from Madrid.[40] These novels depict noble slave protagonists in order
to suggest that slaves possess the moral capacity to be their masters'
equals, and occasionally their superiors; however, in addition to demonstrating how this nobility should not threaten the status quo, these
narratives sidestep how the Creole bourgeoisie might have grappled with
the moral quandary of human bondage in favor of representing slave-
protagonists as embodiments of social antagonisms that eventually
implode or disappear. These reformist narratives cannot be considered
tragedies in any strict sense; in their penchant for pure symbolism, they
refrain, with the possible exception of Avellaneda's Sab, from endowing
their protagonists with a requisite tragic flaw.

   The writers knew enough about the human complexities of plantation
and domestic slavery to avoid exclusively depicting slave protagonists
as symbols of inner torments, as subjects that wholly and without irony
embodied futile struggles with moral dilemmas that were occasionally
not their own. Tellingly, it did not occur to these writers to depict slaves
who were unruly or rebellious simply because they were enslaved. So, to
suggest that slaves not only possessed inner lives but also acted beyond
ethical reproach while being cruelly subjugated challenged the slave-
owning bourgeoisie's paternalist ideology that conveniently attributed
infantilism, innate character flaws, or moral underdevelopment to slaves.
What appears equally puzzling is the writers' failure to extrapolate from
Manzano's circumstances as a man whose freedom del Monte's literary
circle was ultimately responsible for purchasing. What would freedom
have meant for the formerly enslaved poet? After he was liberated and
his entrance was facilitated into the growing community of skilled, free
blacks, what expectations regarding equality could he have reasonably
entertained? The challenges that he faced were there to be gleaned in his
autobiographical writing and correspondence with del Monte. Inadvertently or not, the literary circle's members blinded themselves to these
concerns in ways that I detail below.

THE COLLAPSING FICTION OF THE SUBMISSIVE SLAVE

A literary mission that aims to rally reticent or lackadaisical readers to
its cause is likely to be highly selective in its illustration of injustices.

Antislavery poets and writers did not set out to be objective by providing slave owners with fair and equal literary representation. In their transatlantic efforts at consciousness raising, these antislavery advocates sought to penetrate and tumble the range of moral and psychological defenses with which slave merchants and owners perpetuated the violence of human bondage, and they frequently employed the most horrid and disturbing spectacles of cruelty in order to polarize good and evil and offer readers sentiment as the path to sympathy and redemption. Such spectacles took place wherever slavery existed in the Americas, and abolitionists and reformists disseminated documented descriptions and literary evocations of them in order to strengthen their cases against chattel slavery and rally new members to their causes, but with an important distinction. Whereas abolitionists could engineer conceding the status of parliamentary evidence to select antislavery literary writings, the reformists, socially isolated because of their antislavery convictions, were confined to clandestine literary creation and discussions. As I showed in the previous chapter, the abolitionists' attempts to internationalize the antislavery movement after the triumph of the British Abolition of Slavery Act of 1833 included the plan to gather evidence of the cruelty of slavery in Cuba. Madden undertook this reconnaissance mission in Havana and was influential in del Monte's decision to request Manzano's autobiography and Suárez y Romero's novel for the portfolio that he submitted to the international Anti-Slavery Conference of 1840 that took place in London. While it can be argued that the abolitionists' demand for vivid illustrations of slavery's brutalities influenced the literary circle's conceptions of antislavery literary writing, the propensity toward foregrounding sensational spectacles of cruelty—as politically instrumental as they might have been—does not capture the daily violence of slavery nor uncover some of the more mundane reasons why slave owners felt obliged to resort to extreme violence in order to control their slaves and the free black and mulatto population.

The ideological function of the literary circle's protagonists—that is to say, the reformists' as well as the greater Creole bourgeoisie's subliminal attachment to the idea of the slave as a docile body—should be perceived in light of a number of evolving circumstances. I agree with Fischer that the fantasy of the submissive slave functioned in the

discourses of both pro- and antislavery advocates.⁴¹ However, in what
follows, I focus less on the distinction between how these factions employed the image of the compliant slave and place more emphasis on the
common front that they gradually began to share in a time of crisis. Class
and racial tensions around the question of Cuban slavery, the geopolitical vying between Spain, England, and the United States to determine
the role of slavery in the island's political future, the greater frequency
of localized slave rebellions, and the increasing fear of conspiracies on
and off the island contributed to shifting the Creole bourgeoisie's attachment to the fiction of the submissive slave from its generally subliminal
presence in the routine operations of plantation life to the assumption
of a more conscious, proactive, and decidedly racist stance against black
empowerment that eventually allied the Creole bourgeoisie and colonial
authorities during the reign of terror that characterized the Escalera
conspiracy of 1844. Such a turn corroborates Mary Nyquist's observation that antityrannicism—in our case anticolonial sentiment and activism—in the context of transatlantic slavery "becomes an important
conductor of racialization."⁴² This crisis eventually eliminated the Creole reformists' leadership, thereby repolarizing racial tensions in a way
that allowed Madrid to continue to manage and manipulate slavery and
the political aspirations of the local bourgeoisie; but before describing
and interrogating this outcome in the chapter's next section, I want to
demonstrate how this shift from the subliminal attachment to the fiction of the compliant slave to the panicked awareness in the late 1830s
and early '40s that slaves were not submissive stimulated the colonial
reevaluation of the bodies not only of slaves, but also of the free blacks
and mulattoes among whom Manzano would eventually be counted.

The slave owners' reactions to reformist tendencies that came from
Madrid—complaints similar to those that the count in Madden's poem
"The Sugar Estate" lodged against the colonial legal system—played
their part in the planters' transformation of the image of the slave's body
from docility to looming, hyper-racialized peril. Reform did not emerge
solely as a "radical" movement within the ranks of local bourgeoisie in
the 1830s. At the end of the eighteenth century, Cuban slave owners had
already begun to encounter increasing, but manageable, reformist pressures from slave codes that Madrid had been imposing by royal decree.

For example, in light of breaches to prior codes and in preparation for the dramatic increase in slaves that the liberalization of the slave trade was expected to produce, the Slave Code of 1789 stipulated measures for the instruction, treatment, and occupations of "this category of individuals of the human race," in deference to which slave owners had to reconcile "principles and rules dictated by religion, humanity, and the well-being of the State" and "slavery and public tranquility."[43] In addition to providing for the slaves' religious instruction, food and clothing, work hours (between dawn and dusk), recreation, housing and health, old age, and marriage, the code also laid out measures concerning how slaves should be disciplined. Depending on the seriousness of the offense, masters and overseers were permitted to employ "imprisonment, shackles, chains, mace or stocks, excepting the head, or no more than twenty-five lashes lightly laid on, that do not cause serious contusions or excessive bleeding."[44] Harsher disciplinary measures required a hearing with the presence and participation of the syndic procurator, whose duty it was to advocate for the slave. The code also outlined an incremental scale of fines for masters and overseers for extreme cases of corporal punishment. If these transgressions included "administering excessive corrective penalties, causing slaves serious contusions, excessive bleeding, or mutilation of limbs," criminal charges could be lodged against the slave owner or overseer in a trial that would treat "the injured party" as if he or she "were free"; should the master or overseer be found guilty, then the slave could be confiscated and sold to another owner. If the excesses incapacitated the slave for menial labor, then the master would be required to pay for the slave's maintenance and clothing for the rest of his or her life.[45] As we observed, the twenty-five lashes that Manzano received daily over nine days remained within the legal limit that the slave code established. By contrast, the thrashings that Francisco receives in Suárez y Romero's novel clearly exceed this limit. The Slave Code of 1789, which still held purview in the 1830s, was considered "enlightened," even by the standards of British abolitionists, and it prodded them in London to search for ways to investigate and verify how the royal decree was being administered in Cuba.

Havana's slave owners responded to the royal decree the following year. In their response, they recognized the monarch's "full and complete embodiment of the highest sovereignty" but predicted "dismal consequences" for theirs as well as the king's economic interests if they were obliged to obey every aspect of the code.[46] With the exception of the code's regulation of the slave's workday to daylight hours, which they directly countered with technical explanations of why slaves were required to work overnight during the sugarcane harvest, the document consistently attempts to correct purported misconceptions and request the monarch's intervention because "no abuses opposed to the system of legislation, or religious maxims, or humanity will be found in our sugar refineries."[47] For example, the slave owners denied abusing their slaves since "it behooves owners to treat their slaves well, given that the masters' own sustenance and the very advancement of their haciendas is linked to the labor of those same slaves."[48] Claiming that the distance between the metropolis and the island could distort reports and cause misinterpretations, they assured the monarch that they treated their slaves well. Disingenuously turning the fear of being outnumbered by their slaves into a rhetorical strategy, they asserted that if slave owners were indeed responsible for mistreating their slaves inhumanely, "then vast numbers would not be gaining their freedom" by purchasing it.[49]

With respect to disciplining their slaves, the authors of the response argued that they were "especially vigilant in protecting [their] investment" and then expressed concerns about the consequences that limiting the potential number of lashes that could be administered would have on their authority on the plantations: "Now, slaves can go confidently to their haciendas and the mayorals who govern them, understanding all the while that any authority their owners may have had served for naught, with the full knowledge that twenty-five lashes will be the maximum penalty they will suffer for any infraction they may commit."[50] In setting themselves apart from the allegedly small number of abusive masters, they requested that the fines and criminal charges that the decree stipulated against abuses be limited to the offenders and not applied indiscriminately to the entire group of slave owners.[51] Employing a respectful tone throughout, the slave owners maintain that even though their unregulated policy of "scrupulously humane treatment" and the monarch's decree pursue the same goals, the treatment that the code institutionalizes would cause slaves to "become insolent,

rousing and inciting them against their masters."[52] Through a deceptive take on work injuries, the slave owners assert that "the slaves who,
because they detest their masters, are prone to callously mutilate their
hands or render their arms useless in order to avoid serving their masters,
will endeavor to provoke their superiors solely for the pleasure of seeing
them taken prisoner and treated as common criminals."[53] Despite this
distorted view of the slaves' incapacitating work injuries, the planters'
argument still reveals how their reactions to the slave code's provisions
for "a category of individuals of the human race" inadvertently raises
anxieties about the slaves' agency as legal subjects who can assimilate
the law and take advantage of its loopholes.[54] According to García Rodríguez, the slaves' eloquence and their ability to take advantage of legal
flaws and oversights in the cases that she compiles in her study were
impressive and contributed toward the gradual extension of rights to
slaves from the 1830s to '60s, but the gains were beneficial for only a few
in the overall context of the island's slavery.[55]

In the slave owners' appeal for the king to allow them to administer
more than twenty-five lashes at any one time if the slave's transgression
required it, they turn their attention from a discussion about slaves who
were sufficiently informed about the slave code that they could contest
their masters' authority in specific areas to propagating racist scare tac-
tics at the center of which they define the *bozales* as "barbarians, auda-
cious and ungrateful" who are "prone to desperation, to mayhem, to rob-
bery, to drunkenness, to perfidy, are easily inflamed, and are susceptible
to all classes of vice."[56] The slave owners argue against limits on corporal
punishment, claiming that they could document "the appalling crimes
the slaves so shockingly perpetrate in the countryside any time their
masters subject them to less rigor or treat them too leniently." They end
up situating themselves defensively between the cleverness of plantation
slaves who could check their masters' legal authority from within colonial society and the fear of recently arrived Africans, whom they portray
as savage, rebellious, and prepared to establish maroon settlements from
where they could harass the plantations.[57] These planters insisted that
the threat of an undefined number of lashes was the most persuasive
means of controlling their slaves and that leniency, by contrast, not only
imperiled their authority on the plantations but endangered the security

of the colony in the face of purportedly uncontrollable *bozales* as well. Despite this recourse to a racist depiction of rampaging Africans, the planters failed to convince Madrid to deregulate the code's limits on corporal punishment, so that the same specific prohibitions against excessive punishment appeared in the 1842 Slave Code.[58] In other words, as early as 1790, the year before the outbreak of the slave rebellion that launched the Haitian Revolution, Havana's planters were already postulating their anxiety about uncontrollable slaves and the threat of losing the colony, not as trepidations about Creole slaves who could potentially and increasingly take advantage of colonial laws and their loopholes, but as a fear of recently arrived Africans. This deployment of racial terror as a threat to the smooth functioning of the island's economy and to Cuba's status as a Spanish colony would increasingly become a frequent rhetorical device after the Haitian Revolution in order to dissuade Madrid from its colonial policy of keeping the island well supplied with African slaves for economic and political reasons and to push back against the slave codes' reformist tendencies.

Yet the fear that recently arrived Africans could galvanize and lead uprisings—a suspicion, by the way, that the fiction of the docile slave functioned psychologically to keep at bay—was not without foundation. José Antonio Aponte planned his well-organized but eventually exposed conspiracy of 1812 in a Yoruban *cabildo*.[59] Ironically, the fear of newly arrived African slaves that informed the specter of violent uprisings might not have attained its intensity in Cuba without the unwitting collaboration of colonial authorities. Colonial governments had initially encouraged the establishment of *cabildos de nación*, which were fraternal societies to which distinct African ethnicities belonged for the purposes of entertainment and mutual aid, as a calculated strategy to sow divisions among recently arrived Africans on the basis of language and culture and thereby guard the colony against organized slave rebellions. However, Aponte's conspiracy revealed the extent to which these societies had begun to exchange information about abolition and rebellions elsewhere and to cooperate more closely despite the linguistic, cultural, and ethnic differences on which colonial governments depended in order to foster their mutual segregation. Even more revealing was the fact that Aponte was not the image of the wild, African savage or the unyielding *cimarrón* (maroon) that slave owners fabricated and disseminated as the colony's foremost enemy within but a Cuban-born cabinetmaker and sculptor who owned a workshop and enjoyed a great deal of prestige in the emerging free black and colored class of artisans.[60] Even though it was said that he was an elected leader of the Shango-Tedum *cabildo*, he definitely belonged to a society of free blacks or confraternity that his guild established in 1800 whose religious practices were closer to Catholicism. In any case, the respect that he had garnered in colonial society as a whole was due to his officially recognized status as a member of the free black militiamen—a military arm of the colonial administration that began at the start of the eighteenth century—who had served Spain well during its campaigns in the Gulf Coast during the American Revolution.[61] That Aponte and other free blacks who had acquired prestige through their participation in the militia and began to form a petite bourgeoisie increasingly placed their lot with that of slaves and *bozales* in the first quarter of the nineteenth century resulted from a deep deception, because their meritorious conduct on behalf of the Spanish empire became an object of scrutiny and suspicion for Cuba's colonial authorities.[62] Nonetheless, the realization that planters and the organizers of slave uprisings lived, moved, and interacted within the same social environments increased the colony's paranoia. Such was the growing concern about organized slave rebellions that by 1825, the island's Military Commission was in constant pursuit of free people of color for "uttering 'subversive words,' holding 'secret gatherings,' and committing 'various excesses.'"[63]

By the 1830s, several factors began to destabilize the slave owners' belief that they wielded absolute power over their slaves and to undermine the certainty that they and the colonial government had about managing the free colored population on the island. During this period, tens of thousands of slaves were being introduced into the island annually, and free people of color increased from approximately 30,000 in 1774 to roughly 153,000 in 1841.[64] Given a tense situation in which maintaining and controlling the black presence on the island represented the pivotal point in relations among the colonial government, the proslavery Spanish and Creole bourgeoisies, the reformists, and a population of free blacks and mulattoes that was gaining economic relevance, tipping the balance in favor of any semblance of black empowerment threatened Cuba's colonial status. Suspicions regarding abolitionist activities on and around the island also added to the colonial authorities' heightened state of alert during this decade and until they eliminated the leadership of the free colored population because of its alleged participation in the Escalera conspiracy. According to Antonio Benítez-Rojo, this fear of black empowerment, or of *el peligro negro,* motivated the reformists because they wanted to avoid a situation in which free blacks, who already constituted one-fifth of the population, would ally themselves with an emancipated slave population and increase the black and mulatto presence on the island to 60 percent.[65] The racial polarization of colonial society, which functioned well to ensure Spanish control of the island, intensified during the decade at the same time that the reformist bourgeoisie was helpless to stop the dramatic increase in the number of African slaves that traders illegally introduced into the island while a number of colonial officials received generous kickbacks for ignoring the whole contraband arrangement.

Even though the Creole reformists' long-term goal was to whiten the island's population, so that in a more gradual sense they, too, contributed to the colony's racial polarization, the space that they had opened up for their writers to imagine their slaves' limited social protagonism dwindled as the decade drew to a close. The reformist writers' insistence on prioritizing the redemption of the local bourgeoisie through sentimental literature instrumentalized the slave's body in order to distinguish them as enlightened men of feeling who could potentially lead their class out of the moral quagmire and imperial opportunism of slavery. It is thus possible to see how the gesture of liberating Manzano had more to do with forging a class identity for themselves than with envisioning a political future for emancipated slaves on the island. Their inability to imagine the equality of blacks and whites in a future polity could be perceived in their naive expectation that liberated slaves would remain compliant and forfeit the rights and claims that freedom granted them. Because it was already evident in the 1830s that the free black and colored population had been acquiring greater social status and maneuverability—a situation that only Cirilo Villaverde captured in all its complexity over several decades and published almost half a century later in *Cecilia Val-*

dés—the literary circle's consensus to work imaginatively with enslaved rather than liberated or free protagonists highlights its members' self-serving agenda to denounce slavery because of the effects that it had on their class and on Cuba's racial future. With the exception of Villaverde, this decision to ignore free blacks and mulattoes as significant characters in their narratives meant setting aside observable evidence of colonial society, which, in their circumstances as daily witnesses of human bondage, had given reformists an advantage over abolitionists in depicting the realities of slavery in plantation society.

Similarly, the circle's writers ignored basic, empirically verifiable details in the literary elaboration of sympathy for the plight of slaves. At the start of the decade prior to the Escalera conspiracy, it would have been possible to claim that the cruelties that the antislavery novels depicted were more instrumental for abolitionist and reformist agendas than for complex, local circumstances that required constant vigilance, direct and unstated negotiations between masters and slaves, and, above all, restraint. García Rodríguez asserts that masters and slaves consistently attempted to strike a balance between the demands of production on the plantation and the knowledge that slaves possessed that their labor was essential for the plantations' smooth functioning: "The daily routine on both the ingenio and the cafetal depended on such a delicate equilibrium and not simply on blind obedience to the owner. Contemporary descriptions were overwhelmingly one-sided and distorted in that matter. Even appeals to violence were limited for fear of affecting the uneasy coexistence of the different sectors on the plantation."[66] In order to assure the sugar plantation's daily functioning, it fell upon the overseer and the foreman, or *contramayoral,* to assess the need for restraint or force. Establishing this delicate balance, for example, would have been Sab's daily responsibility on the plantation rather than the unlikely position that he occupied as both an overseer who espoused antislavery rhetoric and an assessor of his master's wealth. Don Saturnino, the overseer who appears toward the end of Manzano's autobiography, did not always carry out the Marchioness de Prado Ameno's orders to punish the slave and, comprehending the abuses that the poet experienced in her household, even facilitated his escape from her home.[67] Admittedly, episodes such as this would have been extremely rare, yet the circle's writers consis-

tently portrayed overseers as barbaric perpetrators of corporal punishment and torture. As García Rodríguez reports, the plantation operated
according to an equilibrium in which it was essential to preserve the
authority of the master and his surrogates and, at the same time, take
matters concerning the slave crews into serious consideration. According to her, confrontations between overseers and slave crews were common, but slaves not only understood that masters saw advantages to
practicing "a certain amount of restraint" because the failure to do so
could involve the loss of workers or a series of legal complications; the
slaves also knew how to manipulate such confrontational situations in
their favor and, in the analysis of an incident that she describes in her
study, García Rodríguez notes that "the slaves clearly were anything but
docile."[68] Such confrontations and the masters' use of restraint in order
to resolve them were a modus operandi.

The most obvious indicator that the suffering and demise of protagonists in the circle's narratives were meant to accomplish goals that went
beyond empirically based portrayals of plantation life was the fact that
slave owners could not afford to treat their slaves as the expendable property that the novels' protagonists seemed to embody. Due in part to pressures on the international slave market that mounted after the British
abolition of the slave trade in 1807 and persisted with the call for an end
to slavery, the price of slaves tripled between 1800 and 1840. According to Moreno Fraginals, reasons for improving the treatment of slaves
at this time rested on sound economic principles: "When the value of
slaves tripled, without a proportional increase in productivity, it was
necessary to adjust the returns from capital invested in the work force,
which could only be done increasing the annual rate of depreciation or
lengthening its term. But extending the period of depreciation was not
simply a question of accounting since it demanded, in a concrete way,
prolonging the useful life of the slave by modifying those factors that
provoked their premature death. This was, in essence, the logic that led
to good treatment."[69] The premature deaths of Petrona, Rosalía, and the
latter's child would not have made economic sense to many of the island's
slave owners. Don Fernando's and his mother's nonchalant "we're out
of a thousand pesos" upon learning of the deaths of the last two would
probably have struck readers as extravagant. Ricardo's obsessive pun-

ishment of Francisco and the time that he and the overseer devoted to persecuting him would have been counterproductive for the plantation's efficient management; relatedly, this mismanagement renders the young patrician's hatred for Francisco intelligible as an idiosyncratic pathology rather than as one of the resources through which masters could psychologically distance themselves from the violence that they perpetrated on their slaves. Nonetheless, this considerable rise in the prices of slaves induced slave owners to consider the economic sense of paying closer attention to, if not modifying, how they treated their slaves. Since slaves could purchase their freedom if they had a source of income, they knew their real value on the slave market and could employ that knowledge to their benefit. The knowledge that the slaves possessed of their economic value and, on this basis, their related disposition toward negotiating the fairness and limits of expectations regarding their tasks were entirely absent from the literary circle's narratives. These authors prized the absolute victimization of their protagonists over evident indicators that demonstrated how slaves and the emerging population of free blacks and mulattoes considered themselves conscious social actors in their respective claims for freedom and equality.

By the end of the 1830s, the Creole bourgeoisie's image of the submissive slave became untenable as reformist writers undertook last-ditch efforts to shore up their class's ability to exercise influence on the question of slavery through literature. Published in Spain three years before the Escalera conspiracy, Avellaneda's *Sab* captures the degree to which the institution of slavery and the fear of slave rebellions threatened to cross the threshold, which the fantasy of the submissive slave constituted, from the local bourgeoisie's disavowal of the colonial crisis that was besieging it to a panicked consciousness that some way of resolving the situation was desperately needed. The novel provides two succinct examples of the Creole bourgeoisie's reactions to the crisis. The first is disavowal. When Sab informs his master, Don Carlos, that he had heard Martina, purportedly the last descendant of Cuba's indigenous population, proclaim that blacks will avenge the disappeared natives, his master stops him from speaking because, as the narrator puts it, Cubans lived in a constant state of alarm. Moreover, after the "frightful and recent example from a neighboring island"—an elliptical reference to Haiti—

they could not listen "without terror" to any talk of the denial and recovery of rights "in the mouth of a man of that wretched color."[70] Don
Carlos, the "benevolent" patrician whose declining fortune forces him
to entertain his daughter's marriage to a member of a new cosmopolitan
bourgeoisie that was making inroads in the local economy, prefers to
bury his head in the sand. He silences Sab rather than discuss the issue
of slavery with a man whose color he refrains from mentioning. The
scene describes the customary handling of the issue of slavery between
master and slave in a context in which power relations are clearly demar-
cated: the slave brings up the question through circumlocution and the
master refuses to recognize the slave as an interlocutor on the subject.
The master's refusal to engage Sab on the question of slavery remains
consistent with an economically eclipsed sector of the local bourgeoisie whose traditional attachment to the fantasy of the submissive slave
underscores its own passivity and increasing obsolescence in the face
of emerging socioeconomic transformations.

The second example of the Creole bourgeoisie's reaction to the island's looming social and political crisis is the pure terror that Sab's
denunciation of slavery produces in Teresa, a distant relative and con-
fidante of Carlota who also lived in the household. In a scene in which
he summons Teresa in order to confess that he loves his mistress, Sab
decries how belonging to "a debased race" automatically disqualifies
him from being loved in return. The realization not only underscores
that he is a mulatto and a slave but frustrates and infuriates him because
"nature has not been any less a mother to us than to you."[71] At this point
in his diatribe, the metaphor of Sab's unrequited love reveals its broader
sociopolitical meaning: "But men's society has not imitated the impartiality of the mother we have in common, who in vain has said to you:
'You are brothers!' Foolish society, which has reduced us to the necessity
of hating it and founding our happiness on its total ruin." However, when
a terrified Teresa asks Sab if he had summoned her in order to confess
his participation in a slave uprising, he answers that the household was
not in danger because any rebellion would be premature: "the slaves pa-
tiently drag their chains: perhaps they need only hear a voice that shouts
to them: 'You are men!' But that voice won't be mine, you can believe
it."[72] Toward the end of the novel, Sab succumbs in a typically Romantic

vein to consumption, but not before arranging to place a winning lottery ticket in Carlota's possession, thus providing his former mistress with the dowry that would assure her marriage to Otway and, by extension, the perpetuation of the Creole bourgeoisie as a class. The protagonist's refusal to rise up against slave owners is not simply an attempt to retain their comforting image of the compliant slave. Teresa's question implies that Sab possesses clandestine agency beyond his apparent subservience, so that the ambiguity that characterizes him throughout the novel suddenly becomes an indication of the threat that he potentially represents for planters and the colony. This interpretation corroborates Paquette's observation that because skilled or privileged slaves were among the leaders of nearly every major slave revolt in the Americas, docility coexisted with militancy.[73]

The 1830s may be characterized as a period that produced an unstable tension between the relentless economic demand for slave labor and the local fear of being outnumbered by blacks. The Creole reformist bourgeoisie and the colonial government differed in their attitudes toward this tension. For the former, the results of the Cuban census of 1841, as debated as they were at the time and afterward, were a source of alarm because it indicated for the first time that there were more slaves than whites on the island.[74] That the Creole bourgeoisie as a whole had little control over the number of African slaves that were being introduced into the island—a condition that distinguished it from the likes of Jefferson and his class—constituted a fundamental part of its colonial experience. Given its double-edged reliance on a source of labor that it could neither regulate directly nor do without, the image of the submissive slave functioned to provide this class with the fantasy of being able to control and project the stability of its economic and political future. Moreover, unlike the bourgeoisies who governed in the United States or constituted the ranks of British abolitionists, the local bourgeoisie witnessed the incipient recognition of the rights of slaves under the aegis of a colonial legal system and slave codes that tended toward reform. By contrast, keeping Cuba well supplied with slaves for economic reasons and maintaining an important black presence in the colony as part of its political agenda against any independence movement did not constitute a contradiction but functioned to the advantage of the colonial government, so long as the latter possessed the military strength to sustain the institution and practices of slavery and protect the colony against slave uprisings. However, the rise of a black petite bourgeoisie of free artisans and others who specialized in many of the trades and services that the colony required generated a set of unknowns that began to preoccupy the local bourgeoisie and colonial government.[75] At a time of increasing racial polarization and segregation between blacks and whites, which the colonial government steadfastly encouraged, a burgeoning class of free blacks and mulattoes meant that the Creole bourgeoisie would need to take this community into account as a political actor in any bid for independence; in other words, some form of equality or the recognition of rights for this class would have to be contemplated and negotiated.[76] The colonial government in turn considered this incipient petite bourgeoisie the natural ally of abolitionists whose work to emancipate slaves in non-British colonies not only would augment the population of free and emancipated blacks and mulattoes but also seemed to corroborate British imperial designs by threatening the very existence of Cuba as a Spanish colony. Given the intrigues, suspicions, and fears of uprising that characterized the colony between 1842 and 1843, Cuba had become a "cauldron of rumor and tension."[77] In the following section, I examine how colonial authorities dealt with perceived threats to their control of the island.

CONSPIRACY AND SILENCE

The Escalera conspiracy carries an unusual name. *Escalera* (ladder) refers to the method that colonial authorities employed to torture alleged conspirators by stretching them across and tying them to ladders in order to whip them and extract information about and confessions regarding the alleged island-wide slave uprising that was being planned. Unlike other conspiracies that were named after their instigators or leaders, the 1844 conspiracy took its name from the method that authorities employed to interrogate mostly free blacks and mulattoes, who were suspected of fomenting a slave rebellion along the lines of Haiti's, as if the technique for extracting confessions was itself the conspiracy's source of infamy. As Paquette, Murray, and others have asserted, a long debate has ensued over whether a conspiracy of such a magnitude had ever existed. Those commentators who claim that the threat of so massive an uprising could not be substantiated in effect purport that the excessive force that authorities displayed in their response to the anxieties that were gripping the island once more exemplified the brutality of the colonial government's oppression. By contrast, proponents of the belief that the conspiracy was real consider the authorities' reaction a practical preemptory response to the life-and-death struggle between masters and slaves that would have been unleashed in the event of an island-wide uprising. After furnishing a description and critique of both views on the conspiracy, Paquette asserts that the Military Commission that Captain-General Leopoldo O'Donnell had established to uncover the slaves' plot did not appreciate how the Escalera conspiracy had not been one but several schemes that had been years in the making and that were moving toward convergence by late 1841—the same year when a controversial census indicated that slaves had begun to outnumber whites.[78] What interest me and occupy my attention in this final section of the chapter are the uses of torture and racial terror to accomplish specific political goals: How did this stretching and flailing of mostly free black bodies across ladders help to secure the island's colonial status? Do the narratives that emerged at the end of the 1830s shed any light on the events that occurred a few years afterward during the colonial government's reign of terror?

Now, in order to describe how the racial terror that led to torture functioned in the context of the Escalera conspiracy, it is necessary to point out the conundrum of violence that slave owners and colonial officials historically produced but of which they claimed to be victims. On the one hand, there existed an exhibitionist, fear-inducing repertoire of practices and punishments to which masters and colonial authorities adhered in order to keep slaves in check and to institute whiteness, both directly and indirectly, as a symbol and instrument of power and authority; on the other, slave owners and colonial authorities were becoming increasingly convinced, especially after the successful uprising in Haiti, that slaves would annihilate the white population, if given the opportunity, and would thus become the avenging "black peril" that many planters feared. As the omniscient narrator in *Sab* puts it, Cubans lived in a constant state of alarm, which is worth recalling because, even though planters and colonial officials wielded immense power over the lives of their slaves, the former were responsible for generating an atmosphere of fear, apprehension, and paranoia by attributing to their slaves the desire to eliminate the white population. Stated differently, the practitioners and attributors of racial terror were one and the same: slave owners and colonial authorities who would insist that public exhibitions of power were necessary in order to control slaves and who, by identifying a retaliatory racial terror with spectral protagonists of a slave conspiracy—which is probably why the conspiracy was not named after anyone in particular—found just cause for resorting to violent oppression and torture. Undoubtedly, there were slaves and free blacks who were inspired by events in Haiti, and local uprisings in which slaves showed themselves to be unruly and unrepentant were on the increase.[79] According to Josep Fradera, the authorities and courts were continuously suppressing local uprisings and challenges to enslavement by individual slaves or small groups of them from 1838 to 1843 in Cárdenas, Trinidad, Cienfuegos, and Manzanillo.[80] As black discontentment grew, so did the "paranoid fear of race revolution among the whites."[81] The colonial government and the planters were convinced that a conspiracy was afoot, and it was this "honest fear of revolutionary violence," according to Paquette, that drove the Military Commission to focus closely on punishment and to mutilate the remains of the executed for strategic public display.[82] Yet the perception that vengeance was all that slaves wanted, which was a way to reduce their desire for freedom to schemes for imposing racial terror, allowed planters and the colonial government to argue that by preempting the outbreak of a massive slave rebellion they were acting in self-defense.

David Murray argues that because an abolitionist conspiracy, backed by the British government, had ultimately proved to be unsubstantiated, the only threat to Cuba's colonial status around 1844 came from the remote possibility of a general slave uprising.[83] According to him, the island's status as a Spanish colony had never been in jeopardy. However, Murray also asserts that because the colonial authorities' tendency to blame external agents for the island's turmoil cannot account for the "extraordinary barbarity of the torture and punishment carried out mainly on the black population," an explanation for this savagery could be found in the paranoia that took hold of the planters and colonial authorities after close to a decade of "real and imagined" abolitionist activity on the island.[84] Perceptions of immediate danger, whereby foreign abolitionists conspired with local antislavery proponents and activists, certainly added to the general consternation. If Madden had raised suspicions during his term as the superintendent of emancipated Africans in Havana from 1836 to 1839, the tireless and occasionally reckless abolitionist zealot David Turnbull, whose parliamentary connections and activities made him a dangerous figure in the eyes of the island's officials and planters, perturbed the latter when he visited Cuba in 1838 and especially during his consular appointment in Havana from 1840 to 1842.[85] Moreover, Turnbull successfully lobbied to have the British government, under a reticent Lord Palmerston, pressure Spain to accept the abolitionist's plan to empower the Court of Mixed Commission in Havana to oblige Cuban planters to prove that their slaves were not newly arrived Africans but legitimately owned according to previous treaties with Britain. Turnbull's goings and comings so rankled planters and authorities that merely being associated with him became a major crime in Cuba.[86] For slave owners and colonial officials, these abolitionists' activities were real and threatened the colony's economic welfare and political future, but the connections between abolitionists, their agents, and potential leaders of antislavery movements on the island were shrouded in intrigues, rumors, and hearsay in such a way that they magnified the paranoia.

The contested 1841 census was controversial because hard data substantiated the growing fear that slaves and free blacks and mulattoes were beginning to outnumber the island's white population. Whether or not all whites accepted its results, the census fed growing anxieties because it acted as an empirical referent for other clandestine or alleged activities. This same year, the Spanish government thought that it had uncovered definitive proof of Turnbull's seditious maneuverings. A letter, written from Havana and published in July in the *Anti-Slavery Reporter*, the mouthpiece of British abolitionism, stated that abolitionist ideas had found fertile ground in Havana and Matanzas. Even though Turnbull had not written the letter, it did express views that he held as British consul in Havana at the time. For the Spanish government, the letter clearly implied that "the fuse of slave revolts had been primed in both cities and needed only a match to set the island alight."[87] According to Paquette, groups of free blacks and mulattoes and some dissident whites had begun to form by 1841–42.[88] However, the hopes that abolitionists held out that these groups might join forces in a more consequential way began to vanish as rumors about a conspiracy began to spread. The Creole reformist bourgeoisie had already shown itself to be reluctant to support any kind of emancipation for slaves and was ambivalent about striking out for political autonomy from Spain. Once Turnbull's ominous return to the island, after having left his duties as consul, began to catalyze various clandestine activities, the reformists retreated from any thought of establishing alliances with free blacks and mulattoes. In fact, it was Domingo del Monte, who had previously furnished Madden with information and texts that the latter employed to debunk the myth of Cuba's enlightened slavery at the World Anti-Slavery Convention of 1840, who now blew the whistle on suspected abolitionist activities on the island. In 1842, rather than directly inform the colonial authorities about these activities, del Monte contacted Alexander Everett, the former United States minister to Spain, whom the Creole patrician had met when the latter visited Cuba in 1840. Everett, an advocate of the U.S. annexation of the island, was wary of British intentions, and he began corresponding with important figures in Washington and London, which eventually led to Washington Irving's delivery of del Monte's information about abolitionist conspiracies to the Spanish government. Del Monte's fear of a slave revolt and racial terror induced him to side with the rest of the Creole bourgeoisie that he had so ardently wished to educate about the need to do away with slavery. Paquette summarizes this mood among the Creoles at the time: "Feeling backed into a corner, the white elite, not just those liberal intellectuals opposed to the slave trade, contemplated desperate measures and desperate alliances to save themselves and the slave property from which they profited. The external forces beyond their control seemed to be heading them to the realization of their omnipresent class and racial fears."[89] In a letter to Everett that he wrote on June 28, 1844, del Monte claimed to have rebuffed an abolitionist agent who attempted to recruit him for the conspiracy, stating that the abolitionist had been mistaken "in judging me capable of committing the madness of sacrificing the tranquility of my country and the existence of my race, to the liberty of blacks."[90] Del Monte's correspondence with Everett, already showing signs that the patrician was on the defensive, should not be overestimated in the effect that it would have on a tensed colonial environment, but his move helped to alert the colonial government to the urgency of acting forcefully against any possible conspiracy.

By 1844, just five years after he wrote what I have thus far considered imaginary scenes of excessive brutality in the context of normal plantation life, the episodes of torture to which Francisco's body was submitted in Suárez y Romero's novel eerily foreshadowed the scourge of thrashings that befell slaves and the free colored population in the first half of that year as Captain-General O'Donnell gave the Military Commission free hand to investigate and root out plots for a general slave uprising. The novel's opening dialogue between Ricardo and the overseer in which the slave owner urgently inquires if the matter of whipping Francisco had been seen to, if the slave had bled profusely, and if he had been left half dead, would have sufficed to reproduce the kinds of exchanges that the overseer, Agustín Contrera, could have had with fellow torturers in March of 1844 as he tied slaves to a ladder, whipped them, and killed seven of them on a plantation in Cárdenas province that belonged to Theodore Phinney.[91] What distinguished the exaggerated viciousness of Francisco's treatment from the equally brutal though mundane use of violence against slaves and the free colored population was the exercise of an absolute colonial authoritarianism that sought to extract specific confessions from tortured victims. The owners of neighboring plantations had angrily accused Phinney of treating his slaves too leniently—a practice that Havana's planters denounced as early as 1790 in their response to the slave code of the previous year—and Lieutenant-Governor Javier Quintairo interceded by praising Contrera for the severity with which he treated slaves and by recruiting him to interrogate them on Phinney's plantation. The horrified slave owner provides a detailed description of how Contrera employed the ladder:

> Stripped naked and lashed to a ladder on the ground with a rope around
> each wrist so tight that the blood could scarcely circulate, and the whole arm
> drawn above the head till the shoulder joints fairly cracked, while the ropes
> were secured to the top of the ladder, the feet and legs stretched in the same
> manner, and fastened to the lower part with a double turn around the loins

and back, binding the whole trunk of the body immoveably to the rounds
of the ladder, in this position, the poor negro was thought to be ready to
commence his declaration.[92]

Such scenes became common. Ramón González employed a similar
method, except that he had his victims tied head down after having them
introduced into a whitewashed room where a bloodied ladder was cen-
trally positioned. An officer by the name of Juan Costa had whipped to
death forty-two free people of color and forty-four slaves by the time he
finished his "investigations."[93] These inquiries were intended to produce
the same kinds of confessions: that a conspiracy among the slaves and
free colored population was afoot, that the British and the abolitionists were involved, and that members of the free colored community
and some antislavery Creoles were in cahoots. David Murray reports
that those who died as a result of being tortured in this manner during
investigations exceeded those who were executed after being sentenced
to death.[94] Physicians were obliged to report that many of the tortured
who died had succumbed to diarrhea. Observers, both foreign and local,
likened the scenes to the Inquisition and Dante's inferno. The narrator's meticulous calculation of the lashes that Francisco received daily
in Suárez y Romero's novel did not approximate the "thousand lashes
[that] were in many cases inflicted on a single negro."[95] Nor did it ever
occur to the young novelist that a small button made of fine wire could
be secured to the end of leather straps in order to inflict extreme pain
and injury.[96] In contrast to the high cost of slaves, the bodies and lives
of free blacks and mulattoes were more expendable in what amounted
to be an island-wide assault on this community.[97]

The harshness with which slaves and the free colored were whipped,
tortured, and executed might suggest that the narrator of Suárez y Romero's novel had been accurate in its assertion that slavery had so thoroughly poisoned the atmosphere that it left "hatred and scorn for the
miserable race of colored people in its wake."[98] The displays of savagery
might also lead us to agree with the young novelist when he wrote to del
Monte in 1839 stating that there were whites who were "zealous enemies
of the Ethiopian race."[99] However, it is also necessary to point out that
the racial hatred to which Suárez y Romero alludes cannot be confined
to individual racists. It is noteworthy that Madden depicts the count

in "The Sugar Estate" as a believer in "the sacred privilege and right / Which ev'ry law accords the skin that's white!"[100] More easily substantiated is the colonial government's consistent and devious policy, which intensified in the 1840s, to encourage and exacerbate the polarization of blacks and whites and thereby stymie any possible alliance among them against abolition and, relatedly, against colonial rule. This policy created a social environment in which racism became key to the survival of the Spanish colony as such. In his analysis of the community of free people of color in Cuba in this period, Paquette demonstrates the presence of competing thoughts about race during the sugar boom, namely, the filtering in of late-eighteenth-century pseudoscientific racism and the proclamation of natural rights for all peoples in an age of democratic revolutions. He also provides a detailed description of the ways in which the period was marked by the increasing segregation of whites and the free colored population in education, employment, trades, and social relations. According to him, the segregation of whites from free people of color intensified during the first half of the nineteenth century to the extent that the latter "found themselves by the early 1840s under fierce attack, separated within society, not integrated into it."[101] Given this calculated policy of racially polarizing colonial society, it is no surprise that those who represented the greatest challenge to this official scheme were intermediary figures that the polarization failed to encompass and contain. We can only hypothesize what kinds of intermediary protagonists del Monte's literary circle might have created had it not been for the attention that they paid for the most part to the oppressed pole of colonial society for didactic literary purposes that had less to do with the objects of this oppression than with the redemption of the Creole bourgeoisie. Once again, the racially and ideologically indeterminate Sab is instructive.

The protagonist of Avellaneda's novel articulates discourses that a racially polarized society could not easily provide to a single individual. He nonchalantly shifts from the matter-of-fact listing of real estate values to a lyrical antislavery denunciation. More significant for the years directly following the publication of Avellaneda's novel in Spain and its banning in Cuba is the protagonist's insistence that even though he was fully aware of the slaves' discontent and yearnings for freedom he would not rise up against his former enslavers. This last admission also reveals his awareness of a clandestine network of conspirators. Yet Sab should not be taken at face value as simply a mulatto. In a move that might appear poststructuralist today, the novelist ends the protagonist's physical description with a "yet without his being a perfect mulatto" and thereby permanently releases his meaning to an elusive noncon- formity. Sab, I would argue, invokes all of those who were becoming increasingly suspect in the widest sense from the purview of a colonial and geopolitical policy of racial polarization that gradually intensified in Cuba during the first half of the nineteenth century. In other words, because being mulatto was not a guarantee of freedom from bondage, Sab's perpetually elusive identity is intelligible as both the potentially treacherous ambivalence of the trusted, submissive slave in times of cri- ses, such as in slave uprisings, and the intermediary status of free blacks and mulattoes, who were neither enslaved nor politically empowered as free colonial subjects, but whose growing economic and social influence meant that they were headed toward becoming an important constitu- ency and player in the colony's future. Proof of Paquette's claim that the fiction of the slave's docility often coexisted with militancy can be found in Miguel Aldama's astonishment when he learned that two privileged Creole slaves from his Santa Rosa plantation—he called one the most trustworthy of all his slaves and the other a respected slave driver—had been executed as the ringleaders of an organized rebellion.[102] Reactions of this sort became frequent as planters discovered how submissiveness not only camouflaged the complexity of their slaves' lives and think- ing but also revealed the tenuousness of the slave owners' belief that they controlled their slaves and the way of life that the latter afforded them. Teresa's unprompted admission to Sab that she was terrified that he might be involved in a slave rebellion hints at the dreaded ability of intermediary figures to cross the psychological threshold, as far as the planter was concerned, from being objects of slavery's controlled violence to becoming the purported protagonists of violent retaliation against their enslavers.

If the Haitian Revolution gave rise to the realization that slaves could successfully rebel and forge an independent state, events in Cuba in the 1840s suggest that free blacks and mulattoes had steadily been acquiring political importance not through armed rebellion but through licit activities, including being loyal to the crown in military campaigns in the region and plying a wide range of trades and commercial activities throughout the island. Even though they were legally free, the free colored population did not receive the treatment that the free white population did under colonial rule. An increasingly authoritarian colonial government actively worked to eliminate any chance for liberal ideas, such as the advocacy of inalienable rights and inherent freedoms, to gain a foothold in the island, which is precisely why Turnbull's alleged statement in the *Anti-Slavery Reporter* about abolitionist successes in Cuba alarmed authorities. Racism and the policy of racial polarization created insurmountable obstacles for the development of a colored petite bourgeoisie, which, hypothetically, should have emerged with the rapid economic growth that already characterized the colony. In light of this policy of radical segregation, where there was enormous pressure on the part of colonial authorities to racialize freedom as white and enslavement as black, intermediating figures whose goings and comings could not always be accounted for became a source of anxiety and paranoia for the government.

The Escalera conspiracy would probably have been named after Plácido, had there been definitive proof that the free mulatto poet, Gabriel de la Concepción Valdés—or Plácido, as he was known more widely— had indeed been the leader of an island-wide conspiracy. Like the conspiracy itself, the extent to which the poet was involved in seditious schemes to overthrow colonial rule continues to be debated. His figure is often cast as either the virtuous, heroic, and civic-minded poet who employed his lyrics to advocate political independence from Spain or the mediocre, obsequious poet who, being almost white, was racist against blacks and who did not even merit the execution to which he had been sentenced.[103] Fischer amply demonstrates how Plácido continues to be one of nineteenth-century Cuba's most difficult public figures to interpret and categorize.[104] What appears more reasonable today are a number of possibilities between both extremes: he may have been involved in a conspiracy, but he was not its leader; he married a woman who was darker than him, which may have raised eyebrows among his critics, but he was not interested in eliminating whites from the island; some of his

more "radical" poetry shows sympathy for independence and local pa-
triotism, but these verses were not very different from similar romantic
poems that young white poets were composing at the time nor were they
the only kinds of poetry that Plácido wrote. Nonetheless, the treatment
that he received at the hands of the Military Commission was certain.
Plácido was the most renowned free man of color on the island and represented, as far as the colonial authorities were concerned, a perturbing
symbol of the visibility of those who enjoyed freedom without equality
and whose growing importance as likely allies of abolitionist strategies
threatened the colonial status quo. He was arrested in Villa Clara in
1843 for suspicious movements in the middle of the island and then subsequently released. By this time, the colonial government was already
considering him a dangerous character, and some government officials
began to call for a suppression of his poetry. In January of 1844, he was
once again imprisoned, and, after a trial in June, he was sentenced to
death. The case that the colonial government built against Plácido rested
on thirty-two government witnesses, some of whom only knew him by
name. From March to the day of his execution, he underwent several
interrogations at the hands of the Military Commission and, under extreme physical and psychological coercion, provided his interrogators
with the names of fifty-five individuals, including del Monte and other
members of the reformist bourgeoisie and literary circle, who in one way
or another had knowledge of or were involved in antislavery conspiracies. Plácido claimed to have rejected del Monte's solicitation of a poem
praising the British government's desire to end slavery.[105] His confession
is a series of disjointed ramblings about events that had taken place over
a number of years and not a coherent description of a plot to overthrow
slavery and the government.[106] Nevertheless, Plácido maintained his
innocence to the very end. The government accused him of fomenting
a race war, which was uppermost in the mind of its officials and agents
as they went about attributing racial terror to their victims, yet far from
the complex racial relations that informed antislavery and anticolonial
sentiments and activities on the island.

The Escalera conspiracy aptly identifies a method of torture, pain,
and bodily harm as the official means for resolving the political and
social tensions that Captain-General O'Donnell considered dangerous

for Cuba's colonial status. In such circumstances, the ladder became
the protagonist of an absolute authoritarianism that the government
deemed necessary for conserving the colony's status quo. The Military
Commission oversaw the torturing of slaves and the free colored so that
they might produce the confessions, accusations, and language of rights
and freedom that the government was intent on documenting as bona
fide evidence of seditious plots and conduct. As an episode of punishment from Manzano's autobiography reveals, torture produces conve-
nient "truths" that calibrate the torturer's desire for satisfaction and
the victim's simultaneous desire for deliverance from pain. It was not
the facticity of the confessions that the colonial government sought,
since these were already predetermined in the latter's bid to justify the
use of torture, but the control over the looming crisis that the absolute
objectification of black and colored bodies lent it. According to Elaine
Scarry, when societies succumb to a crisis of belief—in this case, the
slave owners' collapsed fiction of the submissive slave and, in response,
their retreat from paternalism as a justification for human bondage in favor of overt racism—"the sheer material factualness of the human body
will be borrowed to lend that cultural construct the aura of 'realness'
and 'certainty.'"[107] The devious, barbaric use of ladders as instruments
of torture provided the government's Military Commission with the
"certainty" that they were in full control of black and colored bodies.

Outrage concerning the reign of terror that gripped Cuba in 1844
came from western Europe, especially Great Britain, and the northern United States. Yet the consternation did not diminish the value of
O'Donnell's achievements as far as Madrid was concerned. The rem-
nants of Spain's empire in the 1840s were of supreme importance for its
economy, and he ruthlessly resolved, for the time being, the atmosphere
of uncertainty, paranoia, fear, and hatred through the direct application
of torture to very specific bodies. First, and most obviously, the subjugation and brutalizing treatment of slaves and the free colored population
reasserted the exhibitionist exercise of power that had long characterized colonial rule in the Americas; this treatment, meted out during
the exception to "normal" colonial rule that the Military Commission's
pursuit of conspirators provided, reversed the tendencies toward reform
that characterized the more recent slave codes from Madrid. The debate

over the number of lashes that could be legally administered to slaves became a nonissue in the Slave Regulations of 1844, which only specified that the master, "who in no case should apply the lash himself and who upon ordering it, should incline to moderation rather than excess."[108] The new regulations also elaborated a series of measures to control the free black and colored population as never before. During the colonial government's reign of terror, all adult male free people of color who had been born abroad were given fifteen days to leave Cuba. In addition to the strict vigilance of free people of color on the estates, the 1844 regulations called for the expulsion of all *emancipados* who had completed their civil and religious education and of all foreign-born free people of color. The regulations prohibited "any person of color, free or slave" from disembarking on the island;[109] local authorities were expected to scrutinize the activities of the free colored who rented land in the country and punish their crimes against whites severely. Finally, no people of color were to be employed in apothecaries. In contrast to the slave code two years earlier, the new regulations did not pursue reform but concentrated on the control of a population that hitherto had not received a great deal of the colonial government's attention. The regulations recognized in free people of color the emergence of new though suspect social actors.

Second, the aftermath of the Escalera conspiracy brought abolitionist and Creole reformist antislavery activities on the island to a close. Turnbull had been implicated in the conspiracies, but there was no evidence that he had the backing of the British government or even of the Anti-Slavery Society, both of which learned about the former British consul's abolitionist activism after the investigations of 1844. Even though he had left the island permanently in 1842, except for a brief, unofficial return the following year, his departure marked the end of potential abolitionist collaborations with local antislavery allies. Nevertheless, it was evident that Turnbull had found it to his advantage to represent his actions as official while he was stationed in Havana.[110] British abolitionists worked to create alliances with the Creole reformists in order to undermine and eliminate the slave trade, but the latter withdrew their assistance, fearing the empowerment of the free black population and the risk of a racial conflagration. The Escalera conspiracy permanently disbanded the Creole reformists.[111] Félix Tanco y Bosmeniel, the ardently anticolonial

and antislavery author of *Petrona y Rosalía,* was imprisoned and interrogated as a few others from the literary circle, such as Manuel de Castro
Palomino, had been. Del Monte, José de la Luz y Caballero, and Gómez
de Avellaneda avoided arrest because they were abroad, and other like-
minded Creoles followed suit by leaving the island at the first opportunity. Manzano had erroneously been sent to jail because his name and
color matched those of an accused conspirator, but he stayed there longer than necessary because he was a poet who had been associated with
del Monte and the members of the literary circle. Manzano's year of imprisonment brought the public recitation and publication of his poems
to an abrupt end as the former slave faded into oblivion, leaving no traces
of poetry written after the government's reign of terror. In an ironic twist
for Manzano, who hoped that his poetry would garner recognition and
acclaim in Europe, José Antonio Echeverría wrote to del Monte, who had
by then escaped to Paris, informing him that Manzano had been released
from prison and asking him to warn those French writers who wanted to
write about Manzano's life against committing the grave error of referring to the former slave by name.[112] In the aftermath of the government's
persecution of the free black and mulatto population, anonymity was
the most to which Manzano could aspire after regaining his freedom.

Finally, O'Donnell's enduring accomplishment for the Spanish government was to reassert the polarized racialization of black bodies as
a defining practice for conserving the colony. The Slave Regulations
of 1844 not only marked the transformation of Madrid's acknowledg-
ment that a strong black presence on the island made good economic
and geopolitical sense into specific controls over enslaved bodies; the
regulations also exercised new regulatory power over the free black and
mulatto community. In this sense, O'Donnell was successful at securing
the colony for another two decades until the outbreak of the first war
of independence (also known as the Ten-Years War) in 1868, when the
loyalty of slaves and the free colored population once again became a
crucial issue. The Creole reformists were no less concerned about controlling this black presence than the colonial government was, but their
writings sought to clear a critical space that the authorities deemed untenable because it dangerously linked antislavery sentiments, attitudes,
and activities with anticolonialism. If the reformist "young liberals" al-

ready demonstrated anxiety about the racial constitution of a hypothetically more autonomous Cuban polity, events in 1843 and, especially, in
the first half of the following year caused them to retreat from establishing consequential alliances with free blacks and mulattoes. According
to Murray, British abolitionism and the Escalera conspiracy uncovered
the "narrowness and racism inherent in the creole definition of political
liberty."[113] Del Monte's racist statements against black empowerment
not only marked the triumph of O'Donnell's achievement for the Spanish government; they also represented his desperate efforts, from exile
in France and Spain, to protect family and friends from persecution.
So enduring was the reimposition of polarized racialization as a means
of subjugating the colony that José Martí, who, in his unyielding efforts
to convince compatriots of the necessity of struggling for independence
in the 1890s, would devote what are now considered seminal pages to
passionate arguments for deracializing Cuba as the prerequisite for a uni-
fied struggle against Spain.[114] His claim in chronicles such as "Nuestra
América" (Our America) and "Mi raza" (My race), which he had written
a few years before he died in one of the first skirmishes in Cuba's second
war of independence, that there were no races or only "library-shelf"
ones, are testaments to the importance of reversing a long and periodically intense colonial policy of racial polarization and segregation.[115]

Epilogue

This book began as a reflection on Juan Francisco Manzano's account of his life. What initially intrigued me about the text were the ways in which the former slave and poet was consistently engaged in psychic battles on two fronts, or so it seemed. The more obvious fight was his struggle against the unrelenting, dehumanizing oppression of slavery. It is on this score that his autobiography takes its place among other slave narratives as documented evidence of some of the most atrocious practices that a group of human beings has ever perpetrated on another in the modern period. Such writings can be shocking in the barbarisms that they reveal, and abolitionists who sought to speak on behalf of slaves valued these texts precisely because they believed that the impact that brutal episodes could have on readers would produce the empathy that their faith and the abolition movement required. However, in addition to the violent spectacles that slave narratives detailed, there also existed, side by side, or often relegated to the background in the quest for this impact, a subtler and ubiquitous range of oppressive practices and responses to these that were so mundane as to escape ready notice. Even an account as epic and inspirational as *Narrative of the Life of Frederick Douglass* displays another site of daily struggle that he felicitously called the "tender point" that kept slaves from heading north to escape slavery. In a system that consistently destroyed familial and communal ties, the decision to remain behind, to stay in bondage for the sake of these attachments, cannot be considered a willing or masochistic acceptance of enslavement. Aware of its enormous pull on enslaved subjects, including the extent to which it affected his desire to run away, Douglass respected this decision or outcome. The vast majority of slaves throughout the Americas lived debating their inclinations toward the "tender point" or the "point of no return" that made slavery so unbearable that it propelled the enslaved subject to undertake life-threatening measures to break out of bondage; moreover, they engaged in this internal quarrel, both consciously and unconsciously, from within the confines of their enslavement. In order to evaluate those mundane situations in which the tender point might win out, it seemed to me that my task involved trying to imagine the contexts, conditions, and contingencies that made this option or outcome a reasonable way, even if temporary, to resolve difficult dilemmas. Because Manzano believed that his account was true to life, I was not willing to ignore the obstinacy with which he held on to certain complex attachments, including those that seemed to oppress him the most.

It soon became evident that Manzano was not battling on two fronts and that his struggle against slavery on a daily basis not only required an avoidance of physical pain and discomfort but also an internal fight to come to terms with the failure to avoid being treated as an object, a commodity, and a brute. As Hegel and many after him have shown, there can be no proper understanding of oppression without an appreciation of the role that the unconscious plays in accounting for the ways in which we grapple with power as it presses against us. To a certain degree, then, Manzano's struggles were paradigmatic and possessed characteristics that are analogous to those of victims of oppression in many other contexts. Yet the challenge that Howard McGary made in 1992 for those of us who work on historical slavery to imagine how the concept of "unconscious resistance" might operate has not been sufficiently met. His assertion that instead of privileging someone's intentions, it might serve us better to examine "the conditions that the agent faced when he or she acted or failed to act and the avenues available for reducing oppression" offers an analytical method.[1] Even though this argument was valuable for my reading of Manzano's autobiographical writing, the former slave and poet articulated attachments to his enslavers that seemed to be pure anathema for anyone interested in denouncing slave masters. It piqued my curiosity that while the band of "young liberals" who attended del Monte's literary circle was so drawn to the nuanced eloquence with which Manzano complained about being enslaved and so invested in considering him submissive that these two characteristics featured prominently in the protagonists of the novels that they wrote, Madden, the passionately engaged abolitionist, avoided reflecting on the problem altogether and purposefully mistranslated Manzano's stated affection for his enslavers as gratitude for the education that he received from them. This perceived compliance was a source of inspiration for different political agendas as reformists and abolitionists harnessed it for their respective goals. It is in this sense that the idea of freedom from liberation, as opposed to that of freedom from slavery, begins to account for paternalistic attempts at "liberating" slaves during that first historical era of humanitarianism that Michael Barnett calls "imperial."[2]

Yet there is something genuinely disturbing about the invisible oppressiveness of circumstances that could oblige a subject to express affection for his or her enslavers. Slaves did not willingly submit to oppression but needed to display and master a repertoire of nonthreatening affects in order to survive in and live with slavery. Consequently, to find fault with the victim of oppression, to suggest that the compliant slave exists as a human type, only reinforces the oppressor's upper hand. A viable alternative, therefore, is to enter the enslaved subject's world, to the extent that he or she provides us with an entry, and to find ways to narrate a point of view that would embrace such paradoxes as indicators of human struggles for self-mastery. To take these paradoxes into consideration does not mean depriving Manzano of agency in the constantly negotiated balance between tender points and points of no return, so that external factors in a social context alone may be called upon as adequate explanations for quarrels that he had with himself. On the contrary, interrogating Manzano's stated affection for his enslavers allowed me to demonstrate how the violence and traumas of slavery were not limited to spectacles of physical violence but operated in a mundane and almost imperceptible way in the psychic life of an enslaved subject. The concept of "double consciousness" that Du Bois coined alerts us to the force of this phenomenon. For it is one thing to submit the slave to physical beatings, which produces the effect, as far as the slave master is concerned, of being a visible and exemplary warning to slaves; it is another to induce the slave in mundane ways, especially during the formative years of life, to believe that the only source of stability to which he or she can aspire is the master's terrifying whim. Manzano's induced affection for his enslavers is the result of abject circumstances, not because he is abject, but because of the kind of fiction that he compulsively tells himself—that his was a privileged childhood—in order to avoid contemplating the enormity of his subjugation. Nevertheless, as destructive as the circumstances that rendered this fiction necessary were, this version of his life constituted a first step toward the sublimation and creativity that would allow him to rise above his circumstances and eventually lead him out of bondage. To avoid any confusion, it should be noted that Manzano's tender point was not this induced affection but the love that he felt for his biological mother, whom he occasionally mentions in the account of his life, and for his brother, who appears as the object of his care in the poem "Un sueño" (A dream); the former slave and poet also describes a point of no return in his autobiography when, in attacking an overseer for beating his mother, he risked life and limb to defend her.

In the course of writing this book, I also began to ask myself questions about the relation between the expectations that readers typically have of slave narratives and what Manzano's account had to offer. As in all such narratives, his autobiography denounced slavery by furnishing the kinds of abundant details from lived experiences that would substantiate arguments against the practice. In addition to analysis of some of the atrocities that he experienced, my task also involved the straightforward scholarly work of describing and interrogating how others profited from his life story. As much as abolitionists and reformists wanted to consider themselves morally upright "men of feeling," the surplus value that they extracted from his intellectual and artistic labor for their respective causes was both illicit and extraordinary: the Creole reformists who frequented del Monte's literary circle trafficked in his text as they reflected on how to write a literature of proto-national consciousness; also, because of the patrician's intervention, Manzano's story became the evidence that Madden sought in his mission to uncover the cruelty of Cuban slavery that British abolitionism required as it internationalized its movement. Unbeknown to him, Manzano's account of his life assumed these dimensions, and focusing on the expropriation of his labor brought specificity to my analysis of the afterlife of his writings.

Yet, how do his self-reflections contribute to an understanding of the psychic life of an enslaved subject? And how is this understanding useful for the symbolic, rallying power that is often expected of the slave narrative? With respect to the first question, I believe that my close reading of Manzano's autobiography demonstrates the insidious machinations of oppression in and against which he struggled and highlights his ability to negotiate varying degrees of agency through a clever repertoire of convincing poses, sudden moments of rebellion, craftiness, sublimation though artistic creativity, the composition of verses, and the clandestine method that he employed to teach himself to write. However, my analysis of his life story concentrates for the most part on his self-representation in an effort to show how his self-ascribed melancholy is first and foremost an obstinate engagement with his oppression—and not a permanently demoralizing pathological condition—that leads him to the privileged insight that he is not to blame for the fact that slavery itself forecloses his ability to assume ethical positions. His devastatingly accurate assertion that he would never be considered an honorable man despite his knowledge of "the truth" represents a triumphant denunciation of the immorality that lies at the core of his slave-owning colonial society.

And what of the symbolic rallying power of Manzano's *Autobiography of a Slave*? There is no doubt that abolitionism positioned the slave narrative as a clarion call for an emancipatory discourse and ethics that would serve as a model for subsequent social movements. Because the power of the writing to denounce injustices was key to a successful rallying of advocates and supporters, Manzano's disorderly text almost fails to inspire. Some of the reasons why, which I have already listed, include the self-censorship with which he wrote after being cajoled into writing his autobiography while he was still enslaved, the lack of clarity surrounding who his intended readers were going to be, and the number of mediations through which the text passed before it was eventually published for the first time in English. Even more curious for the abolitionist reader of the time must have been the painstaking effort through which Manzano attempts to create a writing subject and narrator who could rise above his circumstances, not by breaking free of bondage, but by working assiduously through it in order to secure his freedom. In other words, the text makes it abundantly clear that for Manzano, knowledgeable and experienced as he was in a number of economically viable trades, there was no place outside of bondage, and subsequently of discrimination and racial oppression, that would allow him to enjoy absolute freedom. This kind of freedom does not exist for anyone, and even though the rallying power of its utopian imaginary cannot be underestimated for those who were willing to push beyond points of no return, Manzano's life transpires within concentric or overlapping forms of insularity that include slavery, classism, racism, and colonialism. There was no underground railroad leading anywhere for Cuban slaves. His writings do not show any indications of a desire to take to the hills as a runaway, and taking part in a slave uprising to gain his freedom became a moot point by the 1840s when he was already free. To work through slavery in order to achieve one's goals, therefore, was not a view with which abolitionists were familiar, nor, given their goals, would they have wanted to be.

To recognize that one is always embedded in the very systems of power against which one struggles is a difficult challenge for an emancipatory politics. Manzano's account illustrates this, and I approached the problem drawing from an ontological reading of Hegel's master-slave dialectic, Judith Butler's analysis of how power functions in the psyche, and Gabriela Basterra's work on the tragic form of modern subjectivity, while maintaining Du Bois's "double consciousness" and Orlando Patterson's "perverse intimacy" as descriptions and analyses of internalized forms of oppression that required elaboration in my reading of Manzano's writings. Exploring a new attitude toward postcolonial criticism for the contemporary period and basing his assertions on C. L. R. James's turn from the romance plot in the first edition of *The Black Jacobins* (1938) to tragedy in the book's second edition (1963), David Scott posits tragic sensibility as "apt and timely" because of the complex analyses that it can provide for "the relation between actions and their consequences, and intentions and the chance contingencies that sometimes undo them" as we attempt to qualify the critical temporalities with which we identify anticolonial and postcolonial struggles.[3] In addition to Scott's book, Chris Bongie's critique of it, particularly for the "aporetic relation between tragic ethics and liberationist politics with which he leaves his reader at the end," also identifies some of the issues regarding the potential rallying power of

Manzano's autobiography that emerged for me as I undertook my analysis of the account of his life that the former slave and poet finished writing in 1839.[4] Admittedly, even though I focused on writings that surfaced in Cuba's colonial period, I attempted to work out the relation between reading to decipher ethical dilemmas and reading for a prescriptive emancipatory discourse, similar to the one that Scott and Bongie identify with the romance plot of anticolonialism, by recourse to a more modern, anticolonial text—Fanon's *Wretched of the Earth*—in an essay that I have not included here.[5] In their respective books, Scott and Bongie are, among other things, deeply critical of the ways in which certain teleologies and temporalities get ascribed to colonial and postcolonial struggles. It was instructive for me to discover how Fanon's book, in the midst of a decolonization movement, did not relent from pitting "colonizer" and "colonized" in the life-and-death struggle of colonial warfare. By relegating his psychiatric clinical notes to an appendix—notes that demonstrate how the psychic ravages of war affected both sides—Fanon sidelined the analysis of the negative reciprocity of colonial relations for "colonizers" and "colonized" in favor of the unambiguous binary oppositions that war required. His strategic decision to postpone the analysis of the clinical notes, to forward them, as it were, to a postcolonial future, offered me a provisional solution for viewing the relation between the task of analyzing Manzano's self-representation and the call to action that his narrative should inspire. I have chosen the humanist's path toward elucidating the depths and breadth of oppression and the barely perceptible though daily struggle against it, so that the victims of oppression do not get blamed for the misfortune of never having known what it was to possess the freedoms that the rest of their society enjoyed.

At the same time, it is not a revelation to claim that Manzano's situation and strivings cannot be accurately appreciated unless we also examine those of his enslavers, liberators, and all who wished to exercise the perverse intimacy of defining his path toward sublimation and the transcendence of his oppression. Given the circumstances and contingencies in which the poet's flaws and weaknesses came to the fore, it comes as no surprise that the Creole reformists and his abolitionist translator should also possess theirs. This purview is also germane to a critical, humanist undertaking, which does not exonerate del Monte and Madden, who, while agreeing that literature should humanize masters and slaves, could not see beyond their paternalist manipulation of Manzano's predicament and struggles. In slave-owning societies, the human flaws and weaknesses of the powerful are far more consequential for the lives and well-being of the enslaved than the other way around. In the case of the abolitionists, their distance from the enslaved was instrumental. The abolitionist at home is a familiar figure who engages in these activities most frequently from a physical distance. This distance has proven to be both enabling and confining. In the abolition movement, physical distances from plantations allowed abolitionists to present moral arguments against slavery with the intellectual disinterest and objectivity that, in the British context, parliamentary procedure required and valued. What these distances also imply is that the abolitionist is rarely in a position to comprehend the conditions in which the slave suffers and strives for freedom. Debbie Lee, Adam Hochschild, and Ian Baucom demonstrate that, in addition to the expansion of this disinterest beyond legislative activities, there also arose the strong desire to learn more about and speak for the enslaved in areas that included, for example, the poetic imagination, British civil society, and the creation of sympathetic, imaginative witnesses. As I have noted, Madden, the cosmopolitan abolitionist—one who is able to take the cause and mission across boundaries to work not in the "peaceful closets of philanthropy," as he put it, but as a "mercenary" and "soldier"—leads us to an understanding of the limits of disinterest when the latter is challenged by activism in the field.[6] Historically at the heart of this matter for abolitionists at home have been the evolving contexts and complexities through which abolitionists' field reports and romantic literature provided the reader with opportunities to "identify with and *feel for* another human being," which is Lee's phrasing and which I have read as both empathy for another and the production of affect in another's stead.[7] By contrast, even though the Creole reformist bourgeoisie was not separated from its slaves by enormous physical distances and could observe their lives at first hand, its members were more attuned to their own vacillating engagements with colonial rule than to pursuit of a deeper understanding of their slaves' conditions. At the time, they could not imagine how freeing their slaves might also free them from colonial rule—a proposition that would have constituted the inverse of Varela's and Gener's statement to del Monte that they could not heed a transatlantic bourgeoisie's call for the natural and universal rights of men because they believed that slavery enslaved them. The reformists' dream of a whiter Cuba dismissed the future of the colony's black population altogether.

This book began as a reflection on an unusual slave narrative and ends with the assertion that speaking on behalf of the enslaved and the oppressed requires the power to discern and respect the contradictions that inform their humanity.

Mis treinta años (*by Juan Francisco Manzano*)

Cuando miro el espacio que he corrido
desde la cuna hasta el presente día,
tiemblo y saludo a la fortuna mía
más de terror que de atención movido.

Sorpréndeme la lucha que he podido
sostener contra suerte tan impía,
si tal llamarse puede la porfía
de mi infelice ser al mal nacido.

Treinta años ha que conocí la tierra;
treinta años ha que en gemidor estado
triste infortunio por doquier me asalta;

mas nada es para mí la cruda Guerra
que en vano suspirar he soportado,
si la comparo, ¡oh Dios!, con lo que falta.

My Thirty Years (*translated by Richard Robert Madden, 1840*)

When I think on the course I have run,
From my childhood itself to this day,
I tremble, and fain would I shun,
The remembrance its terrors array.

I marvel at struggles endured,
With a destiny frightful as mine,
At the strength for such efforts:—assured
Tho' I am, 'tis in vain to repine.

I have known this sad life thirty years,
And to me, thirty years it has been
Of suff'ring, of sorrow and tears,
Ev'ry day of its bondage I've seen.

But 'tis nothing the past—or the pains,
Hitherto I have struggled to bear,
When I think, oh, my God! On the chains,
That I know I'm yet destined to wear.

Sonnet (*translated by Victor Schoelcher, 1840*)

Quand je considère l'espace que j'ai parcouru
Depuis le commencement jusqu'à ce jour,
Je tremble et je salue ma fortune
Plus ému de terreur que de respect.

Je suis étonné de la lutte que j'ai pu soutenir
Contre un sort tant impie;
Si je puis ainsi appeler les combats
De ma malheureuse existence à partir de ma fatale naissance.

Il'ya trente ans que je connus la terre,
Il'ya trente années qu'en un état plein de larmes
Triste infortune m'assiège de tous côtés.

Mais qu'est-ce que la cruelle guerre
Que j'ai supportée un pleurant en vain
Quand je la compare, o Dieu! à celle qui m'attend.

NOTES

INTRODUCTION

1. Unlike its more contemporary usage in other parts of the Americas, where it is used to connote racial and cultural mixtures, the term "Creole" emerged first in Portuguese as a way to differentiate the African- from the American-born or "Creole" slave. In its Spanish derivation, *criollo* not only came to designate the American-born slave but also distinguished Spaniards born in the Americas from those born in the metropolis. For a summary of the historical definitions of the term in the early modern period, see Bauer and Mazzoti, introduction to *Creole Subjects in the Colonial Americas*.

2. José Antonio Saco, an important intellectual from the sector of the Creole bourgeoisie that was interested in reforming slavery, had summarily been sent into exile in 1834 for daring to challenge this ban.

3. For more about this treaty and conflicting British and Spanish policies concerning the slave trade in Cuba, consult Corwin, *Spain and the Abolition of Slavery in Cuba, 1817–1886*, and especially Blackburn's *The Overthrow of Colonial Slavery, 1776–1848*, 381–417.

4. Davis, "What the Abolitionists Were Up Against," 20.

5. Ibid., 23.

6. Ibid.

7. Lee, *Slavery and the Romantic Imagination*, 32.

8. Baucom, *Specters of the Atlantic*, 194.

9. Lively, *Masks*, 55–56.

10. Ibid.

11. For more about this "imaginative" witness, see Baucom's development of the subject in the second section of *Specters of the Atlantic*, 173–296.

12. Patterson, *Slavery and Social Death*, 50.

13. In positing freedom as a continuum that extends from liberation from coercion to the struggle for self-mastery, I am indebted to Isaiah Berlin's essay "Two Concepts of Liberty" (1958). Employing the words "freedom" and "liberty" interchangeably, Berlin defines "negative" liberty as freedom from the coercion of other persons or institutions; negative liberty—the more frequent understanding of freedom—seeks to answer the

question, in what areas of life can the subject act without interference from others? By contrast, "positive" liberty asks, who or what is the source of control that can determine a subject's action? For Berlin, this liberty is positive since it designates the freedom to be one's own master. See Berlin, "Two Concepts of Liberty," 169–70 and 178–79.

14. W. E. B. Du Bois's seminal concept of "double-consciousness," or "the sense of looking at one's self through the eyes of others, of measuring one's soul by the tape of a world that looks on in amused contempt and pity," constitutes a brilliant rendering of the psychological internalization of oppression. See Du Bois, "Of Our Spiritual Strivings," 8.

15. Douglass, *Narrative*, 57–58. Deborah E. McDowell warns that equating resistance to power with physical struggle runs the risk of suggesting that power relations can be as uncomplicated as the tussle between Douglass and Covey. See McDowell, "Making Frederick Douglass," 52.

16. Ibid., 72.

17. Hegel formulated the master-slave dialectic while he witnessed important revolutions, including the Haitian Revolution, which almost exactly coincided with his development of a theory of self-consciousness and of the subject in *Phenomenology of Spirit*. For more about this "coincidence," see Susan Buck-Morss's important essay, "Hegel and Haiti." The Hegel who designated Africa as ahistorical emerged fully in the 1830s. For Helen Thomas, the later Hegel "identified Christian ideology as *the* world narrative of cultural liberation, hence endorsing, albeit indirectly, the interrelationship between missionary activity and colonialism." See Thomas, *Romanticism and Slave Narratives*, 134.

18. Douglass, *Narrative*, 102.

19. Stephanie Li describes decisions such as that of remaining on the plantation in order to sustain and protect family ties as the "freedom of choice." See Li, *Something Akin to Freedom*, 7.

20. Davis, *The Problem of Slavery*, 564.

21. Buck-Morss argues that although slavery was the "root metaphor" of Western political philosophy, slavery was more than a metaphor for Hegel as he imaginatively witnessed the Haitian Revolution from afar. She posits the metaphor of slavery as a vehicle of irrepressible knowledge, that is, as proof of the specter of human bondage to which Enlightenment thinkers gave rise in the very act of suppressing direct references to chattel slavery in their reflections on freedom. The extent to which these thinkers consciously suppressed this knowledge remains a serious point of contention today. Significantly, Buck-Morss also claims that the metaphor allows us to unify theory and reality and transcend the "confines of academic theory." See Buck-Morss, "Hegel and Haiti," 60.

22. "Lord" and "bondsman" translate Hegel's *Herr* and *Knecht*, with *Herrschaft* as "lordship" and *Knechtschaft* as "bondage." Nonetheless, even though the contemporary usage of "master" and "slave" is not a literal rendering of the German, the power relations and configurations that lord or master and bondsman or slave are meant to designate remain operative. Given its current usage, I employ the term "master-slave" to refer to Hegel's dialectic but retain "lord" and "bondsman" for all other instances.

23. Fredric Jameson reminds us that it is precisely because consciousness and subjectivity cannot be represented as such that we have recourse to this kind of figurative language. See, Jameson, *Singular Modernity*, 55–56.

24. Fischer, *Modernity Disavowed*, 25.

25. Gilroy, *Black Atlantic,* 62.

26. Ibid., 55.

27. Kojève, *Introduction to the Reading of Hegel,* 25. In this light, Manzano's desire to be proficient at his work does not reveal a willingness to be subjugated but a struggle for greater self-consciousness through work as a free laborer.

28. In other words, this vicarious enjoyment of the bondsman's labor means that the lord depends on the former's consciousness and experience in order to appreciate his own. The lord thus loses his status as an independent self-consciousness because, ironically, he is unable to achieve the recognition of an equal, which is required in order for him to enjoy self-certainty. In Hegel's paradigm, it is the realization of his creative power and the desire to transcend his subjugation that lead the bondsman to the subsequent stages of self-consciousness and allow him to outstrip the master's.

1. LIBERALISMS AT ODDS

1. Félix Varela and Tomás Gener to Domingo del Monte, New York, September 12, 1834, in *Domingo del Monte: centón epistolario* 1:367–371. Del Monte was born in Maracaibo, Venezuela, and moved with his family to Cuba in 1810, when he was six years old. Even though his family had sufficient resources to purchase a sugar estate and its hundred slaves, del Monte did not rise to prominence in Cuba's sugarocracy until 1834, when he married his wife, Rosa Aldama y Alfonso, a member of one of the island's wealthiest and most influential families. Del Monte's cohorts were Manuel González del Valle and Vicente Osés. Trained as a lawyer and philosopher, González del Valle attended Havana's Seminario de San Carlos with del Monte where they were both disciples of Félix Varela. Osés was a member of the so-called young liberals that del Monte led against the conservative slave-owning old guard in the early 1830s. For a list of the members of this group of liberal reformists, consult Andioc Torres, "Ensayo introductorio: Cartas para la historia de Cuba" in *Domingo del Monte: centón epistolario,* 1:43–44, and Otero, "Delmonte y la cultura de la sacarocracia," 726.

2. Censorship was an unavoidable part of colonial life, and Tacón was extremely vigilant on this score. In Spain, the captain-general had been a progressive liberal. However, his experience as an *ayacucho*—a veteran of the Spanish American wars of independence—led him, in part, to be one of the most authoritarian and oppressive military rulers that the Spanish government sent to the island. For more on Tacón's political persuasion, see Pérez de la Riva, "Introduction." Also see Gomariz, *Colonialismo e independencia cultural,* 53–54.

3. Félix Varela and Tomás Gener to Domingo del Monte, New York, September 12, 1834, in *Domingo del Monte: centón epistolario,* 1:368; my translation. This Creole consciousness of the gap between European liberalism and the local experience of slavery also constitutes a point of departure for Roberto Schwartz's seminal essay, "Misplaced Ideas: Literature and Society in Late-Nineteenth-Century Brazil."

4. Hegel, *Philosophy of History,* 80.

5. Baucom, *Specters of the Atlantic,* 187.

6. Rojas, *Isla sin fin,* 18–19.

7. Barcia, "Fighting with the Enemy's Weapons," 172.

8. Moreno Fraginals, *El ingenio,* 367.

9. Hochschild, *Bury the Chains,* 87. Hochschild's book falls in the category of recent approaches to abolitionism that examine this movement as foundational for middle-class reform.

10. Nyquist, *Arbitrary Rule,* 362.

11. Davis, *Problem of Slavery,* 41–42. Robin Blackburn corroborates this periodization, stating that few protested the increasing mass enslavement of Africans before 1760 even though slavery had disappeared from northwestern Europe by then. See Blackburn, *Overthrow of Colonial Slavery,* 13.

12. Davis, *Problem of Slavery,* 45–48.

13. Ibid., 262.

14. Ibid., 71.

15. Murray, *Odious Commerce,* 114.

16. Ibid., 139–40. In the 1790s, British and American vessels were the chief rivals for supplying Cuba with slaves. In a controversial treaty that Spain and England signed in 1817, the slave trade was prohibited north of the equator on the coasts of Africa, and the prohibition was extended south of the equator three years later. By 1835, after the two nations signed another treaty against the now contraband Cuban slave trade, slave traders resorted to the use of the United States flag to transport slaves. See Murray, *Odious Commerce,* 14–15; 40–41; and 104.

17. Davis, *Problem of Slavery,* 267–68.

18. Félix Varela and Tomás Gener to Domingo del Monte, New York, September 12, 1834, in *Domingo del Monte: centón epistolario,* 1:235.

19. Saco, "Ideas sobre la incorporación," 118.

20. Moreno Fraginals, *El ingenio,* 112.

21. Moreno Fraginals reports that Captain-General Tacón opposed railway construction in Havana during his administration (1834–38) because he opined that Cuba should not enjoy this technological advance before Spain did. See *El ingenio,* 110. It was symbolic of this competition between the colonial government and the Creole bourgeoisie that some of the public works that Tacón commissioned arose out of his rivalry with the wealthy Creole Claudio Martínez de Pinillos. See Pérez de la Riva, "Introduction," 35.

22. Moreno Fraginals, *El ingenio,* 367–8.

23. For a detailed description of the wealth of del Monte's family, see Andioc Torres, Presentación to *Domingo del Monte: centón epistolario,* 2:xiv. For information about del Monte's and other leading families in Cuba during the nineteenth century—among them, some of the founders of financial institutions such as the New York Sugar Exchange, Spain's Bank of Santander, and the Bank of Bilbao—consult Moreno Fraginals, *El ingenio,* 219–24.

24. The Quakers were one of the first religious groups that made it clear to their followers that slavery was immoral and would not be tolerated by its members. Abolitionism was the first social reform movement that was organized and run by businessmen such as the Quakers. See Hochschild, *Bury the Chains,* 127–28.

25. Moreno Fraginals, *El ingenio,* 111.

26. Ibid.

27. Ibid., 115.

28. Hilton, *Age of Atonement,* 41.

29. According to Moreno Fraginals, the Spanish economy seemed more colonial than metropolitan. See *El ingenio,* 348–49 and 431–32.

30. Ibid., 376–79.

31. Rojas, *Isla sin fin,* 40.

32. Saco, "Carta de un patriota," 32.

33. In his analysis of the origins and development of the concept of civilization, Bruce Mazlish argues that racism began to characterize European civilization during this period and hindered any real understanding of the other. "Race had become destiny," he writes, "and the determinant of civilization." See Mazlish, *Civilization and Its Contents,* 46–47.

34. Corwin, *Spain and the Abolition of Slavery,* 65–66.

35. Murray, *Odious Commerce,* 149.

36. Pérez de la Riva, "Introduction," 42.

37. Moreno Fraginals, *El ingenio,* 377.

38. Del Monte, *La isla de Cuba,* 5–6.

39. Moreno Fraginals, *El ingenio,* 380.

40. Carlos Alonso argues that despite their rhetoric of modernity and change, Spanish American Creoles were generally economically and politically conservative. According to this rhetoric, he writes, "Spain and everything associated with it was placed in a hopelessly archaic and static temporal location by the Creole anticolonial struggle, which is wryly ironic because the liberal and forward-looking policies of the Enlightened metropolitan administrations of the second half of the eighteenth century had been bitterly opposed by the emerging and triumphant Creoles." See Alonso, *Burden of Modernity,* 16.

41. Moreno Fraginals, *El ingenio,* 228–29.

42. Davis, *Problem of Slavery,* 183.

43. Moreno Fraginals, *El ingenio,* 110–11.

44. Saco, "Paralelo," 35–36.

45. Moreno Fraginals, *El ingenio,* 459.

46. Keene, *Beyond the Anarchical Society,* 22.

47. Ibid., 6–7.

48. Ibid., 112.

49. Ibid., 6.

50. Ileana Rodríguez's research shows that many of the young liberals first met at the San Carlos Seminary in Havana, where Félix Varela taught philosophy; some were active politically; most of them came from a middle class that was just emerging; and a few of them, like Anselmo Suárez y Romero and Cirilo Villaverde, were quite poor. In Cuba, they constituted a minority of learned Creoles who were influenced by liberal democratic ideas. See Rodríguez, "Romanticismo literario y liberalismo reformista," 54–56.

51. Alonso, *Burden of Modernity,* 69–70.

52. In a note that del Monte wrote at the bottom of the letter that he received from Varela and Gener, he indicates that the treatise was translated and published in Antonio Bergues's publishing house in Barcelona. The Creole patrician lamented the fact that even though the treatise was advertised in the newspapers and sold in bookstores in

Havana and elsewhere on the island, neither the government nor the public paid the slightest attention to it. See *Domingo del Monte: centón epistolario*, 1:371.

53. Murray, *Odious Commerce*, 128.

54. Fischer, *Modernity Disavowed*, 96–106.

55. As Lisa Surwillo illustrates in her reading of *Haley,* a Spanish theatrical adaptation of parts of *Uncle Tom's Cabin,* the use of oblique references to slavery in Spain was still being successfully practiced in the 1850s. See Surwillo, "Representing the Slave Trader."

56. Bueno, *La crítica literaria cubana*, 32. Bueno suggests that this eclecticism was foundational for Spanish-American literary criticism, not because of ignorance or superficiality but because of the urgency with which it had been necessary to strengthen an initially weak literary production. See Bueno, *Las ideas literarias*, 5.

57. Andioc Torres, Presentación, 2:x.

58. Saco, "Análisis," 174.

59. Rodríguez, "Romanticismo literario y liberalismo reformista," 44.

60. Ibid., 46.

61. Andioc Torres, Presentación, 2:xi n. 12.

62. The letter appears in *Domingo del Monte: centón epistolario*, 1:322–26.

63. Corwin, *Spain and the Abolition of Slavery*, 63–64.

64. Andioc Torres, Presentación, 2:xxx.

65. González del Valle, *La vida literaria en Cuba*, 24.

66. Bueno, *La crítica literaria cubana*, 35.

67. Leante, "Dos obras antiesclavistas cubanas," 184.

68. Ibid. Leante reports that this was the word that del Monte used.

69. Anselmo Suárez y Romero to Domingo del Monte, Ingenio Surinam, April 11, 1839, in *Domingo del Monte:centón epistolario*, 2:347.

70. Vera-León, "Juan Francisco Manzano," 19–20.

71. Ramos, "Cuerpo, lengua, subjetividad," 225.

72. Leante, "Dos obras antiesclavistas cubanas," 188.

73. McGary, "Paternalism and Slavery," 21 and 34.

74. Bueno, *La crítica literaria cubana*, 45.

75. Ibid., 42.

76. Ibid., 9.

77. Otero, "Delmonte y la cultura de la sacarocracia," 728.

78. Andioc Torres, Presentación, 2:xxxiv.

79. See the appendix for the entire sonnet, Richard Robert Madden's 1840 translation of it into English, and the translation of it into French by Victor Schoelcher that same year.

80. McBride, *Impossible Witnesses*, 89.

81. Franco, "Estudio Preliminar," 27.

82. It would be illuminating to investigate the story behind the multiple translations of Manzano's sonnet as the composition made its way into powerful abolitionist circles in London and Paris. Madden was the first to translate the poem into English. A translation of the poem into French appears in the French abolitionist Victor Schoelcher's *Abolition de l'esclavage; examen du préjugé contre la couleur des africains et des sang-mêlés*

(Paris, 1840). Schoelcher probably picked up the poem during his brief visit to the Caribbean in the late 1830s. The sonnet was also translated into German.

83. Schulman, Introduction to *Autobiography,* 14.

84. Lee, *Slavery and the Romantic Imagination,* 31–33.

85. Fischer comes across an analogous use of the term *mal nacido* in her analysis of verses by the Cuban poet Plácido, who was executed in the Escalera conspiracy of 1844. See her *Modernity Disavowed,* 89.

86. Rodríguez interrogates the suitability of the term "Romanticism," which accompanied the rise of certain European nationalisms, for nationalist sentiments in Cuba's colonial context. Consult her "Romanticismo literario y liberalismo reformista," 35–56. For thorough analyses of the development of the literary field in Spanish America during this period, see González-Stephan, *Fundaciones,* and Ramos, *Desencuentros de la modernidad en América Latina.*

87. Bueno, *Las ideas literarias de Domingo Delmonte,* 11.

88. Hegel, *Phenomenology of Spirit,* 117.

89. Ibid., 118.

90. Ibid., 118–19.

91. Ibid., 118.

92. Lawson, "Oppression and Slavery," 8.

93. Davis, "What the Abolitionists Were Up Against," 23.

94. Ibid.

95. Alonso, *Burden of Modernity,* vi.

96. Ibid., 66.

97. Haskell, "Capitalism and the Origins of Humanitarian Sensibility, Part 1," 113.

98. Ibid., 120.

99. Ibid., 124.

2. IN SPITE OF HIMSELF

1. Manzano completed the original text in 1839, and Madden's first English translation of it appeared a year later. The second part of the autobiography, which Manzano also delivered to Domingo del Monte in 1839, was mysteriously lost while Ramón de Palma, a member of the latter's literary circle, was editing it. Cuba's Biblioteca Nacional holds the first and only part of the original autobiography. For more about the issues that surrounded the authorship and editing of the account, consult William Luis's comprehensive, recent edition of Manzano's writings, *Autobiografía del esclavo poeta y otros escritos.* Hereafter, I cite the text as *Autobiography* and employ the bilingual edition of the autobiography that Evelyn Picon Garfield translated and Ivan A. Schulman edited. In this edition, the English translation is printed on recto pages.

2. Oliver, *Colonization of Psychic Space,* xxii.

3. See, in particular, chapter 3 of Basterra's *Seductions of Fate.*

4. For more details about Elkins's assertion, consult his *Slavery: A Problem in American Institutional and Intellectual Life.*

5. Andrews, "Representation of Slavery," 82.

6. Escott, *Slavery Remembered,* 73.

7. Ibid., 78.

8. Moreno Fraginals, *El ingenio,* 267–268.

9. McGary, "Resistance and Slavery," 46. See in particular his analysis of the notion of "unconscious resistance," 41–48.

10. Manzano, *Autobiography,* 97.

11. After the juice is extracted from the sugar cane, the dried stalks, or *bagasse,* are reused for fuel.

12. Manzano, *Autobiography,* 101.

13. Ibid., 103.

14. Ibid.

15. Ibid.

16. Ibid.

17. Ibid., 49–51. Fray Luis de Granada was a sixteenth-century Spanish Dominican clergyman.

18. Ibid., 65. A *décima* is a classic Spanish ten-line poem that is written in octosyllabic form and rhyming abbaaccddc.

19. Ibid.

20. Ibid., 103.

21. Ibid., 103–105.

22. Ibid. Some years later, Don Nicolás Cárdenas, Manzano's former master, began to frequent the literary circle's meetings at del Monte's home. According to a letter from José Miguel Angulo y Heredia to del Monte, dated on May 7, 1836, Cárdenas also contributed a small sum toward Manzano's manumission. See *Domingo del Monte: centón epistolario,* 2:20.

23. Molloy, "From Serf to Self," 51.

24. Equiano, *Interesting Narrative,* 64. For more on the subject of the talking book, consult Henry Louis Gates Jr., "James Gronniosaw and the Trope of the Talking Book."

25. Douglass, *Narrative of the Life of Frederick Douglass,* 33. Douglass recognizes that he enabled himself as a literate subject at the same time that he was oppressed: "In learning to read, I owe almost as much to the bitter opposition of my master, as to the kindly aid of my mistress. I acknowledge the benefit of both." See ibid., 34.

26. Molloy, "From Serf to Self," 53.

27. Manzano, *Autobiografía del esclavo poeta,* 125. Here I consult William Luis's edition of Manzano's writings for the latter's correspondence and poetry. The translations of the quotes from this correspondence are mine.

28. Ibid.

29. Ibid. Manzano plays on the expression *dejar algo en el tintero,* which means to leave something unstated.

30. McBride, *Impossible Witnesses,* 93.

31. Manzano's attempt to rescue his self-representation from the objectification that the abolitionist slave narrative seemed to require was a common practice in Douglass's writing. Demonstrating the frequency with which Douglass employed slavery's paraphernalia in a series of speeches that he gave in Britain and the United States in the 1840s, not to allude to his former enslavement, but to underscore his autonomy, Celeste-Marie Bernier argues that he made use of this physical evidence "to both reclaim his

subjectivity and dissociate his own body from the status of slave object." See Bernier, "From Fugitive Slave to Fugitive Abolitionist," 210.

32. Juan Francisco Manzano to Domingo del Monte, Havana, June 25, 1835, in Manzano, *Autobiografía del esclavo poeta*, 125. Manzano's choice of the word *rodando*, or "stumbling along," could hardly be more appropriate because it captures his anxiety about the arbitrariness of life in bondage.

33. Ibid., 125; my italics. Being cautious about not writing her name in his letter, Manzano alludes to the Marchioness de Prado Ameno when he mentions "the one who has given me reason to moan."

34. These poems can be found in Manzano, *Autobiografía*, 152 and 175–90.

35. For more on the history of the slave codes in Cuba, consult Barcia, "Fighting with the Enemy's Weapons."

36. Butler, *Psychic Life of Power*, 2.

37. Ibid., 9.

38. Ibid., 8.

39. Basterra precisely states that "if 'we subjects' cooperate with power, it is because both 'subject' and 'objective necessity' bear the paradoxical status of 'necessary fictions.' They are fictions, we have constructed them, but we cannot do without them because they constitute what we are." See Basterra, *Seductions of Fate*, 90 and 103–105.

40. Manzano, *Autobiography*, 47 and 61.

41. Ibid., 45.

42. Ibid., 133.

43. Ibid., 45 and 47. Luis's edition illustrates that Manzano's text is less intelligible here due to additions that were made on the original writing by someone who corrected it.

44. Ibid., 47.

45. Lawson, "Oppression and Slavery," 6–9.

46. Manzano, *Autobiography*, 49.

47. Ibid., 51.

48. Ibid. For an insightful reading of this silence, see Casanova-Marengo's chapter on Manzano's autobiography in *El intersticio de la colonia*, chapter 2.

49. Manzano, *Autobiography*, 47.

50. Ibid., 123.

51. Ibid., 125–27.

52. Ibid., 109.

53. Ibid., 65 and 123.

54. Sweeney, "Atlantic Countercultures and the Networked Text," 410.

55. Ibid., 411.

56. Ibid., 412. Yet, in a poem like "La esclava ausente" (The absent slave), Manzano also partook of a literary practice among the members of del Monte's circle in which the principal voice of protest was often that of a female slave. William Luis argues that this voice probably made for a clearer representation of slavery's inequalities. See Luis's "Nicolás Azcárate's Antislavery Notebook," 338.

57. Manzano, *Autobiography*, 111.

58. Bontemps, *The Punished Self*, 142–43. Nevertheless, it is crucial to point out that while "Creole" in the context of the United States denotes racially mixed parent-

age, this is not necessarily the case in the context of the Spanish-speaking Caribbean, where *criollo* primarily means born and raised in the Americas. Moreover, slave labor was stratified: being African and newly arrived typically meant laboring in the fields and sugar mill, whereas Creole slaves constituted by far the majority of the house slaves. Highlighting racial and racist distinctions, Manzano and others (both masters and slaves) employed the term *mulato* to distinguish him from slaves of purer African ancestry.

59. Manzano, *Autobiography*, 131.

60. Juan Francisco Manzano to Domingo del Monte, Havana, December 11, 1834, in Manzano, *Autobiografía del esclavo poeta*, 123.

61. Starobin, Preface to *Blacks in Bondage*, xx.

62. Gomariz, *Colonialismo e independencia cultural*, 54.

63. See Draper, "Voluntad de intelectual," 112–13, and Fischer's chapter on Cuban wall painting in *Modernity Disavowed*, 57–76.

64. Draper, "Voluntad de intelectual," 104–106.

65. Butler, *Psychic Life of Power*, 11.

66. Ibid., 12.

67. Ibid., 15.

68. Manzano, *Autobiography*, 59.

69. Ibid., 63.

70. Ibid., 101.

71. Freud, "Mourning and Melancholia," 584.

72. Ibid., 585.

73. Manzano, *Autobiography*, 59 and 61.

74. Freud, "Mourning and Melancholia," 585.

75. Butler, *Psychic Life of Power*, 3.

76. Freud, "Mourning and Melancholia," 585.

77. Ibid., 586.

78. Ibid.

79. Manzano, *Autobiografía*, 307.

80. Manzano, *Autobiography*, 65.

81. Ibid.

82. McGary and Lawson, "Philosophy and American Slavery," xxv.

83. Manzano, *Autobiography*, 127.

84. Ibid., 67.

85. Ibid., 69.

86. Ibid., 105.

87. Ibid., 89.

88. Ramos, "*The Law Is Other*," 6–7.

89. Ibid., 9.

90. Wilcox, "The Body into Print," 9.

91. Sweeney, "Atlantic Countercultures and the Networked Text," 408.

92. Draper, "Voluntad de intelectual," 109–10.

93. Sweeney, "Atlantic Countercultures and the Networked Text," 406.

94. Baucom, *Specters of the Atlantic*, 177–78.

95. De Man, "Autobiography as De-Facement," 69.

96. Molloy, "From Serf to Self," 43.

97. Ramos, "*The Law Is Other*," 13–14.

3. BEING ADEQUATE TO THE TASK

1. For example, Thomas Bender's edited collection of essays, *The Antislavery Debate: Capitalism and Abolitionism as a Problem of Historical Interpretation*, ed. and intro. Thomas Bender (Berkeley: University of California Press, 1992), provided John Ashworth, David Brion Davis, and Thomas L. Haskell with the opportunity to engage one another on the relationship between capitalism and humanitarianism. As Christopher L. Brown demonstrates in *Moral Capital: Foundations of British Abolitionism* (2006), this debate among historians remains vibrant, and engagements with it have recently entered other areas of scholarship, such as in Baucom's *Specters of the Atlantic*.

2. See Mrs. Pringle's letter to the Society in Mary Prince, *History of Mary Prince*, 130–31. Prince's life story was published in England in 1831.

3. Consult Ramos's analysis of the emergence of the slave as a juridical subject in "*The Law Is Other*: Literature and the Constitution of the Juridical Subject in Nineteenth-Century Cuba." According to Jane G. Landers, it was loyalty to the Spanish crown that determined whether Indians and Africans possessed a legal personality. See her *Atlantic Creoles*, 7.

4. Baucom, *Specters of the Atlantic*, 208.

5. It should also be noted that proslavery advocates in Cuba promoted the idea that Africans were better off as slaves on the island than in their homelands. See, for example, Juan Bernardo O'Gavan's arguments in Torres-Cuevas and Reyes, *Esclavitud y sociedad*, 143–44. That any government or group should give credence to such arguments attests to the degree to which this racist paternalism had been commonplace.

6. Madden, *Address on Slavery in Cuba*, 3. Also see Madden, "Appendix 7: Laws for the Protection of Slaves in Cuba," 193.

7. Madden, Preface to *Poems by a Slave*, 37, hereafter cited as "Preface."

8. Benjamin, "Task of the Translator," 254.

9. Ibid., 257.

10. Ibid., 258.

11. Ibid., 254.

12. Ibid.

13. Ibid., 260.

14. Ibid.

15. Ibid., 261.

16. Molloy, "From Serf to Self," 54.

17. The son of an eminent Catholic manufacturer from Dublin, Madden was born in 1798. He studied medicine and became a doctor after several years of traveling and apprenticeships in Britain, France, and Italy. In 1828 he married Harriet T. Elmslie, the youngest daughter of an English proprietor of several estates in Jamaica, and in 1831 he joined the abolitionist cause and became an active member of the British Anti-Slavery Society. Given the degree to which abolitionism is associated with British and American Protestantism, it is worth investigating—as Sweeney expresses it—"Madden's liberal,

transnational *Catholic* assault on the pro-slavery stance of many first-generation Irish Americans." See Sweeney, "Atlantic Countercultures," 403. Madden attached the appendix, "Necessity of Separating the Irish in America from the Sin of Slavery," to his translation of Manzano's writings.

18. These and other biographical details are taken from Madden's memoirs, *The Memoirs from 1798 to 1886 of R. R. Madden,* which his son, Thomas More Madden, edited and published in 1891. Hereafter, I refer to this source as *Memoirs.*

19. Thomas More Madden, *Memoirs,* 62.

20. Ibid., 70.

21. Ibid., 71. Madden's memoirs cites this letter but does not indicate to whom it was written.

22. Ibid.

23. Ibid., 72.

24. According to the treaty of 1817, captains and ships' masters who were caught with contraband slave cargoes were to be tried, and if they were found guilty, sentenced to ten years of imprisonment in the Philippines. Their illegal cargo would be immediately declared free, thereby creating the juridical category of the *emancipados*—a class of Africans who were taken from captured slave ships—and the need for the office of superintendent, whose responsibility was to ensure that their status as free men, women, and children was maintained and protected in Cuba. The treaty also created mixed courts that were composed of an equal number of judges from England and Spain. For more details about this treaty as well as the history of Spanish and British relations leading up to it and beyond, consult Corwin, *Spain and the Abolition of Slavery,* 28–36.

25. Aware of the pressures that British and American abolitionists were bringing to bear on chattel slavery and the international slave trade, Cuban planters rushed to increase the number of slaves coming into Cuba. A similar phenomenon had occurred in Jamaica. English proprietors had been warned of the coming of abolition since 1788 and had taken measures to ensure their labor supply on the island. Jamaica, which had 200,000 slaves in 1787, doubled that number by 1807. See Corwin, *Spain and the Abolition of Slavery,* 26.

26. Thomas More Madden, *Memoirs,* 77. The slave barracks are called *barracones.* In Spanish, *bozal* refers to the recently arrived African slave, who was sometimes fitted with a muzzle or *bozal* in order to discipline him or her. The term was employed to distinguish the pure African from the black slave, or *negro criollo* who, like Manzano, was born and raised on the island. Among themselves, the slaves typically employed the term *negro de nación* to refer to an African-born slave.

27. In his memoirs, the complexity of this situation is ignored, so that in its place we find the following description of his stay in Havana: "Here, for upwards of three years, he continued to devote all the energies of his character to the battle of right against might, in the vindication of the cause of humanity and liberty which it was his privilege to maintain almost single-handed with the Cuban slave-traders, then supported by the Spanish authorities." See Thomas More Madden, *Memoirs,* 76.

28. Corwin, *Spain and the Abolition of Slavery,* 62.

29. Buxton's letter is dated October 23, 1835. A copy of it appears in Thomas More Madden, *Memoirs,* 203–204.

30. Ibid., 204.

31. Ibid.

32. Ibid., 77. This phrasing appears in Madden's report, "Conditions of Slaves in Cuba," which he appended to the portfolio of materials that he submitted to the Anti-Slavery Society. See Madden, "Appendix 6: Condition of Slaves in Cuba," 184.

33. Ibid., 67.

34. Ibid.

35. Davis, "What the Abolitionists Were Up Against," 23.

36. Madden, "Preface," 37.

37. Luis, *Literary Bondage*, 38.

38. Del Monte began to rethink his position in 1838 when his hopefulness for reform in Madrid had changed to fear and rage. See Andioc Torres, "Presentación," 2:xxxiv.

39. Without contradicting the aforesaid, it is also feasible that del Monte and the members of his circle could not fathom Manzano's academically incorrect Spanish as the proper basis on which to generate the conditions for literary sensibility between themselves and the abolitionist. If they considered academically correct Spanish as a marker of "civilization," then the decision to correct Manzano's writings must also be seen as their promotion of a purportedly civilizing sensibility over and above an appreciation for the difficulty and perseverance with which the poet-slave acquired the writing skills that he possessed at the time.

40. See Mullen, Introduction to *The Life and Poems of a Cuban Slave*, 9. The accusation is spelled out in Madden's pamphlet *A Letter to W. E. Channing, D.D. on the Subject of the Abuse of the Flag of the United States, in the Island of Cuba, and the Advantage Taken of Its Protection in Promoting the Slave Trade.*

41. The *Amistad* was a slave-trading vessel on which its human cargo of Africans, mostly from Sierra Leone, revolted as the vessel was navigating between Cuban ports on July 1, 1839. Forced to navigate east, the overpowered crew tricked the Africans into thinking that they were heading back to Africa and ended up near Montauk on Long Island. The ship was later towed to New London, Connecticut, and kept there until U.S. courts could decide whether the Africans who had been transported on board were property or free men. The *Amistad* affair rallied abolitionists on both sides of the Atlantic and brought pressure on the Spanish government. In 1841, the U.S. Supreme Court decided in favor of the Africans who, through the sale of their handicrafts, collective efforts of several organizations, and private donations, were repatriated.

42. Osagie, *Amistad Revolt*, 11–12.

43. Madden, *Address on Slavery in Cuba*, 1.

44. Kadish, "Translation in Context," 37.

45. De Man, "Autobiography as De-Facement," 69.

46. Suárez y Romero, Advertencia to *Francisco*, 3.

47. The antislavery portfolio that the abolitionist received from del Monte contained Manzano's *Apuntes autobiográficos* (Autobiographical notes) and thirteen of his poems; *Francisco*, Suárez y Romero's novel, and some letters that have been attributed to the young novelist; short prose and verse compositions by Tanco y Bosmeniel, Pedro José Morillas, José Zacarías González del Valle, and Rafael Matamorros y Téllez; and, finally, two separate interviews of del Monte that Madden undertook—the first on the state of religion in Cuba (November 1838) and the other on the slave trade with respect to the

island (September 1839). For more information about the contents of the portfolio, consult Luis, *Literary Bondage*, 36–37.

48. Henceforth, I refer to this book as *Poems and Life*. In all likelihood, the model for Madden's eclectic portfolio was the abolitionist Thomas Clarkson's influential publication of *An Essay on the Slavery and Commerce of the Human Species, Particularly the African, Translated from a Latin Dissertation* in 1786. Clarkson defended the mentioned dissertation in 1785 and received first prize for it at the University of Cambridge. The essay included footnotes citing classical authors in Latin, an imaginary scene in Africa, an imaginary conversation with an African, and eyewitness accounts of slavery's abuses. Even Clarkson's habit of referring to unnamed but trustworthy witnesses and sources was useful for Madden's portfolio. With its wealth of sworn testimonies, statistics, and documents, Clarkson's *Abstracts of the Abridgement of Evidence* (1791) also provided an important model. Madden dedicated his volume to Joseph Sturge, a "friend and faithful follower" of Clarkson.

49. Manzano's handwritten autobiography remained in del Monte's possession until his death in Madrid in 1853. Del Monte's son, Leonardo, passed the manuscript on to Vidal Morales, who eventually handed it over to the Biblioteca Nacional José Martí in Havana. See Luis, *Autobiografía del esclavo poeta y otros escritos*, 30.

50. Ibid., 30–31. For a detailed analysis of the changes made to Manzano's text, see 30–58.

51. De Man, "Autobiography as De-Facement," 71.

52. Madden, *Poems and Life*, 39.

53. Ibid.

54. Ibid.

55. Ibid., 39. According to Mullen, the "Spaniard" who reviewed Madden's translation was none other than Suárez y Romero. See Mullen's introduction to *The Life and Poems of a Cuban Slave*, 13.

56. Benjamin, "Task of the Translator," 260.

57. Ibid., 253.

58. Manzano, *Autobiography*, 59.

59. Davis, "What the Abolitionists Were Up Against," 23.

60. Manzano, *Autobiography*, 123.

61. Madden, "Life of the Negro Poet," 103.

62. Manzano, *Autobiography*, 125 and 127.

63. Madden, "Life of the Negro Poet," 103.

64. Brown, *Moral Capital*, 114–16.

65. Thomas, *Romanticism and Slave Narratives*, 201–203.

66. Ibid., 202–203. See Henry Louis Gates Jr.'s analysis of this kind of duplicity in Wheatley's "On Being Brought from Africa to America" in his *The Trials of Phillis Wheatley*, 87–90.

67. Thomas, *Romanticism and Slave Narratives*, 98.

68. Wordsworth, "To Toussaint L'Ouverture," lines 9–14.

69. Thomas, *Romanticism and Slave Narratives*, 92. Thomas explains that the gradual avoidance of references to abolitionism was due to the movement's loss of respectability after 1792, when William Pitt's government created a climate of fear and suspicion as it

attempted to deal with the challenges of the French Revolution and the radicalisms that
it was said to be exporting, such as parliamentary reform in Britain.

70. Madden, *Poems and Life,* 38.

71. Ibid., 37.

72. Almeida, "Translating a Slave's Life," paragraph 9.

73. Ibid.

74. Madden, "Appendix 5: Evils of the Cuban Slave-Trade," 176.

75. Continuing to draw inspiration for his poetry from the reports that he filed, Madden provides a more detailed description of the middle passage and the holds of slave
ships in ibid., 177–80.

76. Madden, "Appendix 7: Laws for the Protection of Slaves in Cuba," 195. Contradicting the language of the many in Cuba and America who "see no hardships in slavery," Madden writes in "Appendix 5: Evils of the Slave Trade": "What do these gentle-
men know of slavery? They eat and drink, no doubt, in the houses of the opulent planters
in the towns, and they reason on the strength of the goodness of their entertainments,
that the slaves of their hosts are treated like their guests" (180).

77. Madden describes the planters' moral alibi, stating that "even the miscreants in
Cuba, who are steeped to the very lips in slave-trade interests, foreigners and Spaniards,
admit that the traffic is wholly unjustifiable—they condemn it freely, but they pray you
to acquit their honour because the interests of the country require it to be carried on,
and they have a very favourable opinion of the profitableness of it." See "Appendix 5:
Evils of the Cuban Slave-Trade," 178.

78. Madden, "Appendix 6: Conditions of Slaves in Cuba," 182.

79. The collection of Manzano's published poems that Madden translated included,
"A la muerte" (To death), "A la calumnia" (To calumny), "Oda a la religión" (Religion.
An Ode), "Treinta años" (Thirty years), "La cucuyera" (The cucuya, or firefly), "Al reloj adelantado" (To the clock that runs fast), and "Un sueño. A mi Segundo hermano"
(The dream. Addressed to my younger brother). Manzano published two collections of
poems well before del Monte launched his literary circle and Madden arrived in Cuba.
One of his unpublished poems, "La visión del poeta compuesta en un ingenio de fabricar
azúcar" (The poet's vision, composed in a sugar factory), dramatically juxtaposes the
melancholy consciousness of subjugation and the poetic voice's transportation to a neoclassical idyll and merits further study.

80. The citations of Manzano's poems in Spanish are taken from Luis, *Autobiografía,*
135–99; Madden's translations are to be found in *Poems and Life,* 110–23. The translations
of Manzano's verses in parentheses are mine.

81. Benjamin, "Task of the Translator," 253.

82. Madden, "Preface," 37.

83. My translation.

84. Madden included in the index an interview (probably with del Monte) on the
state of religion in Cuba, an argument (supported with research by authorities within
the Catholic church) for the Irish to refrain from supporting slavery, and a brief reas-
sessment of Bartolomé de Las Casas, the sixteenth-century Spanish critic of the enslavement and genocide of indigenous communities in the Americas.

85. My translation.

4. FREEDOM WITHOUT EQUALITY

1. "Thomas Jefferson to John Holmes," http://www.loc.gov/exhibits/jefferson/159 .html.

2. It is worth noting that Jefferson, in the same letter, also linked the emancipation of slaves in the United States to their expatriation.

3. Barreda, *Black Protagonist*, 38.

4. Fischer, *Modernity Disavowed*, 114–20.

5. Barreda, *Black Protagonist*, 45.

6. Draper, "Voluntad de intelectual," 107; my translation.

7. Casanova-Marengo, *El intersticio de la colonia*, 31.

8. Anselmo Suárez y Romero to Domingo del Monte, Ingenio Surinam, Güines, July 7, 1839 in *Domingo del Monte: centon epistolario*, 2:379.

9. In Cuba, the use of black vernacular in the literary field would not become an important phenomenon until the 1920s and '30s with the emergence of *afrocubanismo*. Nicolás Guillén's *Motivos de son*, a collection of eight black vernacular poems, still managed to shock the island's literary establishment in 1930 when they were published in the influential daily *Diario de la Marina*. It is worth noting that the new appreciation for Afro-Cuban contributions to national culture by an influential literary avant-garde minority probably helped to create the climate for interest in Manzano's autobiography, which was published for the first time in Cuba in 1937, almost a century after he wrote it.

10. Miller, "Rebeldía narrativa," 422–26.

11. Tanco y Bosmeniel, *Petrona y Rosalía*, 17; the translations of this text are mine.

12. Ibid., 46.

13. Ibid., 47.

14. Ibid., 48.

15. Gómez de Avellaneda, *Sab*, 104. The translations of the text are mine.

16. Sommer, *Foundational Fictions*, 123.

17. Casanova-Marengo, *El intersticio de la colonia*, 57; my translation.

18. I have taken the equivalency of twelve thousand *arrobas* as thirty thousand pounds from Nina M. Scott's translation of Avellaneda's novel in Sab *and* Autobiography, 29.

19. Moreno Fraginals, *El ingenio*, 302.

20. Gómez de Avellaneda, *Sab*, 121. As in *Petrona y Rosalía*, the narrative voice in *Sab* saves its harshest criticism for the young patrician when Carlota realizes that Otway's soul was not superior, privileged, nor rich in sentiment and emotions. See Gómez de Avellaneda, *Sab*, 133.

21. Ibid., 106.

22. It would have been much more customary for a slave to be given the responsibilities of the *contramayoral*, or black foreman, who was, García Rodríguez reports, "comparable to a pivotal pulley, enjoying the trust of his superiors but, at the same time, counting on the acquiescence of the plantation slave community." See García Rodríguez, *Voices of the Enslaved*, 24.

23. *Sab* is the most sophisticated novel to have been written about Cuba at that time. In my analysis, I have mainly concentrated on the protagonist's racial vagueness as an ideological sign. However, in addition to her autobiography and other writings, Avel-

laneda's novel has also inspired a current of studies that examine her proto-feminist stance and thinking. See, for example, Sommer's list of such studies in her *Foundational Fictions*, 355–56n1. Abundant connections between abolitionism and the women's suffrage movement have been made in Anglo-American scholarship, but Avellaneda's writings are the only ones, to my knowledge, that draw parallels between slavery and the limited rights of bourgeois women in Cuba and Spain.

24. In addition to an Oedipal reading of the relationship between mother and son in *Petrona y Rosalía* and, especially, in *Francisco,* an analysis of the suppression of this complex in the literary circle's didactic narratives would be worthwhile. According to Ricardo, the grave crime for which Francisco must be mercilessly punished is for having impregnated Dorotea, who is his mother's prized personal slave.

25. Suárez y Romero, *Francisco,* 15. The translations of quotations from this novel are mine.

26. As the transcriber of Manzano's autobiography into standard written Spanish, Suárez y Romero was more familiar with the poet's account than were the majority of the circle's members. His novel borrows freely from the autobiography to the extent that he gives Francisco Manzano's nickname of "Pico de oro" (Golden beak) and has the protagonist mention his affection for Doña Dolores Mendizábal. See Suárez y Romero, *Francisco,* 16 and 47. The novelist also creates his protagonist by drawing on Manzano's detailed descriptions of melancholy.

27. Ibid., 41. The Cuban peasant, often associated with tobacco production and a particular form of rural life and autochthonous music, is known as a *guajiro.*

28. Ibid., 12–13.

29. Ibid., 87.

30. See, in particular, the first four chapters of Kutzinski's *Sugar's Secrets.*

31. Anselmo Suárez y Romero to Domingo del Monte, Ingenio Surinam, April 11, 1839, in *Domingo del Monte: centón epistolario,* 2:346; my translation.

32. Ibid., 2:347.

33. Moreno Fraginals, *El ingenio,* 298.

34. Anselmo Suárez y Romero to Domingo del Monte, Surinam Plantation, Güines, July 7, 1839, in *Domingo del Monte: centón epistolario,* 2:379; my translation.

35. Ibid., 2:378.

36. Suárez y Romero, *Francisco,* 7.

37. Ibid., 42.

38. Ibid., 101–102.

39. Ibid., 8, 38, and 101–102.

40. At this juncture, the Creole bourgeoisie did not perceive its ambivalent attitude toward political autonomy as a shortcoming but as the flexibility that it required in order to achieve its immediate goals. For example, the colonial authority's violent reaction to the alleged Escalera conspiracy achieved important socioeconomic gains for the Creole bourgeoisie as well as for its local Spanish rival: it rid the island of abolitionist infiltrations, imprisoned some reformists or drove them into exile, and substantially weakened the wealth and incipient political aspirations of the free black and mulatto communities. Slavery and the wealth that it provided would thus remain intact.

41. See Fischer, *Modernity Disavowed,* 118–19.

42. Nyquist, *Arbitrary Rule,* 366.

43. García Rodríguez, *Voices of the Enslaved,* 47. I cite from the Slave Code or "Royal Decree and Instructional Circular for the Indies on the Education, Treatment, and Work Regimen of Slaves" of May 31, 1789, and from the excerpt of the 1842 Slave Code that García Rodríguez provides in her book.

44. Ibid., 50.

45. Ibid., 51–52.

46. Ibid., 55.

47. Ibid., 62.

48. Ibid., 57–58.

49. Ibid., 63.

50. Ibid., 66 and 68.

51. Ibid., 71.

52. Ibid., 69.

53. Ibid., 68.

54. García Rodríguez reports that greater awareness of slaves' rights, especially with respect to the master's ability to transfer ownership of his slaves, began in the 1830s. By the 1860s, a combination of the slaves' numerous grievances and favorable public opinion resolved this issue, recognizing the slaves' claims. See García Rodríguez, *Voices of the Enslaved,* 42.

55. Ibid., 42–43.

56. Ibid., 66.

57. Ibid.

58. Nevertheless, the maximum of twenty-five strokes per session was often exceeded, which means that the physical distance from the metropolis that the slave owners cited as the reason why distorted and misinterpreted information about the treatment of slaves often reached the monarch's ear facilitated the masters' regular noncompliance with various aspects of the slave codes. See Paquette, *Sugar Is Made with Blood,* 67.

59. For an analysis of the Aponte conspiracy and the book of propaganda that belonged to him, see Fischer, *Modernity Disavowed,* 41–56.

60. Ibid., 44.

61. Landers, *Atlantic Creoles,* 148.

62. Landers's study of Cuba's black militiamen provides several examples of respected figures who directly experienced the contradiction between the upward mobility that participation in military campaigns provided and the insulting treatment that they received at the hands of Cuba's local officials. These militiamen's ample experience in revolutionary wars, including Spain's struggle against Napoleon, and the support that they gave to the Liberal Constitution of 1812 that the embattled Spanish government established in Cádiz provided these free blacks and mulattoes with a broad, transatlantic view of various struggles for freedom. She reports that the three thousand men of color who had joined Cuba's militia by 1770 constituted more than a quarter of the island's armed forces and that, according to the 1776 census, two-thirds of all free men of color in Havana between the ages of fifteen and fifty belonged to the militia. Ibid., 140–42.

63. Paquette, *Sugar Is Made with Blood,* 126.

64. Ibid., 36 and 39.

65. Benítez-Rojo, *Repeating Island,* 122.

66. García Rodríguez, *Voices of the Enslaved,* 15.

67. Manzano, *Autobiografía,* 339.

68. García Rodríguez, *Voices of the Enslaved,* 21.

69. Moreno Fraginals, *El ingenio,* 329; my translation.

70. Gómez de Avellaneda, *Sab,* 168–69.

71. Ibid., 206.

72. Ibid., 206–207.

73. Paquette, *Sugar Is Made with Blood,* 70.

74. According to Paquette, the 1841 census revealed that the slave population was 436,495 or 43.3% of the population and that the white population numbered 418,291 or 41.5% of the population. Ibid., 298n43.

75. Paquette reports that free blacks and mulattoes entered the colony's skilled trades "out of all proportion to their numbers" and that they "literally served whites from the womb to the grave." Ibid., 39.

76. The first half of the nineteenth century saw increasingly rigid boundaries between whites and free people of color in realms such as education, and the state supported the worsening of these relations. Ibid., 113 and 119.

77. Ibid., 179.

78. Ibid., 249.

79. Ibid., 209–11.

80. Fradera, *Colonias para después de un imperio,* 282.

81. Murray, *Odious Commerce,* 173.

82. Paquette, *Sugar Is Made with Blood,* 240.

83. Murray, *Odious Commerce,* 177.

84. Ibid., 173.

85. It is worth pointing out that it was his tense relationship with British merchants in Cuba that caused Turnbull to be removed from his consular post. Ibid., 140.

86. Ibid., 157.

87. Ibid., 152–53.

88. Paquette, *Sugar Is Made with Blood,* 249.

89. Ibid.

90. Del Monte to Everett, June 28, 1844, cited in Paquette, ibid.

91. Ibid., 226.

92. Cited in Paquette, ibid.

93. Ibid., 220–21.

94. Murray, *Odious Commerce,* 174.

95. Reported by Dr. Wurdemann of South Carolina and cited in Paquette, *Sugar Is Made with Blood,* 227.

96. Ibid., 220.

97. Ibid., 227.

98. Suárez y Romero, *Francisco,* 12–13.

99. Anselmo Suárez y Romero to Domingo del Monte, Ingenio Surinam, April 11, 1839, in *Domingo del Monte: centón epistolario,* 2:346.

100. R. R. Madden, "The Sugar Estate," I.14.

101. Paquette, *Sugar Is Made with Blood,* 118.

102. Ibid., 215.

103. Ibid., 256–57.

104. Fischer, *Modernity Disavowed,* 77–84.

105. Paquette, *Sugar Is Made with Blood,* 260.

106. Ibid., 261.

107. Scarry, *Body in Pain,* 14.

108. Paquette, "Appendix II: Slave Regulations of 1844," 273.

109. Ibid., 274.

110. Murray, *Odious Commerce,* 171.

111. Before being expelled from Cuba, Turnbull provided Lord Palmerston with a list of nineteen Creoles with whom he had enjoyed regular contact. They represented the most important figures of Cuba's intellectual and literary elite and included del Monte, José de Luz y Caballero, Félix Tanco y Bosmeniel, Cirilo Villaverde, Manuel de Castro Palomino, Ramón de Palma, José Zacarías González del Valle, José Luis Alfonso, and others. They ranged in age between twenty-four and forty-five and were mostly lawyers by training, with many of them having been students at the San Carlos Seminary where Félix Varela had taught. See Paquette, *Sugar Is Made with Blood,* 176.

112. Lewis Galanes, *Poesías de J. F. Manzano,* 33.

113. Murray, *Odious Commerce,* 179.

114. In *Insurgent Cuba,* Ada Ferrer demonstrates how a powerful language of antiracism emerged during Cuba's first war of independence and intensified in the years after the abolition of slavery in Cuba (1886) and the beginning of the second war of independence in 1895.

115. See my "Against 'Library-Shelf Races': José Martí's Critique of Excessive Imitation," in *Geomodernisms: Race, Modernism Modernity,* ed. Laura Doyle and Laura Winkiel (Bloomington: Indiana University Press, 2005), 151–69.

EPILOGUE

1. McGary, "Resistance and Slavery," 46.

2. Barnett, *Empire of Humanity,* 7. In a history of occidental humanitarianism in which he tries to steer clear of romantic and cynical readings of humanitarianism, Michael Barnett assigns abolitionism to the first period of this history, which he calls "imperial humanitarianism" and which he designates as running from the late eighteenth century to World War II (7). According to him, the fundamental paradox of humanitarianism is that it derives from "the best tradition of emancipatory ethics" at the same time that it operates through interventions that presume the dominance of and governance by humanitarians (11–12).

3. Scott, *Conscripts of Modernity,* 210.

4. Bongie, *Friends and Enemies,* 268.

5. Aching, "No Need for an Apology: Fanon's Untimely Critique of Political Consciousness," *South Atlantic Quarterly* 112, no. 1 (2013): 23–38.

6. Richard Robert Madden, *Address on Slavery in Cuba,* 1.

7. Lee, *Slavery and the Romantic Imagination,* 32.

BIBLIOGRAPHY

Aching, Gerard. "Against 'Library-Shelf Races': José Martí's Critique of Excessive Imitation." In *Geomodernisms: Race, Modernism Modernity*, ed. Laura Doyle and Laura Winkiel, 151–69. Bloomington: Indiana University Press, 2005.

———. "No Need for an Apology: Fanon's Untimely Critique of Political Consciousness." *South Atlantic Quarterly* 112, no. 1 (2013): 23–38.

Almeida, Joselyn. "Translating a Slave's Life: Richard Robert Madden and the Post-Abolition Trafficking of Juan Manzano's *Poems by a Slave in the Island of Cuba*." In "Circulations: Romanticism and the Black Atlantic," ed. Paul Youngquist and Frances Botkin, special issue, *Romantic Circles* (October 2011). Accessed November 24, 2013. http://www.rc.umd.edu/praxis/circulations/HTML/praxis.2011.almeida.html.

Alonso, Carlos. *The Burden of Modernity: The Rhetoric of Cultural Discourse in Spanish America*. Oxford: Oxford University Press, 1998.

Andioc Torres, Sophie. "Ensayo introductorio: Cartas para la historia de Cuba." In *Domingo del Monte: centón epistolario*, vol. 1, 1–44. La Habana: Imagen Contemporánea, 2002.

———. Presentación to *Domingo del Monte: centón epistolario*, vol. 2, v–xxxiv. La Habana: Imagen Contemporánea, 2002.

Andrews, William L. "The Representation of Slavery and the Rise of Afro-American Literary Realism, 1865–1920." In *African American Autobiography: A Collection of Critical Essays*, ed. William L. Andrews, 77–89. Englewood Cliffs, N.J.: Prentice Hall, 1993.

Barcia, Manuel. "Fighting with the Enemy's Weapons: The Usage of the Colonial Legal Framework by Nineteenth-Century Cuban Slaves." *Atlantic Studies* 3, no. 2 (2006): 159–81.

Barnett, Michael. *Empire of Humanity: A History of Humanitarianism*. Ithaca, N.Y.: Cornell University Press, 2011.

Barreda, Pedro. *The Black Protagonist in the Cuban Novel*. Translated by Page Bancroft. Amherst: University of Massachusetts Press, 1979.

Basterra, Gabriela. *Seductions of Fate: Tragic Subjectivity, Ethics, Politics*. New York: Palgrave Macmillan, 2004.

Baucom, Ian. *Specters of the Atlantic: Finance Capital, Slavery, and the Philosophy of History.* Durham, N.C.: Duke University Press, 2005.

Bauer, Ralph, and José Antonio Mazzoti. *Creole Subjects in the Colonial Americas: Empires, Texts, Identities.* Chapel Hill: University of North Carolina Press, 2009.

Benítez-Rojo, Antonio. *The Repeating Island: The Caribbean and the Postmodern Perspective.* Translated by James E. Maraniss. Durham, N.C.: Duke University Press, 1992.

Benjamin, Walter. "The Task of the Translator." In *Theories of Translation: An Anthology of Essays From Dryden to Derrida,* ed. Rainer Schulte and John Biguenet, 71–82. Chicago: University of Chicago Press, 1992.

Berlin, Isaiah. "Two Concepts of Liberty." In *Liberty,* 166–217. Ed. Henry Hardy. Oxford: Oxford University Press, 2002.

Bernasconi, Robert. "Will the Real Kant Please Stand Up: The Challenge of Enlightenment Racism to the Study of the History of Philosophy." *Radical Philosophy* 117 (2003): 13–22.

Bernier, Celeste-Marie. "From Fugitive Slave to Fugitive Abolitionist: The Oratory of Frederick Douglass and the Emerging Heroic Slave Tradition." *Atlantic Studies* 3, no. 2 (2006): 201–24.

Blackburn, Robin. *The Overthrow of Colonial Slavery 1776–1848.* London: Verso, 2000.

Bongie, Chris. *Friends and Enemies: The Scribal Politics of Post/Colonial Literature.* Liverpool: Liverpool University Press, 2008.

Bontemps, Alex. *The Punished Self: Surviving Slavery in the Colonial South.* Ithaca, N.Y.: Cornell University Press, 2001.

Brown, Christopher Leslie. *Moral Capital: Foundations of British Abolitionism.* Chapel Hill: University of North Carolina Press, 2006.

Buck-Morss, Susan. "Hegel and Haiti." In *Hegel, Haiti, and Universal History,* 21–75. Pittsburgh: University of Pittsburgh Press, 2009.

Bueno, Salvador. *La crítica literaria cubana del siglo XIX.* La Habana: Editorial Letras Cubanas, 1979.

———. *Las ideas literarias de Domingo Delmonte.* La Habana: Comisión Nacional Cubana de la UNESCO, 1954.

Butler, Judith. *The Psychic Life of Power: Theories in Subjection.* Stanford, Calif.: Stanford University Press, 1997.

Casanova-Marengo, Ilia. *El intersticio de la colonia: Ruptura y mediación en la narrativa antiesclavista cubana.* Madrid: Iberoamericana/Vervuert, 2002.

Castañeda, Eduardo. "Francisco: El héroe y el abolicionismo reformista." Introduction to Anselmo Suárez y Romero, *Francisco, el ingenio o las delicias del campo,* 9–25. Colección Biblioteca Básica de Autores Cubanos. La Habana: Instituto del Libro, 1970.

Corwin, Arthur F. *Spain and the Abolition of Slavery in Cuba, 1817–1886.* Austin: University of Texas Press, 1967.

Davis, David Brion. "The Preservation of English Liberty I." In *The Antislavery Debate: Capitalism and Abolitionism as a Problem in Historical Interpretation,* ed. Thomas Bender, 65–103. Berkeley: University of California Press, 1992.

———. *The Problem of Slavery in the Age of Revolution.* Ithaca, N.Y.: Cornell University Press, 1975.

———. "What the Abolitionists Were Up Against." In *The Antislavery Debate: Capitalism and Abolitionism as a Problem in Historical Interpretation*, ed. Thomas Bender, 17–26. Berkeley: University of California Press, 1992.

Del Monte, Domingo. *Domingo del Monte: centón epistolario*, vol. 1, ed. Sophie Andioc Torres. Colección Biblioteca de Clásicos Cubanos. La Habana: Imagen Contemporánea, 2002.

———. *La isla de Cuba tal cual está*. New York: Whittaker, 1836.

De Man, Paul. "Autobiography as De-Facement." In *The Rhetoric of Romanticsm*, 67–81. New York: Columbia University Press, 1984.

Douglass, Frederick. *Narrative of the Life of Frederick Douglass: An American Slave*. New York: Dell Publishing, 1997.

Draper, Susana. "Voluntad de intelectual: Juan Francisco Manzano entre las redes de un humanismo sin derechos." *Chasqui* 30, no. 2 (2001): 102–15.

Du Bois, W. E. B. "Of Our Spiritual Strivings." In *The Souls of Black Folk*, 7–15. New York: Vintage Books, 1990.

Elkins, Stanley. *Slavery: A Problem in American Institutional and Intellectual Life*. Chicago: Chicago University Press, 1976.

Equiano, Olaudah. *The Interesting Narrative of the Life of Olaudah Equiano; Written By Himself*. Ed. Robert J. Allison. Boston: Bedford Books, 1995.

Escott, Paul D. *Slavery Remembered: A Record of Twentieth-Century Slave Narratives*. Chapel Hill: University of North Carolina Press, 1979.

Fischer, Sibylle. *Modernity Disavowed: Haiti and the Cultures of Slavery in the Age of Revolution*. Durham, N.C.: Duke University Press, 2004.

Fradera, Josep M. *Colonias para después de un imperio*. Barcelona: Ediciones Bellaterra, 2005.

Franco, José Luciano. "Juan Francisco Manzano, el poeta esclavo y su tiempo." In Juan Francisco Manzano, *Autobiografía, cartas y versos de Juan Francisco Manzano*, 9–32. Cuadernos de Historia Habanera. La Habana: Municipio de la Habana, 1937.

Freud, Sigmund. "Mourning and Melancholia." In *The Freud Reader*, 584–89. Ed. Peter Gay. New York: W. W. Norton, 1995.

García Rodríguez, Gloria. *Voices of the Enslaved in Nineteenth-Century Cuba*. Foreword by Ada Ferrer. Translated by Nancy L. Westrate. Chapel Hill: University of North Carolina Press, 2011.

Gates, Henry Louis, Jr. "James Gronniosaw and the Trope of the Talking Book." *Southern Review* 22 (1986): 252–72.

———. *The Trials of Phillis Wheatley: America's First Black Poet and Her Encounter with the Founding Fathers*. New York: Basic Civitas Books, 2003.

Gilroy, Paul. *The Black Atlantic: Modernity and Double Consciousness*. Cambridge, Mass.: Harvard University Press, 1993.

Gomariz, José. *Colonialismo e independencia cultural: La narración del artista e intelectual hispanoamericano del siglo XIX*. Madrid: Editorial Verbum, 2005.

Gómez de Avellaneda, Gertrudis. *Sab*. Ed. José Servera. Madrid: Cátedra, 1997.

———. *Sab and Autobiography*. Trans. and ed. Nina M. Scott. Austin: University of Texas Press, 1993.

González del Valle, José Zacarías. *La vida literaria en Cuba (1836–1840)*. La Habana: Publicaciones de la Secretaría de Educación, 1938.

González-Stephan, Beatriz. *Fundaciones: canon, historia y cultura nacional: La historiografía literaria del liberalismo hispanoamericano del siglo XIX*. Madrid: Iberoamericana, 2002.

Gutiérrez Alea, Tomás. *La última cena*. DVD. New Yorker, 2007.

Habermas, Jürgen. "Hegel's Concept of Modernity." In *The Philosophical Discourse of Modernity: Twelve Lectures*, 23–44. Translated by Frederick Lawrence. Cambridge, Mass.: MIT Press, 1987.

Haskell, Thomas L. "Capitalism and the Origins of the Humanitarian Sensibility, Part 1." In *The Antislavery Debate: Capitalism and Abolitionism as a Problem in Historical Interpretation*, ed. Thomas Bender, 107–35. Berkeley: University of California Press, 1992.

Hegel, G. W. F. *Phenomenology of Spirit*. Translated by A. V. Miller. Oxford: Oxford University Press, 1977.

———. *The Philosophy of History*. Mineola, N.Y.: Dover Publications, 2004.

Henke, Lewis. *All Mankind Is One*. De Kalb: Northern Illinois University Press, 1974.

Hilton, Boyd. *The Age of Atonement: The Influence of Evangelicalism on Social and Economic Thought, 1785–1865*. Oxford: Oxford University Press, 2001.

Hochschild, Adam. *Bury the Chains: Prophets and Rebels in the Fight to Free an Empire's Slaves*. New York: Mariner, 2006.

Hugo, Victor. *Bug-Jargal*. Trans. and ed. Chris Bongie. Peterborough, Ontario: Broadview Press, 2004.

James, C. L. R. *The Black Jacobins: Toussaint L'Ouverture and the San Domingo Revolution*. 2nd ed. New York: Vintage Books, 1989.

Jameson, Fredric. *A Singular Modernity: Essay on the Ontology of the Present*. London: Verso, 2002.

Jefferson, Thomas. "Thomas Jefferson to John Holmes." Monticello, April 22, 1820. http://www.loc.gov/exhibits/jefferson/159.html.

Johnson, Sarah E. *The Fear of French Negroes: Transcolonial Collaboration in the Revolutionary Americas*. Berkeley: University of California Press, 2012.

Kadish, Doris Y. "Translation in Context." In *Translating Slavery: Gender and Race in French Women's Writing, 1873–1823*, ed. Doris Y. Kadish and Françoise Massardier-Kenney, 26–61. Kent, Ohio: Kent State University Press, 1994.

Keene, Edward. *Beyond the Anarchical Society: Grotius, Colonialism and Order in World Politics*. Cambridge: Cambridge University Press, 2002.

Kojève, Alexandre. *Introduction to the Reading of Hegel: Lectures on the* Phenomenology of Spirit. Ed. Allan Bloom. Trans. James H. Nichols, Jr. Ithaca, N.Y.: Cornell University Press, 1969.

Kutzinski, Vera M. *Sugar's Secrets: Race and the Erotics of Cuban Nationalism*. Charlottesville: University of Virginia Press, 1993.

Landers, Jane G. *Atlantic Creoles in the Age of Revolutions*. Cambridge, Mass.: Harvard University Press, 2010.

Lawson, Bill E. "Oppression and Slavery." In Howard McGary and Bill E. Lawson, *Between Slavery and Freedom: Philosophy and American Slavery*, 1–15. Bloomington: Indiana University Press, 1992.

Leante, César. "Dos obras antiesclavistas cubanas." *Revista Iberoamericana* 227, no. 4 (1976): 175–88.

Lee, Debbie. *Slavery and the Romantic Imagination*. Philadelphia: University of Pennsylvania Press, 2002.

Lewis Galanes, Adriana. *Poesías de J. F. Manzano, esclavo en la isla de Cuba*. Madrid: Editorial Betania, 1991.

Li, Stephanie. *Something Akin to Freedom: The Choice of Bondage in Narratives by African American Women*. Albany: State University of New York Press, 2010.

Lively, Adam. *Masks: Blackness, Race and the Imagination*. Oxford: Oxford University Press, 2000.

Luis, William. Introduction to Juan Francisco Manzano, *Autobiografía del esclavo poeta y otros escritos*. ed. William Luis, 13–69. Madrid: Iberoamericana, 2007.

———. *Literary Bondage: Slavery in Cuban Narrative*. Austin: University of Texas Press, 1990.

———. "Nicolás Azcárate's Antislavery Notebook and the Unpublished Poems of the Slave Juan Francisco Manzao." *Revista de Estudios Hispánicos* 28 (1994): 331–51.

Madden, Richard Robert. *Address on Slavery in Cuba Presented to the Anti-Slavery Convention by R. R. Madden, Esq., M.D.* London: Johnston & Barrett, 1840.

———. "Appendix 3: Necessity of Separating the Irish in America from the Sin of Slavery." In *The Life and Poems of a Cuban Slave*, ed. Edward J. Mullen, 150–67. Hamden, Conn.: Archon Books, 1981.

———. "Appendix 5: Evils of the Cuban Slave-Trade." In *The Life and Poems of a Cuban Slave*, ed. Edward J. Mullen, 176–81. Hamden, Conn.: Archon Books, 1981.

———. "Appendix 6: Conditions of Slaves in Cuba." In *The Life and Poems of a Cuban Slave*, ed. Edward J. Mullen, 182–92. Hamden, Conn.: Archon Books, 1981.

———. "Appendix 7: Laws for the Protection of Slaves in Cuba." In *The Life and Poems of a Cuban Slave*, ed. Edward J. Mullen, 193–205. Hamden, Conn.: Archon Books, 1981.

———. *A Letter to W. E. Channing, D.D. on the Subject of the Abuse of the Flag of the United States, in the Island of Cuba, and the Advantage Taken of Its Protection in Promoting the Slave Trade*. Boston: Ticknor, 1839.

———. "Life of the Negro Poet." In *The Life and Poems of a Cuban Slave*. ed. Edward J. Mullen, 80–107. Hamden, Conn.: Archon Books, 1981.

———. Preface to Juan Francisco Manzano, *Poems by a Slave in the Island of Cuba, Recently Liberated; Translated from the Spanish by R. R. Madden, M.D. . . .*, in *The Life and Poems of a Cuban Slave*, ed. Edward J. Mullen, 37–39. Hamden, Conn.: Archon Books, 1981.

———. "The Slave-Trade Merchant; A Poem, Descriptive of the Cuban Speculators in Stolen Men." In *The Life and Poems of a Cuban Slave*, ed. Edward J. Mullen, 41–51. Hamden, Conn.: Archon Books, 1981.

———. "The Sugar Estate; A Poem, Illustrative of Life and Death in Cuban Slavery." In *The Life and Poems of a Cuban Slave*, ed. Edward J. Mullen, 53–77. Hamden, Conn.: Archon Books, 1981.

Madden, Thomas More, ed. *The Memoirs from 1798 to 1886 of R. R. Madden*. London: Ward and Downey, 1891.

Manzano, Juan Francisco. *Autobiografía, cartas y versos de Juan Fco. Manzano.* Intro.
   José L. Franco. Cuadernos de Historia Habanera. La Habana: Municipio de La Ha-
   bana, 1937.
———. *Autobiografía del esclavo poeta y otros escritos.* Ed. William Luis. Madrid:
   Iberoamericana, 2007.
———. *Autobiography of a Slave / Autobiografía de un esclavo.* Intro. Ivan A. Schulman
   and trans. Evelyn Picon Garfield. Detroit: Wayne State University Press, 1996.
Martí, José. "My Race." In *José Martí: Selected Writings,* ed. and trans. Esther Allen,
   318–21. New York: Penguin, 2002.
———. "Our America." In *José Martí: Selected Writings,* ed. and trans. Esther Allen,
   288–96. New York: Penguin, 2002.
Mazlish, Bruce. *Civilization and Its Contents.* Stanford, Calif.: Stanford University Press,
   2004.
McBride, Dwight A. *Impossible Witnesses: Truth, Abolitionism, and Slave Testimony.* New
   York: New York University Press, 2001.
McDowell, Deborah E. "Making Frederick Douglass and the Afro-American Narrative
   Tradition." In *African American Autobiography: A Collection of Critical Essays,* ed. Wil-
   liam L. Andrews. Englewood Cliffs, N.J.: Prentice Hall, 1993.
McGary, Howard. "Paternalism and Slavery." In Howard McGary and Bill E. Lawson,
   Between Slavery and Freedom: Philosophy and American Slavery, 16–34. Bloomington:
   Indiana University Press, 1992.
———. "Resistance and Slavery." In Howard McGary and Bill E. Lawson, *Between
   Slavery and Freedom: Philosophy and American Slavery,* 35–54. Bloomington: Indiana
   University Press, 1992.
McGary, Howard, and Bill E. Lawson. "Philosophy and American Slavery: An Introduc-
   tion." In *Between Slavery and Freedom: Philosophy and American Slavery,* xvii–xxv.
   Bloomington: Indiana University Press, 1992.
Miller, Marilyn. "Rebeldía narrativa, resistencia poética y expresión 'libre' en Juan Fran-
   cisco Manzano." *Revista Iberoamericana* 71, no. 211 (2005): 417–36.
Molloy, Sylvia. "From Serf to Self: the Autobiography of Juan Francisco Manzano." In
   At Face Value: Autobiographical Writing in Spanish America, 36–54. Cambridge: Cam-
   bridge University Press, 1991.
Moreno Fraginals, Manuel. *El ingenio: complejo económico social cubano del azúcar.* Bar-
   celona: Editorial Crítica, 2001.
Mullen, Edward J. Introduction to *The Life and Poems of a Cuban Slave,* 1–40. Trans. and
   ed. Richard Robert Madden. Hamden, Conn.: Archon Books, 1981.
Murray, David. *Odious Commerce: Britain, Spain and the Abolition of the Cuban Slave
   Trade.* Cambridge: Cambridge University Press, 2002.
Muthu, Sankar. *Enlightenment against Empire.* Princeton, N.J.: Princeton University
   Press, 2003.
Nyquist, Mary. *Arbitrary Rule: Slavery, Tyranny, and the Power of Life and Death.* Chicago:
   University of Chicago Press, 2013.
Oliver, Kelly. *The Colonization of Psychic Space: A Psychoanalytical Social Theory of Op-
   pression.* Minneapolis: University of Minnesota Press, 2004.

Osagie, Iyunolu Folayan. *The Amistad Revolt: Memory, Slavery, and the Politics of Identity in the United States and Sierra Leone.* Athens: University of Georgia Press, 2000.

Otero, Lisandro. "Delmonte y la cultura de la sacarocracia." *Revista Iberoamericana* 56, no. 150–53 (1990): 723–31.

Pagden, Anthony. *The Fall of Natural Man: The American Indian and the Origins of Comparative Ethnology.* Cambridge: Cambridge University Press, 1986.

Paquette, Robert L. "Appendix II: Slave Regulations of 1844." In *Sugar Is Made with Blood: The Conspiracy of La Escalera and the Conflict Between Empires over Slavery in Cuba,* 273–74. Middletown, Conn.: Wesleyan University Press, 1988.

———. *Sugar Is Made with Blood: The Conspiracy of La Escalera and the Conflict between Empires over Slavery in Cuba.* Middletown, Conn.: Wesleyan University Press, 1988.

Patterson, Orlando. *Slavery and Social Death: A Comparative Study.* Cambridge, Mass: Harvard University Press, 1982.

Pérez de la Riva, Juan. "Introduction." *Correspondencia reservada del Capitán General Don Miguel Tacón, 1834–1836.* La Habana: Consejo Nacional de Cultura, 1963.

Prince, Mary. *The History of Mary Prince: A West Indian Slave; Related by Herself.* Ed. and intro. Moira Ferguson. Ann Arbor: University of Michigan Press, 1997.

Ramos, Julio. "Cuerpo, lengua, subjetividad." *Revista de crítica literaria latinoamericana* 19 (1993): 225–37.

———. *Desencuentros de la modernidad en América Latina: Literatura y política en el siglo XIX.* México: Fondo de Cultura Económica, 1989.

———. "*The Law Is Other*: Literature and the Constitution of the Juridical Subject in Nineteenth-Century Cuba." *Annals of Scholarship* 11, no. 1/2 (1996): 1–35.

Rodríguez, Ileana. "Romanticismo literario y liberalismo reformista: El grupo de Domingo Delmonte." *Caribbean Studies* 20, no. 1 (1980): 35–56.

Rojas, Rafael. *Isla sin fin: contribución a la crítica del nacionalismo cubano.* Miami: Ediciones Universal, 1998.

Saco, José Antonio. "Análisis por don José Antonio Saco de una obra sobre el Brasil, intitulada *Notices of Brazil in 1828 and 1829 by Rev. Walsh, author of a Journey from Constantinople, etc.*" In *Esclavitud y Sociedad: Notas y documentos para la historia de la esclavitud negra en Cuba,* ed. Eduardo Torres-Cuevas and Eusebio Reyes, 171–74. La Habana: Editorial de Ciencias Sociales, 1986.

———. "Carta de un patriota, o sea clamor de los cubanos." In *Ideario reformista,* 13–33. La Habana: Publicaciones de la Secretaría de Educación, 1935.

———. "Ideas sobre la incorporación de Cuba en los Estados Unidos." In *Ideario reformista,* 71–118. La Habana: Publicaciones de la Secretaría de Educación, 1935.

———. "Paralelo entre la isla de Cuba y algunas colonias inglesas." In *Ideario reformista,* 35–70. La Habana: Publicaciones de la Secretaría de Educación, 1935.

Scarry, Elaine. *The Body in Pain: The Making and Unmaking of the World.* Oxford: Oxford University Press, 1985.

Schulman, Ivan A. Introduction to Juan Francisco Manzano, *Autobiography of a Slave / Autobiografía de un esclavo,* 5–38. Trans. Evelyn Picon Garfield. Detroit: Wayne State University Press, 1996.

Schwartz, Roberto. "Misplaced Ideas: Literature and Society in Late-Nineteenth-Century Brazil." In *Misplaced Ideas: Essays on Brazilian Culture,* ed. John Gledson, 19–32. London: Verso, 1992.

Scott, David. *Conscripts of Modernity: The Tragedy of Colonial Enlightenment.* Durham, N.C.: Duke University Press, 2004.

Sommer, Doris. *Foundational Fictions: The National Romances of Latin America.* Berkeley: University of California Press, 1991.

Starobin, Robert S. Preface to *Blacks in Bondage: Letters of American Slaves,* ed. Robert S. Starobin, v–xxii. Princeton, N.J.: Markus Wiener Publishers, 1994.

Suárez y Romero, Anselmo. *Francisco, el ingenio o las delicias del campo.* Intro. Fernando Díaz Ruiz. Sevilla: Editorial Doble J, 2007.

Sun-Joo Lee, Julia. *The American Slave Narrative and the Victorian Novel.* Oxford: Oxford University Press, 2010.

Surwillo, Lisa. "Representing the Slave Trader: *Haley* and the Slave Ship; or, Spain's *Uncle Tom's Cabin.*" *Publications of the Modern Language Association of America* 120, no. 3 (2005): 768–82.

Sweeney, Fionnghuala. "Atlantic Countercultures and the Networked Text: Juan Francisco Manzano, R. R. Madden and the Cuban Slave Narrative." *Forum of Modern Language Studies* 40, no. 4 (2004): 401–14.

Tacón, Miguel. *Correspondencia reservada del Capitán General Don Miguel Tacón, 1834–1836.* Intro. Juan Pérez de la Riva. La Habana: Consejo Nacional de Cultura, 1963.

Tanco y Bosmeniel, Félix M. *Petrona y Rosalía.* La Habana: Editorial Letras Cubanas, 1980.

Thomas, Helen. *Romanticism and Slave Narratives: Transatlantic Testimonies.* Cambridge: Cambridge University Press, 2004.

Torres-Cuevas, Eduardo, and Eusebio Reyes. *Esclavitud y sociedad: notas y documentos para la historia de la esclavitud negra en Cuba.* La Habana: Editorial de Ciencias Sociales, 1986.

Trouillot, Michel-Rolph. *Silencing the Past: Power and the Production of History.* Boston: Beacon Press, 1995.

Vera-León, Antonio. "Juan Francisco Manzano: el estilo bárbaro de la nación." *Hispamérica* 20, no. 60 (1991): 3–22.

Wilcox, Kristin. "The Body into Print: Marketing Phillis Wheatley" *American Literature* 71, no. 1 (1999): 1–29.

Williams, Eric. *Capitalism and Slavery.* Chapel Hill: University of North Carolina Press, 1991.

Wordsworth, William. "To Toussaint L'Ouverture." In *William Wordsworth: The Major Works,* 282. Ed. Stephen Gill. Oxford: Oxford University Press, 2000.

Zambrana, Antonio. *El negro Francisco.* Intro. Salvador Bueno. La Habana: Editorial Letras Cubanas, 1979.

Zamir, Shamoon. *Dark Voices: W. E. B. DuBois and American Thought, 1888–1903.* Chicago: Chicago University Press, 1995.

uses of sentiment in, 12; transatlantic
network of, 60

Anti-Slavery Reporter, 185, 191

Aponte, José Antonio, 174–75

Arriaza y Spervilla, Juan Bautista, 77

Ashworth, John, 219n1

La Aurora, 48

Autobiografía de un esclavo (Manzano):
attachment to masters, 73, 74, 81–82,
84–89, 90, 96, 128–30, 142, 198, 199, 200;
on autobiographical writing, 122–23,
152; and British Anti-Slavery Society,
11; and composing *décimas*, 75; counterproductive nature of resistance, 24;
and creativity, 94, 97, 98, 99, 200, 201;
and credibility, 78, 99–100, 124, 127, 152,
161, 201; criteria for selecting episodes,
80, 99, 104; deciphering resistance to
enslavement in, 15, 71, 81; defense of
biological mother, 200; and del Monte
literary circle, 13, 14, 67, 71, 79, 83, 102–
103, 124, 148, 151, 160, 197–98, 200; del
Monte's role in Manzano's writing of,
4–5, 67, 77–78, 79, 80, 102, 104, 119, 125,
126, 148, 169, 203–204, 215n1, 221n39;
depression described in, 71, 73, 94; fragments of, 124; handwritten original of,
124, 222n49; and hunger, 128, 129; idealization of childhood in, 82–85, 88, 89,
95, 200; injuries described in, 71–73, 94;
on internal resistance to slavery, 20, 81;
and internal struggle for self-mastery,
22, 26; liberationist agendas using, 2–3;
Madden's translation of, 24–25, 80, 85,
102, 107, 109–13, 116, 119–23, 124, 126–30,
137, 164, 169, 199, 200, 203–204, 215n1;
and Manzano's anxiety about self-
exposure, 78–79, 80, 216n29; and Manzano's awareness of enslavement, 66,
88; and Manzano's writing for Creole
reformists, 2, 3–6; and Manzano's writing process, 4, 5, 23–24, 77–78, 79, 80,
102, 104, 123–26, 127, 152, 215n1, 217n32,
217n43; as model for autochthonous
literary expression, 2, 14, 24; paradoxi-

cal character traits in, 70–71, 79, 88–89;
psychological struggle against oppression in, 18; publication of, 124, 201,
224n9; and punishments, 5, 72, 73, 74,
75, 78, 79, 85, 86, 94, 97, 98, 128, 152, 171,
177, 193; readership of, 101–103, 124, 127,
201, 202–203; and reading skills, 76, 77,
80; reciting of *décimas*, 75, 216n18; representations of emotional state in, 81;
self-representation in, 14–15, 17, 24, 25,
66, 67, 68, 70–71, 78, 80, 83, 87, 89, 91–92,
93, 94, 95–98, 99, 100, 101, 105, 125, 201,
203, 216n31, 225n26; as slave narrative,
23, 67, 197, 200; Suárez y Romero's
transcription of, 119, 124, 151, 155, 164,
225n26; suppressed information in, 5,
78, 85, 124, 152, 201, 216n29; translations
of, 3, 22, 112–13, 119, 123, 124, 221n39; and
truth, 99–100, 105, 124–26, 127, 152, 161,
165, 198, 201; unconscious resistance in,
24, 66–68, 198; and work ethic, 90–91;
and writing skills, 71, 74, 75–77, 81, 89,
99, 119; wrongful accusation of crime,
71–72, 74

autochthonous literary expression: Manzano's autobiography as model for, 2,
14, 24

Azcárate, Nicolás, 124

Azougarh, Abdeslam, 124

Balzac, Honoré de, 56–57, 155

Barnett, Michael, 199, 228n2

Barreda, Pedro, 151

Basterra, Gabriela, 24, 63, 67, 83, 85, 202,
217n39

Baucom, Ian, 11, 12–13, 29, 55, 103, 109, 204,
219n1

Bender, Thomas, 219n1

Benítez-Rojo, Antonio, 176

Benjamin, Walter, on translation, 24,
110–12, 121, 122, 125, 127, 141, 144, 145

Bergues, Antonio, 213n52

Berlin, Isaiah, 209n13

Bernier, Celeste-Marie, 216n31

Birkett, Mary, 131

223n75; Manzano's autobiography as parliamentary evidence against, 2; slave traders as agents of slavery's inhumanity, 9; and Spain's geopolitical agenda, 38, 39–41, 43, 44, 47, 63, 115, 147, 170, 174, 176

slavery: abolitionists' moral arguments against, 9, 11, 12, 34, 109, 115, 137–38, 169, 204; Britain's abolition of, 34, 114; close examination of, 68; Comte on, 27; conceptions of, 17; debates on, 31, 32–35, 41, 212n11; fissures within hegemony of, 98; heroic versus mundane struggle against, 69; as metaphor, 18–19, 210n21; moral alibis for, 66, 70, 137, 150, 151, 223n77; oppressive practices of, 69; political slavery, 33; as regulation of personal domination, 14; simultaneously legal and immoral character of, 41; struggle for freedom from within, 26; Wheatley's critique of, 131; writing against, 22, 23. *See also* bondage

slavery in Cuba: abolition of, 3; abolitionists gathering evidence on cruelty of, 4, 5, 9, 10–11, 12, 108–109, 110, 116, 127, 133, 146, 164, 169, 200; class and racial tensions surrounding, 170; colonial government's prohibition of public discussion of, 3, 8, 22, 23, 27, 35, 57, 60–61, 124, 132, 145, 150, 209n2, 211n2; and competing struggles for freedom, 1; contingent relationship with colonialism, 23, 25, 47, 148, 149, 151; Creole reformist bourgeoisie's critique of, 3, 6–9, 13, 23, 25, 28, 29, 30, 35, 42–43, 46, 59, 61, 104, 105, 149, 169, 199, 204–205, 209n2, 211n3; in Cuban literature, 9, 148; del Monte literary circle's literature on, 49, 52, 149–50; and economic liberalism, 31; as enslavement of whites in Cuba, 23, 28, 30, 32, 33, 34, 38, 41, 42–43, 62, 144, 145, 147, 159, 166, 205; gradual elimination of, 8, 9; and labor demands, 114, 181, 220n25; Madden on, 132–37, 140, 144, 223nn76–77; in Manzano's "Mis treinta años," 54, 57,

58; in Manzano's poetry, 81; moral issues surrounding, 62, 63–64; proslavery advocates, 219n5

slaves: African slaves, 88, 154, 155, 173–75, 185, 218n58, 220n26; avoiding speaking ill of masters, 5; conceptions of freedom, 1, 2, 13–14; counterproductive actions of, 65; Creole reformist bourgeoisie's using slave's desire for freedom for their cause, 14, 43; Creole slaves, 88, 174, 218n58, 220n26; in Cuban literature, 9, 148; demand for increased productivity on plantations, 8; essentialist characterizations of, 65, 66; figure of submissive slave, 68; fondness for enslavers, 70; fugitive slaves, 69; as helpless victims, 5, 17; lack of visibility as moral subjects, 67; and legal concept of *partus sequitur ventrum*, 82, 87, 101; legality of autonomous voice of, 109; meaning of term, 17; muzzling of, 155–56; myth of slaves' blame for enslavement, 68; negation of moral development of, 70; as overseers, 224n22; prices of, 178, 179; as property, 35, 44, 50, 58, 74, 80, 83, 84, 161; as protagonists in del Monte literary circle's writings, 25; relationships with other slaves, 16–17, 210n19; resistance against internal oppression, 15–16, 20; rights of, 173; Sambo figure as stereotype of, 68; sentimental view of, 10, 11, 12; slavery as social death, 77, 79, 125; and Spanish language, 154–56; subjectivity in struggle for freedom, 22; written testimony of, 100. *See also* master-slave relations

Smith, Adam, 10

Sociedad Económica de Amigos del País, 8–9, 45, 46, 47, 48, 52

Sommer, Doris, 158, 161–62, 225n23

Spain: ambivalent abolitionism policy of, 120; bourgeoisie of, 40–42; colonial policies of, 48, 119; Creole reformist bourgeoisie's advocating white immigration policy, 6, 39; Creole reformists' degrees of political autonomy from, 2,

Tanco y Bosmeniel, Félix: on absence of
black characters in literature, 150; and
Escalera conspiracy, 194–95; *Petrona
y Rosalía,* 25, 148, 156–57, 160, 166, 178,
224n20, 225n24; short prose and verse
compositions of, 221n47; and Turnbull,
228n111
Ten-Years War, 195
Thomas, Helen, 130, 131, 210n17, 222n69
Tocqueville, Alexis de, 110
Toussaint L'Ouverture, François-Domi-
nique, 132
Trist, Nicholas, 121
Turnbull, David, 40, 185–86, 191, 194,
227n85, 228n111

La última cena (The last supper; film), 155
United States: and *Amistad* case, 24, 107–
108, 144; Creole reformist bourgeoisie
on Cuba's annexation as slaveholding
territory, 8, 36, 42, 47, 158, 186; and Cuban slave trade, 37, 170, 212n16; definition of Creole in, 217n58; and economic
ties to Cuba, 31, 37; slave narratives
in, 3; slavery in, 147–48, 224n2; and
transatlantic antislavery propaganda
network, 60
universal appeal, of Manzano's "Mis
treinta años," 60, 61, 71
universal extension of rights: and debates
on slavery, 23, 28, 30, 31, 35, 41, 43, 44,
74, 144, 145, 189, 205; and Enlightenment, 31; and freedom for whites,
23, 35

Varela, Félix: on abolitionism, 29; collaboration on journal, 46; correspondence
with del Monte, 27, 28, 147, 213n52; and
San Carlos Seminary, 211n1, 213n50,

228n111; on slavery's enslavement of
whites in Cuba, 28, 30, 32, 33, 34, 38, 41,
62, 147, 205
Vassa, Gustavus. *See* Equiano, Olaudah
Vera-León, Antonio, 49
Victoria (queen of England), 121
Villaverde, Cirilo: *Cecilia Valdés,* 148, 176–
77; and San Carlos Seminary, 213n50;
and Turnbull, 228n111
Voltaire, 32

wage labor, 13, 106, 202, 211n27
Wheatley, Phillis, 101, 130–31, 141
white immigrant labor, Creole reformist
bourgeoisie on, 6, 7, 39, 149, 158, 167, 176,
181, 205
Wilcox, Kristin, 101
Williams, Eric, 106–107
Williams, Helen Maria, 131
Williams, Lee, 124
Wordsworth, William, 11, 131–32
World Anti-Slavery Convention (1840),
109, 121, 134–35, 169, 186

Yearsley, Anne, 131
young liberals: antislavery writings of, 61;
characteristics of, 213n50; and colonial
policies on slavery, 13, 14; conception of
freedom, 14; connections with Spanish
royal court, 45; critical texts of, 46; del
Monte as, 6, 211n1; disavowal in contact
with slaves, 54–55, 63–64; discussions
of European literature, 48, 51; Manzano
associated with, 91; and Manzano's
autobiography, 102, 103, 104–105, 112,
197–98; and philanthropic compassion,
59–60; racial concerns of, 195–96; as
reformist slaveholders, 61, 62; on translations of Comte, 110

BLACKS IN THE DIASPORA

Herman L. Bennett, Kim D. Butler, Judith A. Byfield, and
Tracy Sharpley-Whiting, editors

FOUNDING EDITORS:
Darlene Clark Hine, John McCluskey, Jr., and
David Barry Gaspar

GERARD ACHING is Professor of Africana and Romance studies at Cornell University and currently directs its Africana Studies and Research Center. His previous publications include *The Politics of Spanish American* Modernismo*: By Exquisite Design* (1997) and *Masking and Power: Carnival and Popular Culture in the Caribbean* (2003). Professor Aching has recently begun a project on just war theory in the early colonial period in the Americas.

CPSIA information can be obtained at www.ICGtesting.com
Printed in the USA
LVOW08*1717260815

451620LV00013B/105/P